IMAGES
of America

LORAIN
OHIO

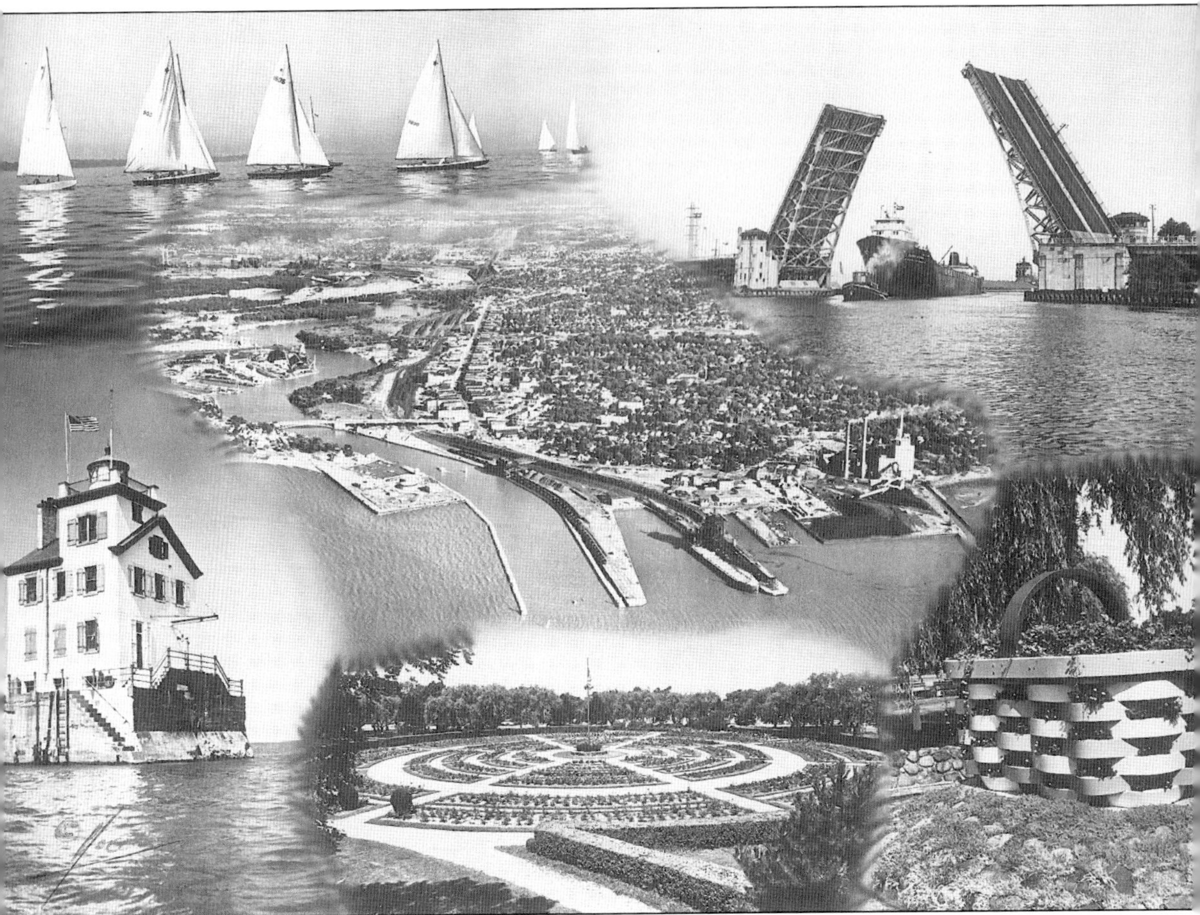

Lorain is an international city because of all the ethnic groups that have come to work in Lorain and made the city what it is. When Tom Johnson was looking for a location for his new steel plant he wanted a site where the coal from Pennsylvania, West Virginia, and southern Ohio, plus the iron ore from the Mesabi Range on Lake Superior, could be brought together economically. He decided on Lorain, and the slogan, "Where Coal and Iron Meet," was adopted. A collage was developed that would show some of the major sites in Lorain. Pictured above from the top left are sailboats on Lake Erie, the largest bascule bridge in the world (until recently), a picture of the Lorain harbor, the Lorain lighthouse, the famous rose garden in Lakeview Park, and the distinctive basket built in Lakeview Park.

IMAGES
of America

LORAIN
OHIO

The Black River Historical Society

ARCADIA
PUBLISHING

ISBN 978-0-7385-0178-9

Published by Arcadia Publishing
Charleston, South Carolina

Printed in the United States of America

Library of Congress Catalog Card Number: 9963796

For all general information contact Arcadia Publishing at:
Telephone 843-853-2070
Fax 843-853-0044
E-mail sales@arcadiapublishing.com
For customer service and orders:
Toll-Free 1-888-313-2665

Visit us on the Internet at www.arcadiapublishing.com

We wish we could have a picture of each person and thing that made Lorain a great city.
This book is dedicated to the people of Lorain, past and present,
and to the volunteers of the Black River Historical Society.

Created by a committee of dedicated volunteers: Publisher Coordinator: Carolyn Sipkovsky; Editors, researchers, and writers: Rodney Beals, John McGarvey, Burton Nesbitt, Carolyn Sipkovsky, and Frank Sipkovsky; Initial picture selection: Al Doane, Eloise Stilgenbauer, Robert Stilgenbauer Sr., and Pauline Stone; Photographer of backup pictures: Roger Brownson; Proofreaders: Phyllis Pfaff and David Rosso.

Photographs are from the collection of the Black River Historical Society and have been taken by many photographers.

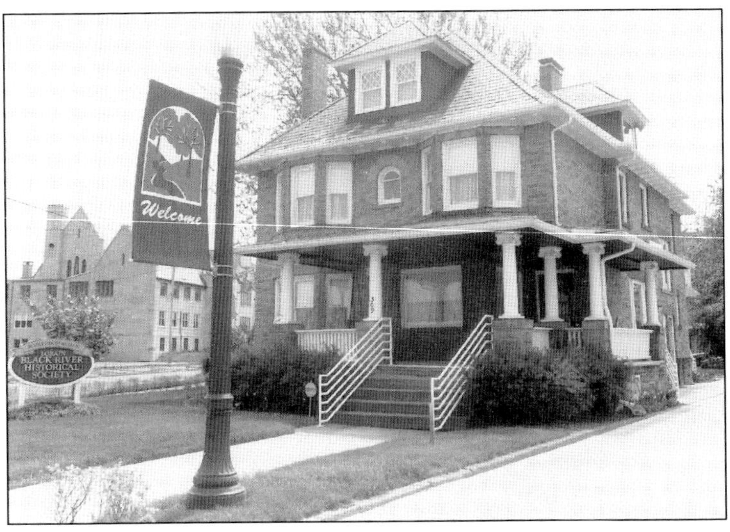

The Moore House
Home of the Black
River Historical Society
309 Fifth Street
Lorain, OH 44052-1611

CONTENTS

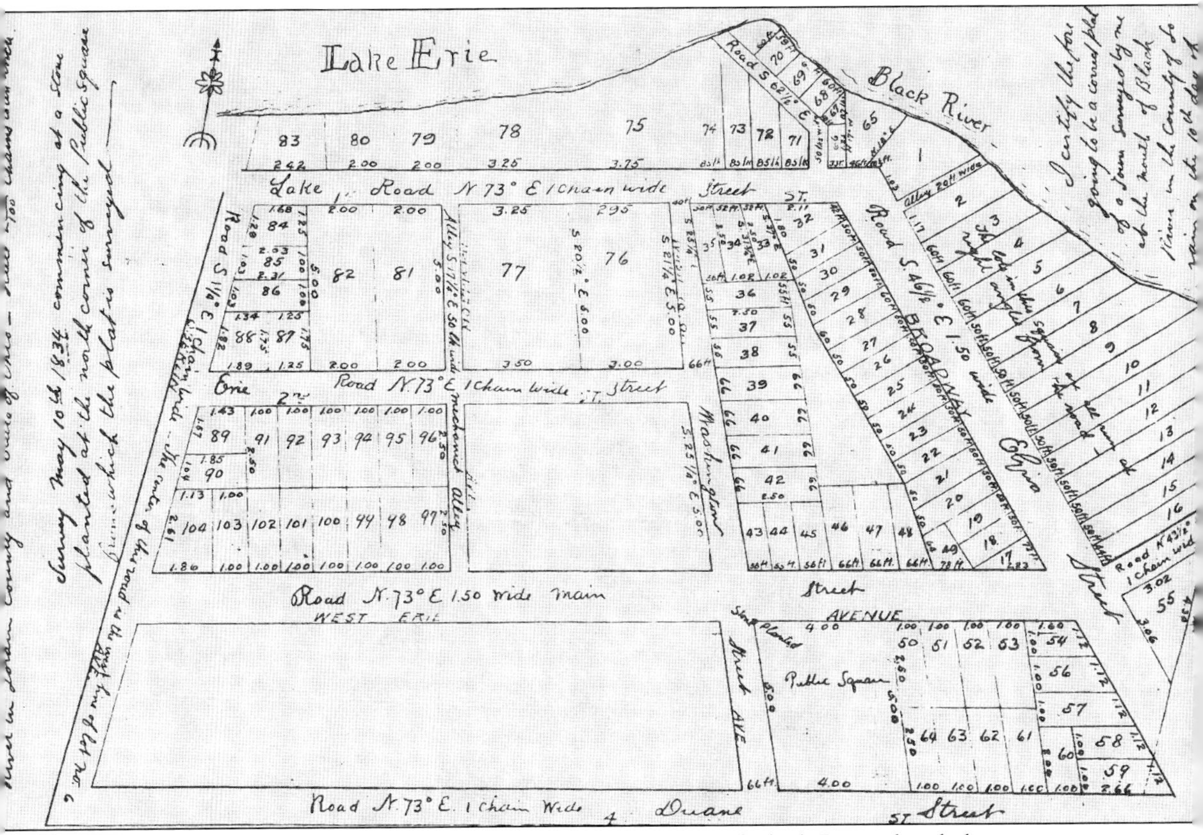

This is the plat for Charleston, Ohio, 1834. The citizens of Black River decided it was time to organize a town and certify it with the State of Ohio. In 1834 John Reid, one of its leading citizens, had a survey done that outlined an area from the Black River, Lake Erie, Oberlin Avenue and Fourth Street. It was sent to the county court house in Elyria, Ohio, to be officially recorded there and with the state. The plat asked that the town be renamed Charleston.

Introduction

Over 10,000 years ago the area that is now known as northwestern Ohio was covered with ice from the glacier that was hundreds of feet thick. That glacier ground out and formed the Great Lakes and leveled the hills into plains.

About 1,000 years ago the glacier had long since left, and forests covered the area. They were so thick that the normal way for humans to travel was by use of the water routes. Only 500 years ago Native Americans moved through the area, including the Delaware, Wyandot, Seneca, and Erie tribes. The Wyandots often lived in the area of a river they named the Canesadooharie, which means River of Black Pearls.

Early Europeans came to the area around 1533, when a French trader named Louis Vagard carved the date 1533 and his name in sandstone in the southern part of Lorain County. Much later, David Zeisberger, a Moravion missionary, started to establish a settlement at the mouth of Black River after he and his Christian Native Americans were forced to leave their settlement in Gnadenhutten. The Wyandots came and told them to leave the area and they moved to the Sandusky area.

Ohio became a state in 1803 and in 1804 Connecticut opened the land in northeastern Ohio for settlement by veterans of the Revolution. That caused many people to move to the area. In 1807 Azariah Beebe came from Vermont as a scout for Nathan Perry Jr. and established the first permanent settlement on the east side of the mouth of Black River. John Reid settled on the west bank of Black River in 1811 and built a trading post. Eventually, a post office was established that was named the "Mouth of Black River." Later the name of the post office was shortened to just "Black River."

By 1819 the first ship built here was the *General Huntington*, and that was the start of many shipyards on the banks of the Black River. The town was soon known for its shipbuilding.

The town was a shipping port for goods brought by wagon from the south to the port for transportation to the Lake Erie markets. To provide better transportation it was decided to build a plank road from the lake, south to Elyria. This toll road followed what is now Broadway to about Fifth Street, and continued south behind the present buildings to connect with Elyria Avenue near Seventeenth Street, where it went on eventually to Elyria, and by 1850, all the way to Medina, Ohio.

By 1834 the business people of the town, led by John Reid, decided that it was time to organize the town. A plat of the town was drawn and sent to the Elyria courthouse and forwarded to the

State of Ohio. The plat listed the name of the town as Charleston. Within three years, the first steamboat was built in the town. Circuit-riding preachers built the first churches.

S.O. Edison built the first blast furnace in 1860 at the foot of Ninth Street. It lasted for only a few years before it burned to the ground. The town was beginning to diversify into different industries. In this same decade the town served as a way station on the Underground Railroad. Escaped slaves often were taken by ship to Canada.

With the coming of the first railroad, the B&O in 1871, the town really began to grow. The town council hired its first police officer, the city school system was founded, and commerce was gaining a foothold.

In 1874 the town council petitioned and became incorporated as the City of Lorain. The name was taken from the county. Heman Ely founded Elyria. He had visited the Province of Lorraine in France and thought it was very much like this area, so he chose to name the county Lorain County. An election was held in town and Conrad Reid became the first mayor of Lorain. He and his wife ran the *Reid House*, a hotel where the *Spitzer Plaza* is now located at the corner of Erie Avenue and Broadway. He died in 1883 and three month later, the hotel burned to the ground.

During the 1880s industry began to take Lorain seriously. In 1881 the Nickel Plate Railroad was the first east-west railroad to come through town. The Hayden Brass Works built a large plant on Elyria Avenue near Eighteenth to Twentieth Streets, which created 400 jobs. By 1888 Captain Thew, a ship captain on the lakes, developed a better way of loading and unloading ships. He developed an improved gear system for a steam shovel, and that started the Lorain Thew Shovel Company that became known worldwide.

During the 1890s Lorain grew tremendously. Tom Johnson owned a steel plant in Johnstown, Pennsylvania. When that famous flood occurred, much of his plant was destroyed. He decided to rebuild at a place where the coal from Pennsylvania and the ore from the Mesabi Range could meet. After visiting all the ports of Lake Erie, he decided to build his plant in Lorain. Construction of the Johnson Steel Rail Co. started in 1894. In just ten years, the population of the city tripled.

In 1894 the American Stove Works built a plant in Lorain. Here, they made heaters and furnaces. In St. Louis the company became famous for the brand name *Magic Chef*. Mr. Meacham of Lorain invented the Lorain Oven Heat Regulator, which was the first thermostat for kitchen ovens.

Three years later the American Shipbuilding Company built a yard and launched hundreds of ships before it closed in 1984. The yard built the first steel-hulled ship on the Great Lakes, the *Superior City*, and many 1,000-foot long lake freighters. During the Second World War, the navy had the yard build the U.S.S. *Lorain*, a frigate.

Lorain continued to grow during the following decades. During the Second World War, the industries of Lorain geared for the war. Many men went into the service. Admiral Ernest J. King became Commander of the Fleet and was responsible for all U.S. Navy troops around the world. Loften Henderson became a hero when he was killed as he lead his torpedo squadron against the Japanese fleet at the Battle of Midway. Charles Berry was a marine in the invasion of Iwo Jima. When a grenade landed in the foxhole where he and his comrades were, he jumped on it as it exploded. His heroic action saved the other men from death.

The Ford Motor Company built a huge assembly plant in Lorain in 1958. Many kinds of Ford cars and trucks were assembled at the plant over the next decades until the *Thunderbird* car line was shut down in 1997. Ford still uses the plant for van production.

As basic industry has shifted in America, the city has been able to keep up. The growth of tourism and the use of the resources on Lake Erie continue to provide growth.

One

Our Beginnings

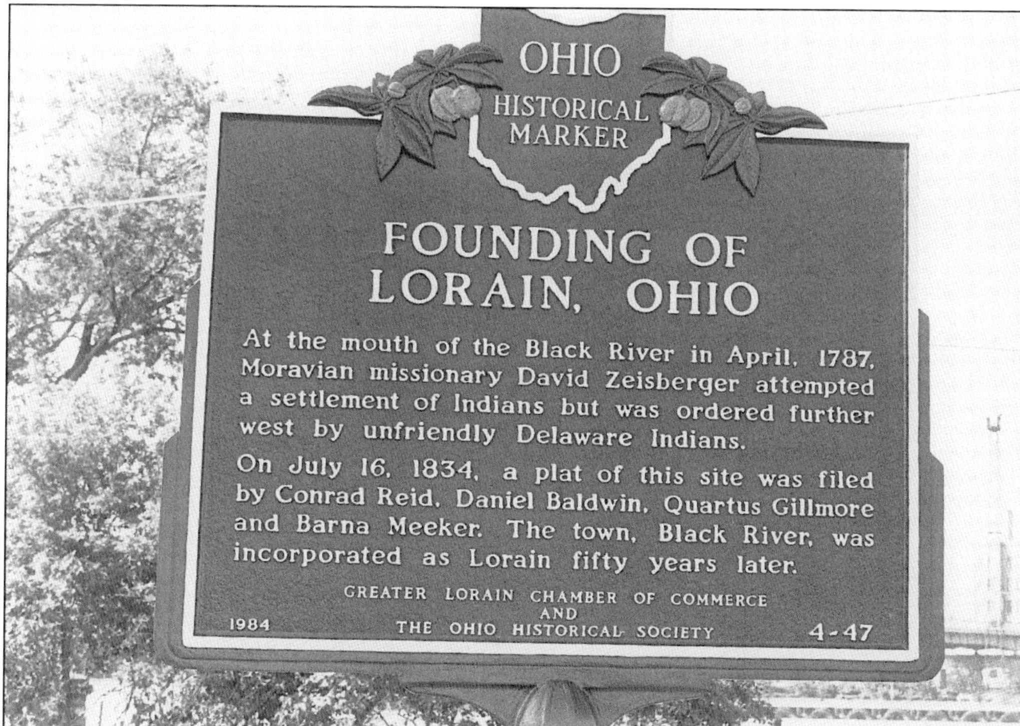

The first temporary settlement at the mouth of Black River was made in 1787, when David Zeisberger brought some converted Native Americans to settle here. He and his friends had been driven out of Gnadenhutten, south and east of Akron, and he was looking for a new settlement that would be safe. They had only been there three days when members of the Wyandot tribe told them they had to move on. They abandoned their cabins and walked on until they reached the Sandusky area.

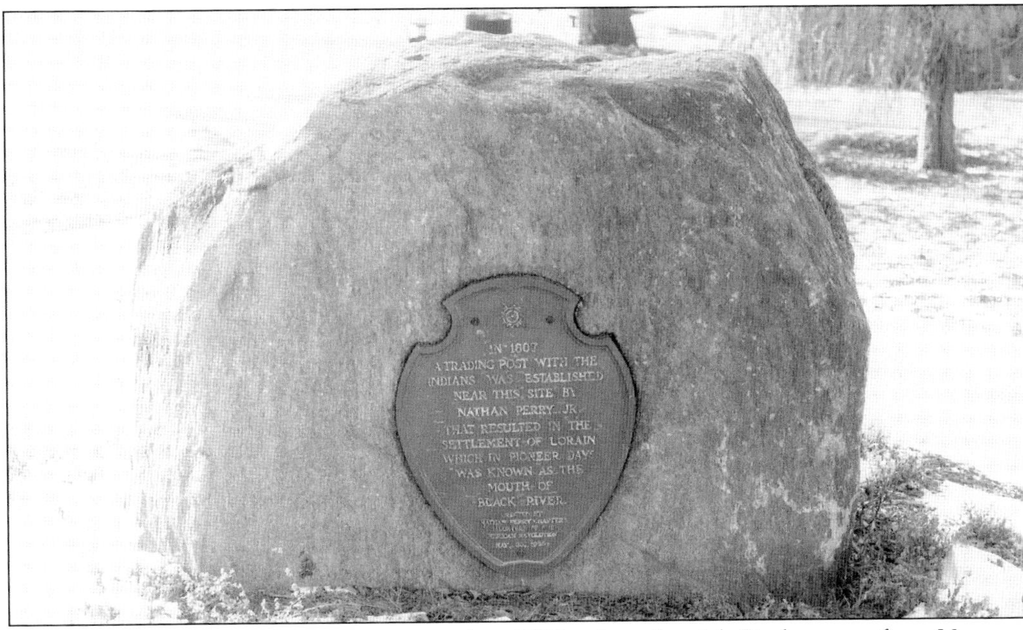

The first permanent settlement was started in 1807, when Azariah Beebe came from Vermont to the mouth of Black River. He was an advance scout for Nathan Perry Jr. Nathan soon joined Azariah and they built a trading post on the east side of Black River. Perry traded goods with Native Americans. Since then, Lake Erie erosion has caused the exact location of the trading post to be about 100 feet out in the lake.

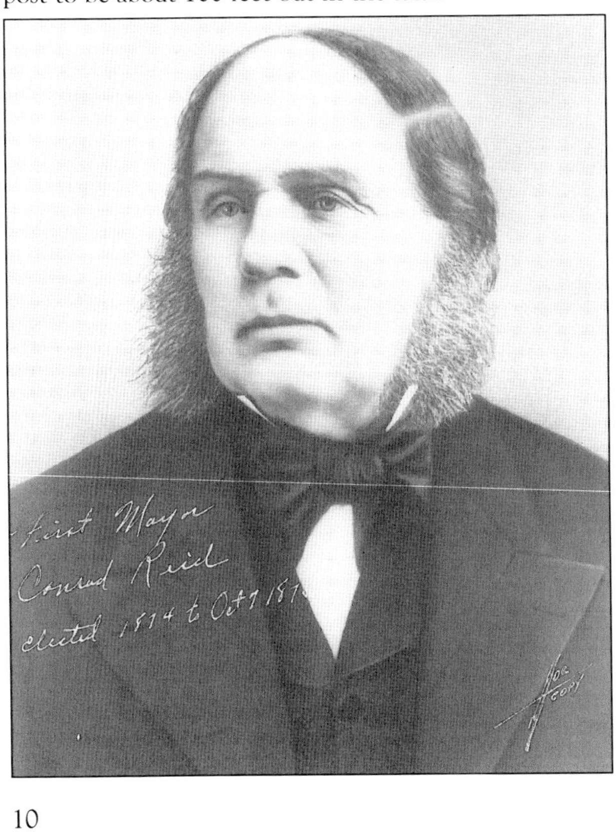

John Reid and his family decided to settle on the west side of Black River in 1811. He built a trading post and started a thriving business. He was soon authorized to establish a post office, and mail to the area was addressed to the "Mouth of Black River." By 1835 John's son, Conrad Reid, built a hotel at the southeast corner of Broadway and Erie Avenue. It served as the town center for years. Conrad became the first mayor of the City of Lorain in 1874; he died in 1883. The Reid House was destroyed by fire just three months later.

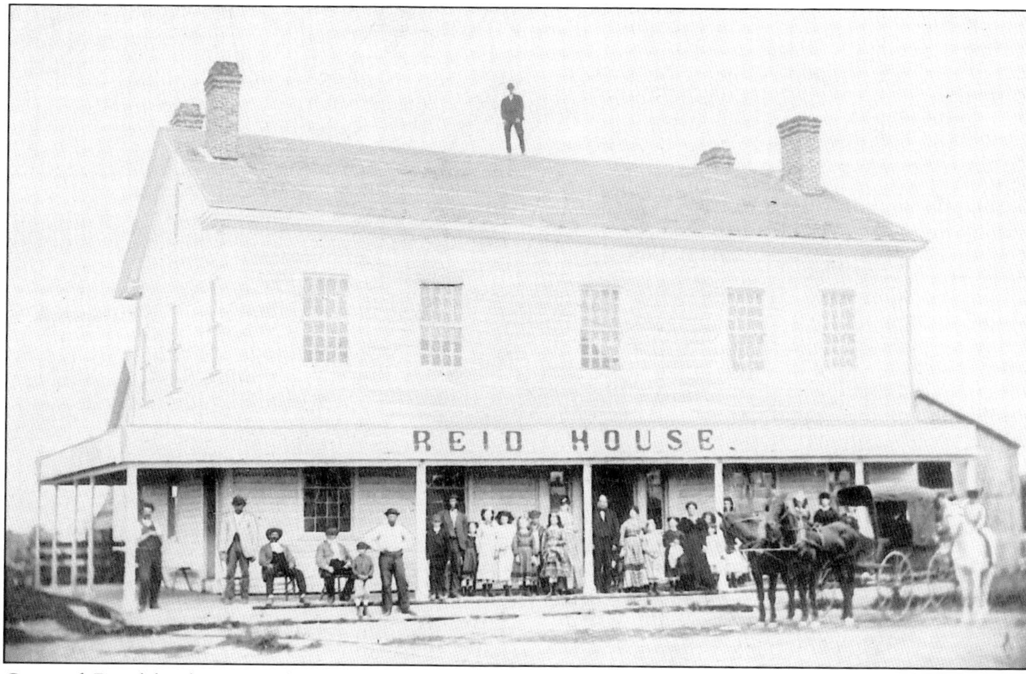

Conrad Reid built a new hotel, the Reid House, at the corner of Erie Avenue and Broadway. The hotel served as the center of town for years. At this time, a team of oxen often dredged the river. A ferry crossed north of the present bridge, and William Jones built little ships on North Broadway. At the time, he lived in the house that later became City Hall. Oak timbers for vessels were brought in from the forests around town.

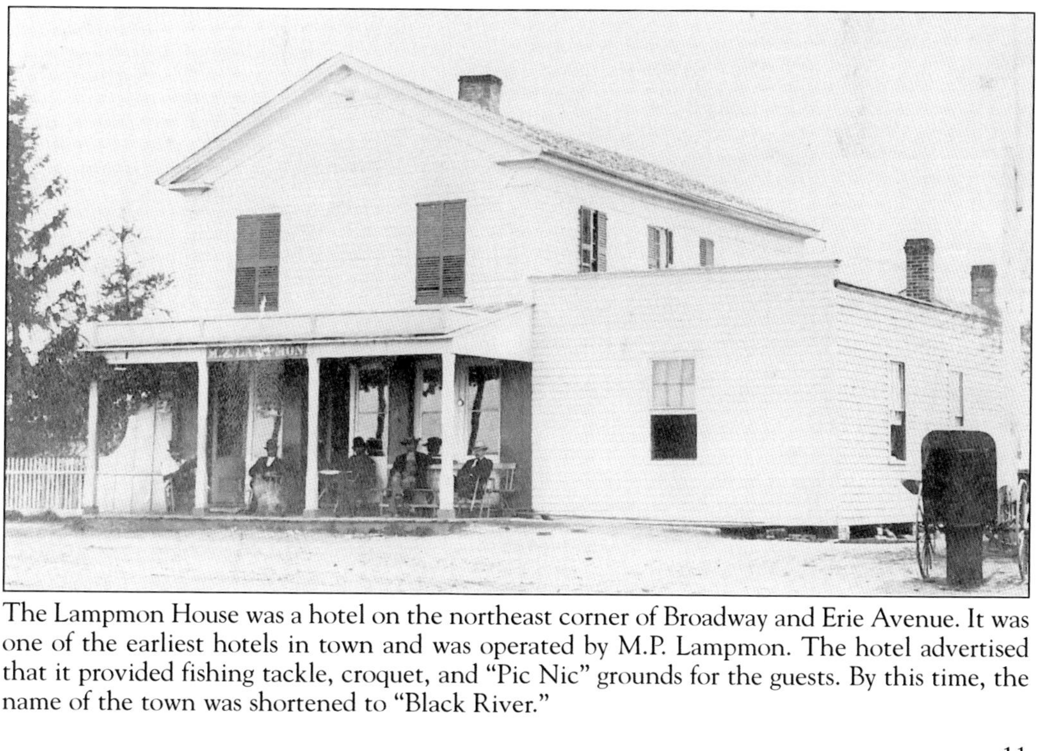

The Lampmon House was a hotel on the northeast corner of Broadway and Erie Avenue. It was one of the earliest hotels in town and was operated by M.P. Lampmon. The hotel advertised that it provided fishing tackle, croquet, and "Pic Nic" grounds for the guests. By this time, the name of the town was shortened to "Black River."

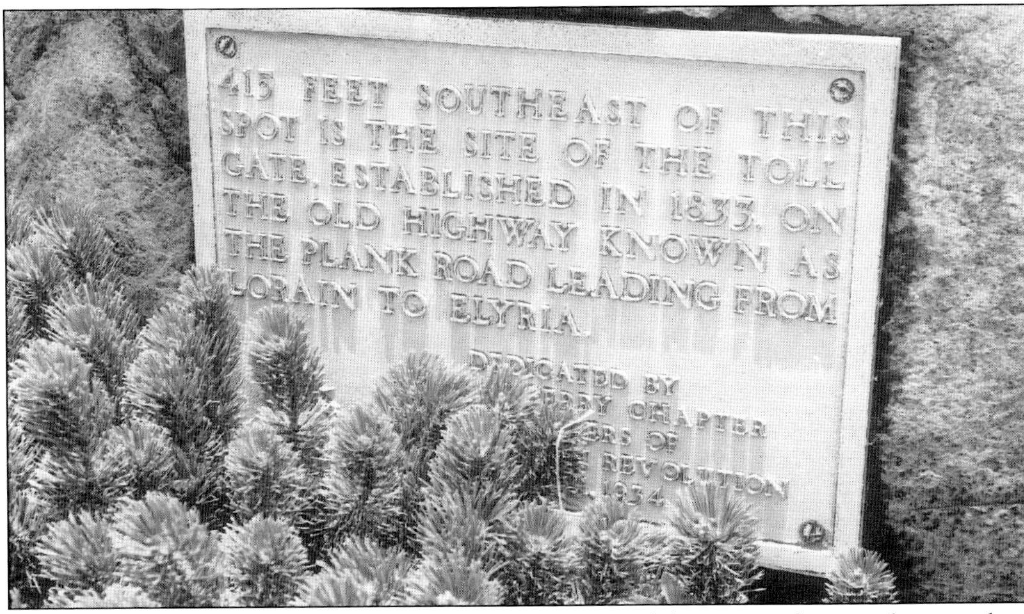

Trade was building from south of town as communities and farms sent their produce north to the port. The traffic was heavy enough that by 1833 a toll road was built from Broadway, east of today's business blocks, and connected with Elyria Avenue. From there it continued to Elyria and, eventually, all the way to Medina, Ohio. It helped to ensure the town of Black River as an important port on Lake Erie. The monument is located across from the *Morning Journal* at the triangle of Broadway, Elyria Avenue, and Seventeenth Street.

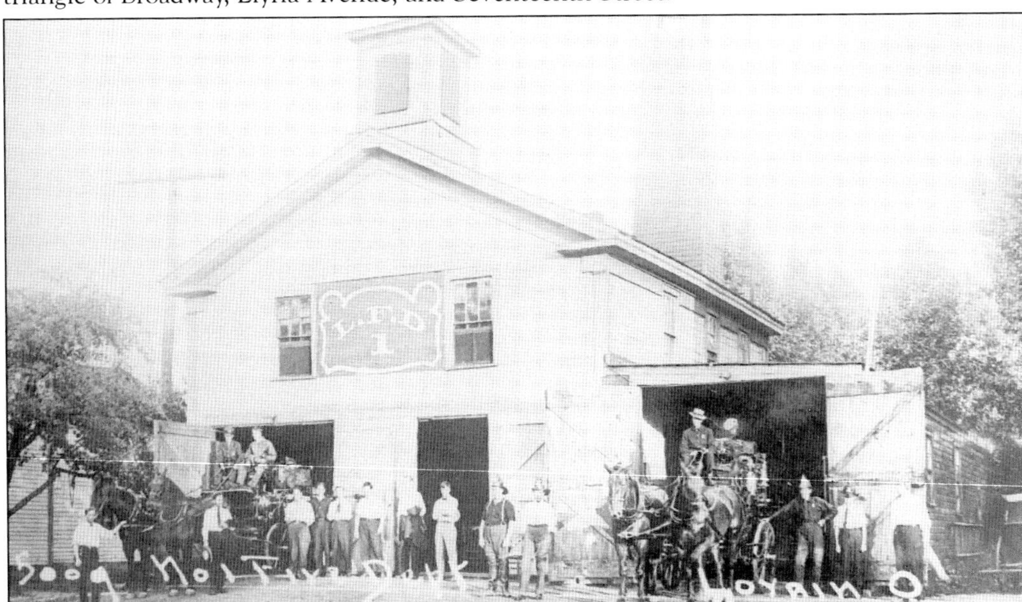

As the town continued to grow, police and fire services were required. The first fire station was built on Fourth Street, near Washington Avenue. The wooden structure had a high tower in the back where hoses were hung after use to let them dry. The first "fire engines" were hand pumps that two men would operate. Horses were used to draw the larger engines until the 1920s, when motorized engines were purchased.

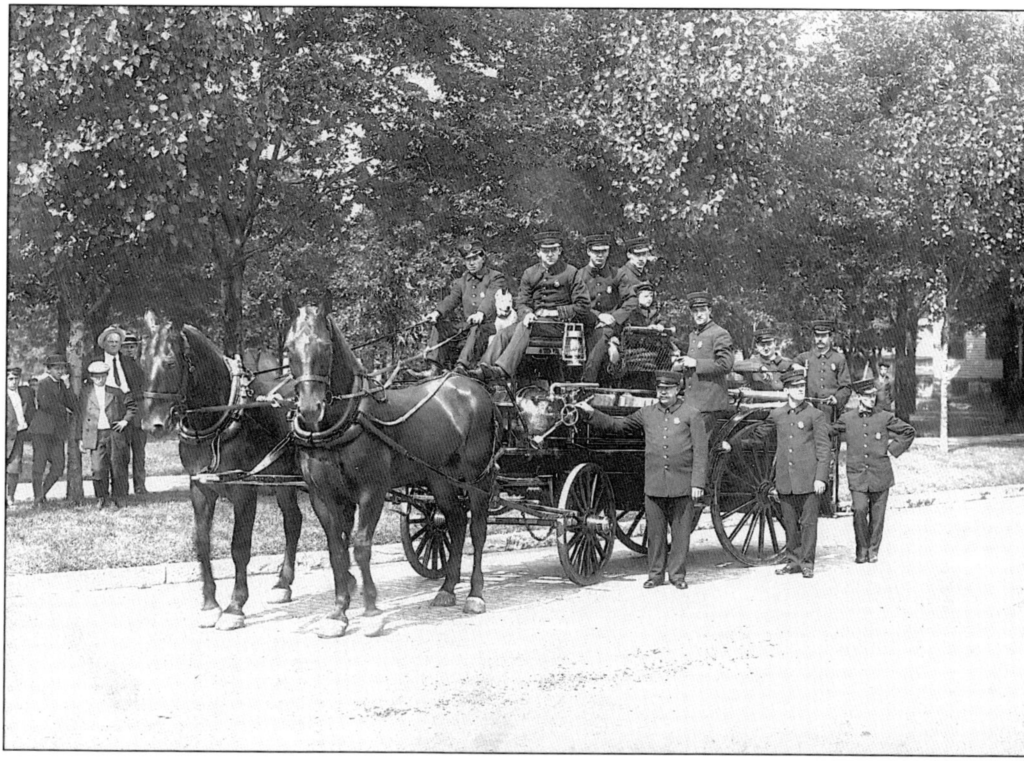

By 1903 the town had grown so much that new engines were added and more stations were built. This picture is of Number One Hose Company and includes Joe Claus, G.A. Conn (on the seat), Gus Bobel, and Chief Essex. Note the mascot on the seat. The horse on the right is "Dolly." Whenever the fire bells rang, Dolly would dash from wherever she was and place herself in the correct position, in front of the engine and ready to be harnessed. She would then dash off to the fire.

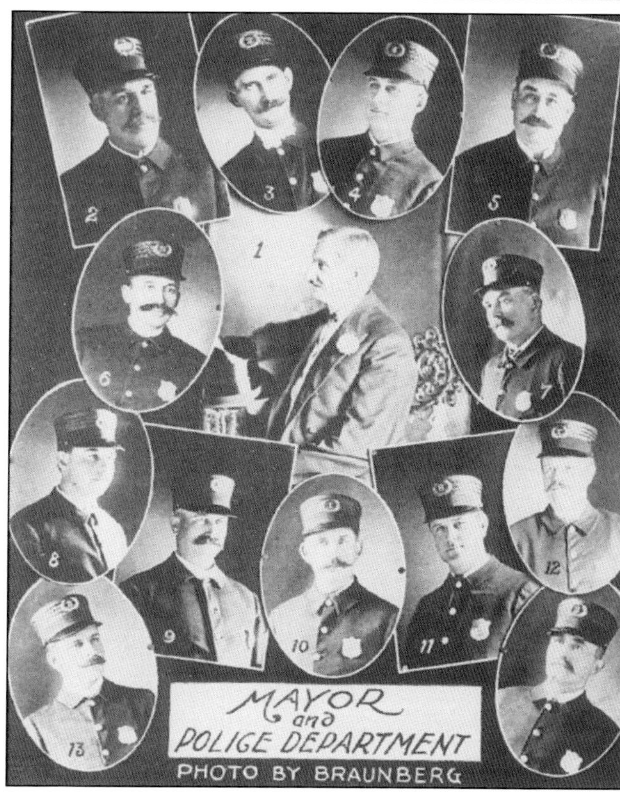

The first policeman in town was hired in 1874. By 1903 the department had many officers. Notice the mustaches worn by many of the officers, which was the style in those days. Lorain Mayor J.F. King is pictured in the center. Only the mayor is identified.

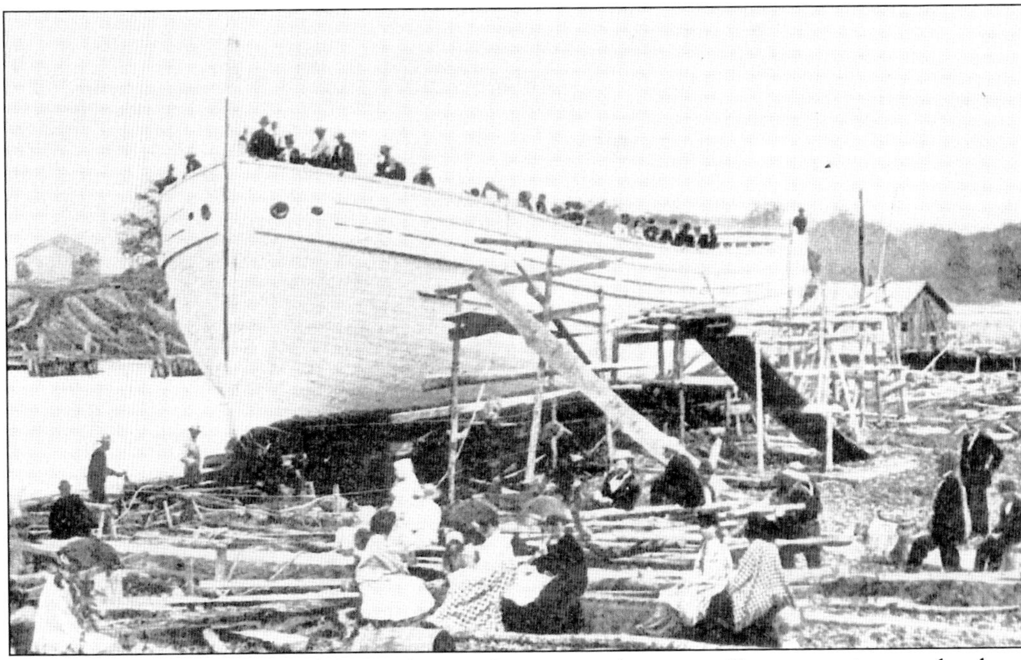

Shipbuilding became one of the earliest industries in the town. Transportation on land was difficult, and ships provided an easier means of moving supplies. There were many shipyards at different times. Some were on the west side of the river, and some were on the east. Oak was plentiful around town for shipbuilding material. Of course, the ships were sailing vessels. In the picture is the launching of the first ship built in Lorain. It was quite a celebration!

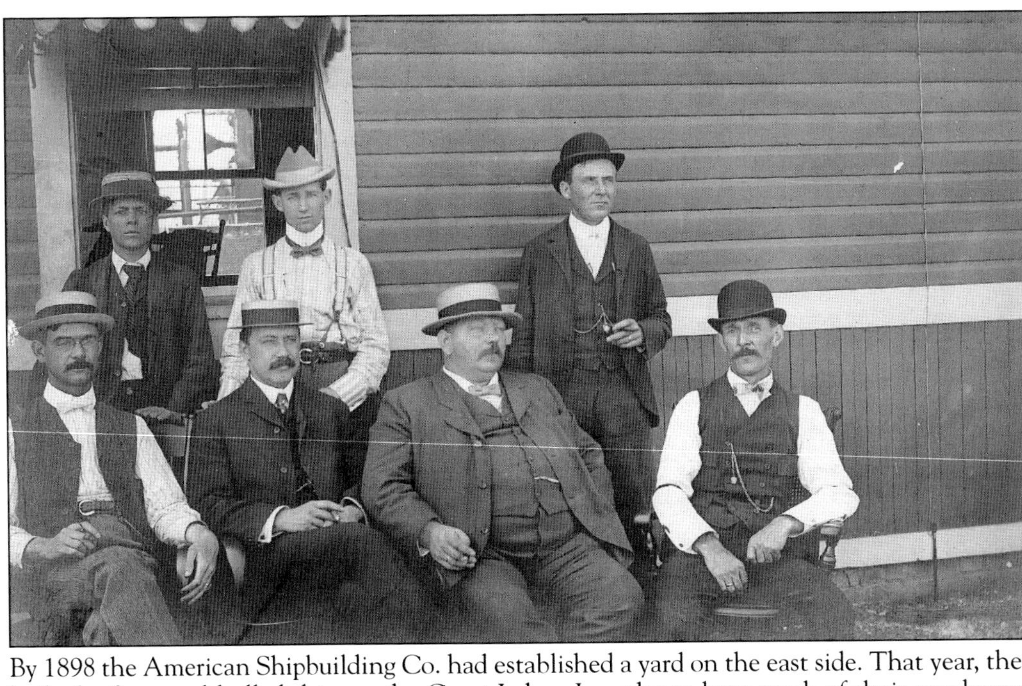

By 1898 the American Shipbuilding Co. had established a yard on the east side. That year, they built the first steel-hulled ship on the Great Lakes. In order to keep track of their employees, they formed the Time and Payroll Office. Pictured are some of the employees in 1900.

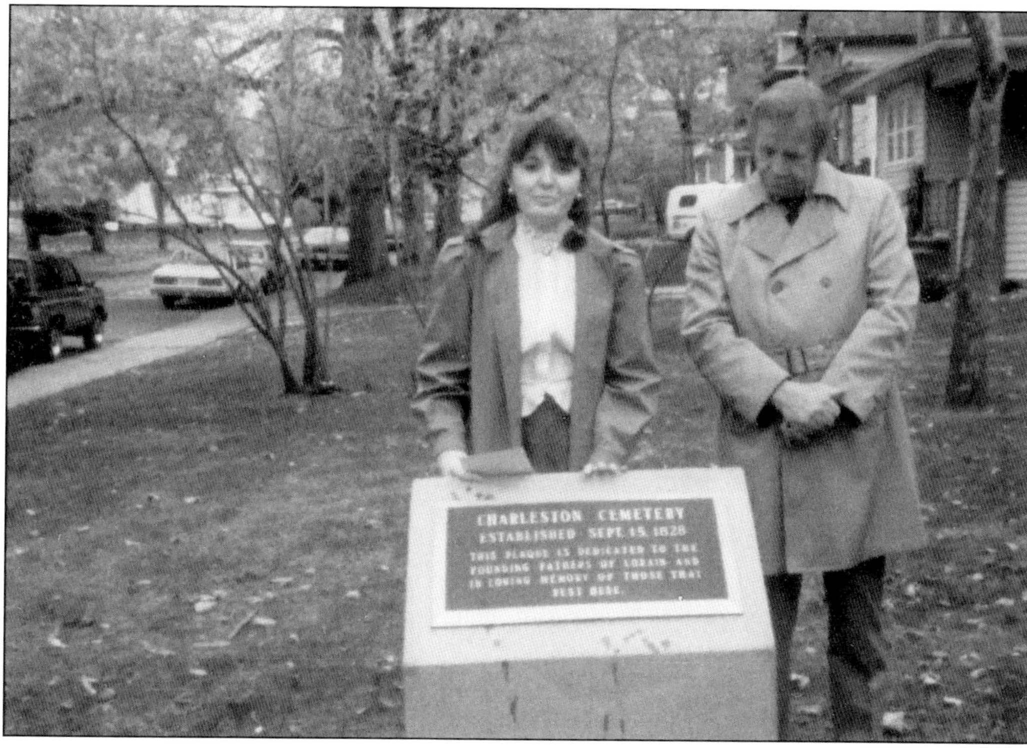

Because there was no cemetery in the town, the first burials from the town were taken south to the Amherst Cemetery. By 1828 the town dedicated its first cemetery on Sixth Street, between Hamilton Avenue and Oberlin Avenue. People were buried there until the plot was filled, and then the new Elmwood Cemetery was dedicated on North Ridge Road. The Charleston cemetery went into disrepair until 1985, when Diane Wargo investigated the plot, and located and dug up some of the gravestones. Pictured above are Diane Wargo and Mayor Alex Olejko. Below is the dedication plaque.

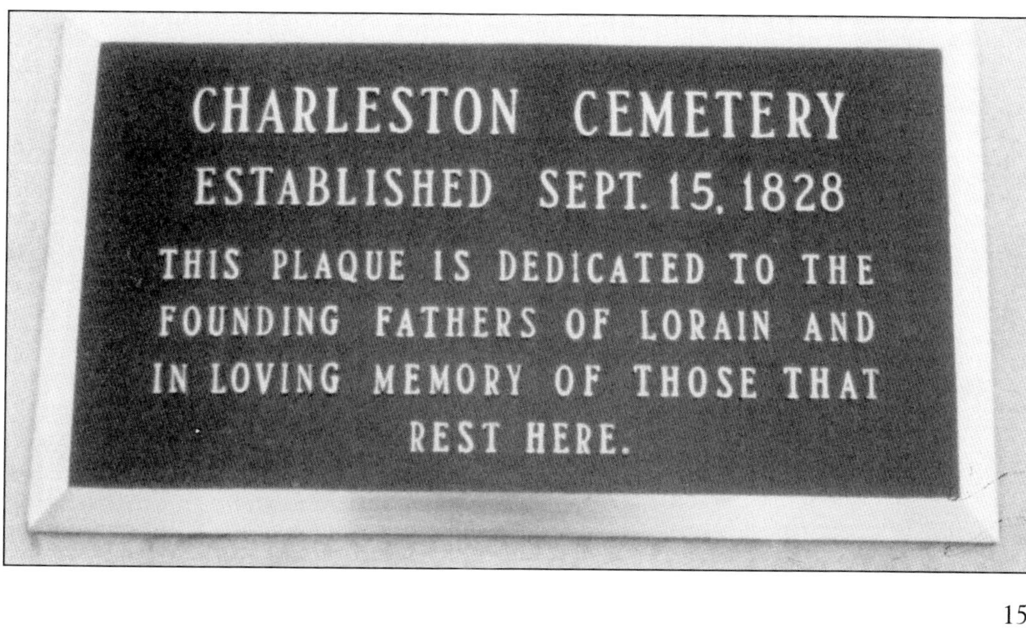

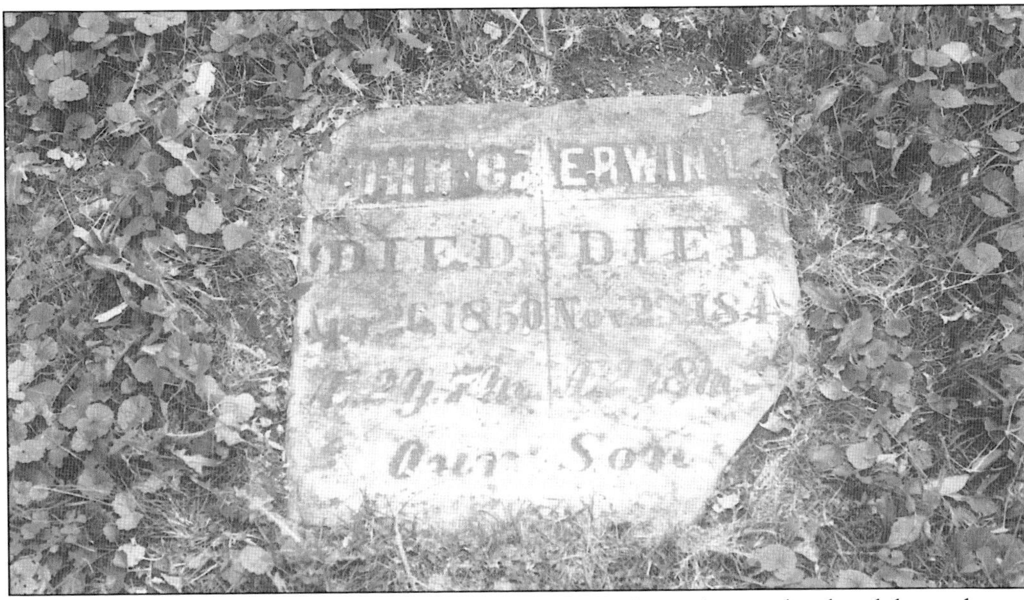

Diane Wargo and helpers went over the entire cemetery plot with a steel rod and drove the rod into the ground to find where old tombstones might be buried. They were able to find quite a few graves that had been lost over the years. The above picture shows a stone that marked the burial of two people from the 1840s and 1850s.

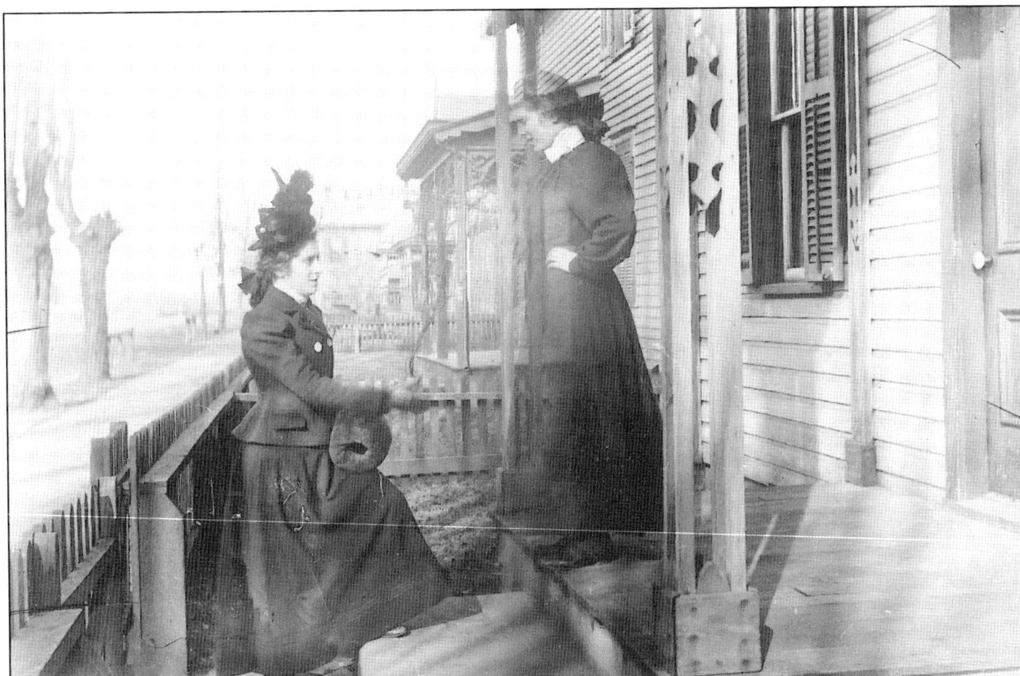

Life in early Lorain was more personal than in modern times. Neighbors visited neighbors. Everyone knew everyone else. This picture is from a glass-plate negative and shows an old ceramic door handle and the dress style of the day. Note the elaborate hat and fur-piece to keep hands warm that is worn by the lady (standing by the wooden fence) as she visits a resident.

Two

Our Businesses

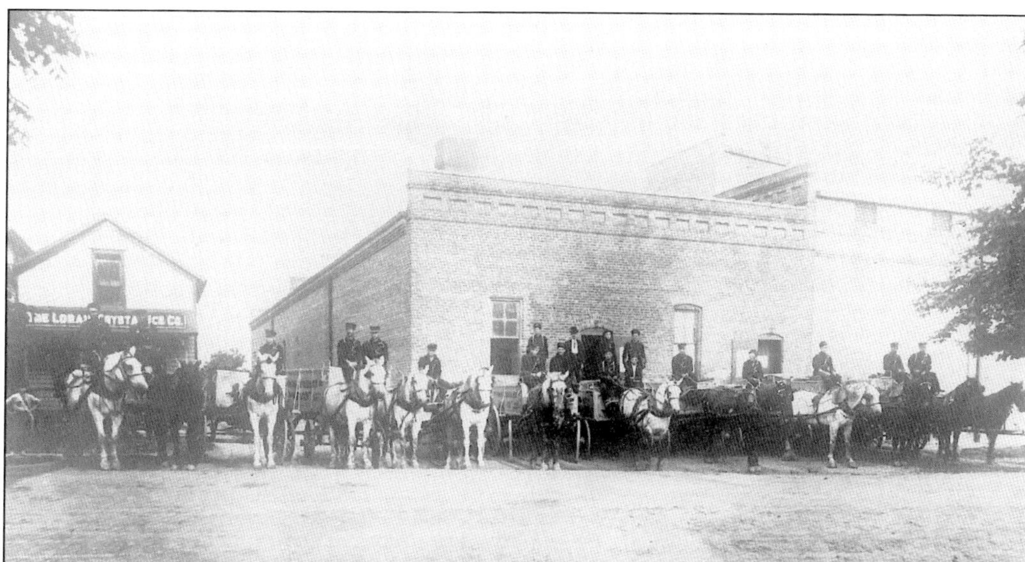

Because there was no refrigeration, people kept food cool by using ice in iceboxes. During the winter, men would cut chunks from the river. Sawdust was put between the layers of ice so they could be easily chipped apart later. The ice was stored until delivery was made by the horse-drawn wagons that took the ice to customers. The Lorain Crystal Ice Co. was located at the foot of Oberlin Avenue and First Street.

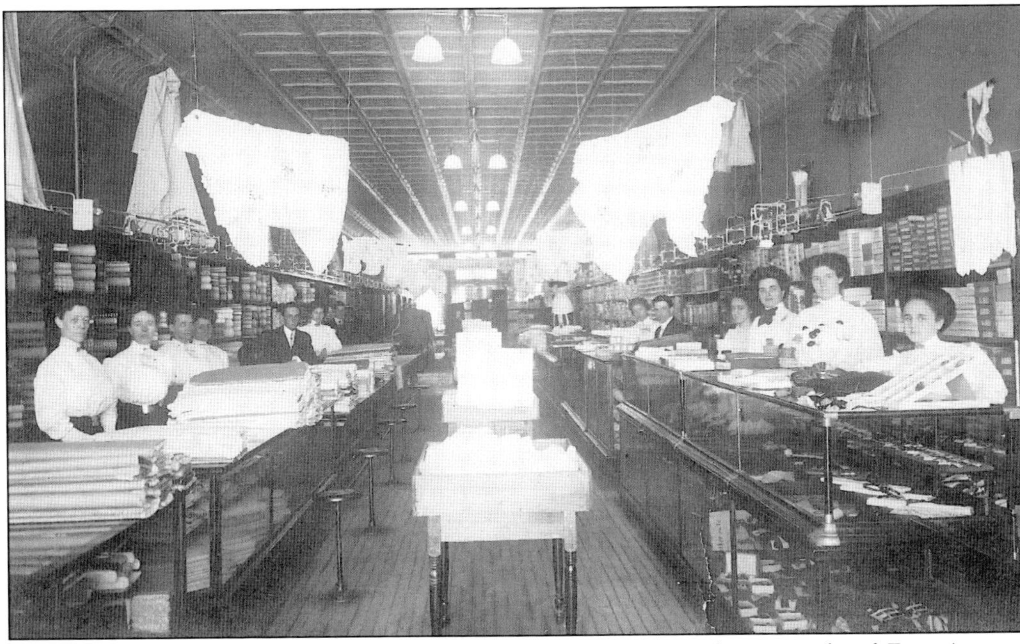

In early Lorain, most of the businesses were located on Broadway, north of Erie Avenue. As the town grew, more businesses lined Broadway farther south. The N.B. Hurst store was located near the Opera House on Broadway, near Fourth Street. This store opened *c.* 1892 and sold dry goods. Shelves were well stocked and clerks would gather the items you were interested in purchasing.

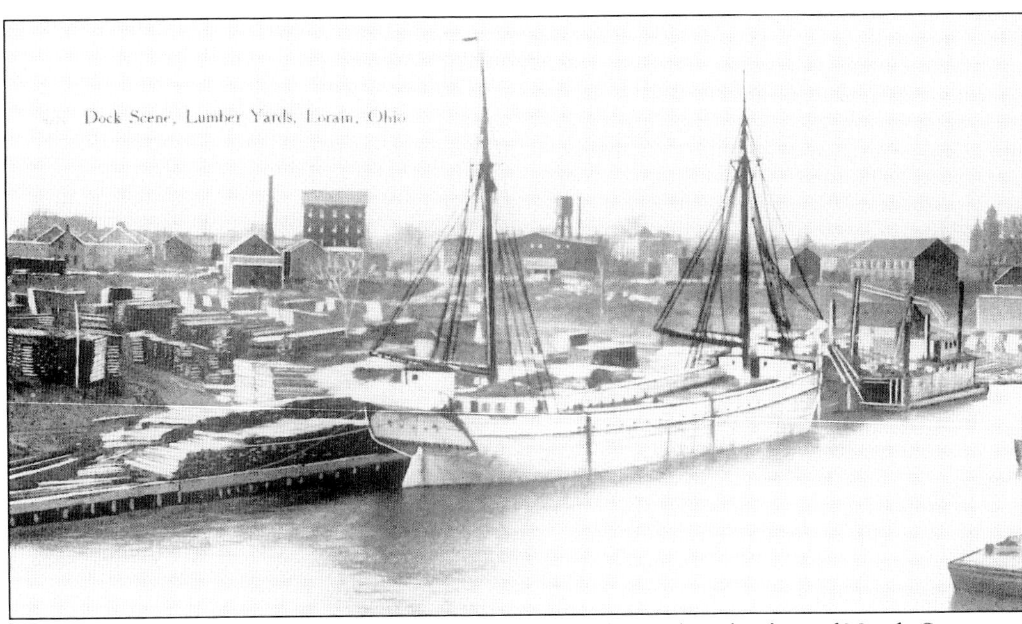

The Lorain Lumber and Manufacturing Company was located at the foot of Ninth Street and served the town for many years. Leonard Moore, who later became mayor of the town in 1916, was the secretary/treasurer. Note the wooden ship docked by the yard as it unloads its cargo.

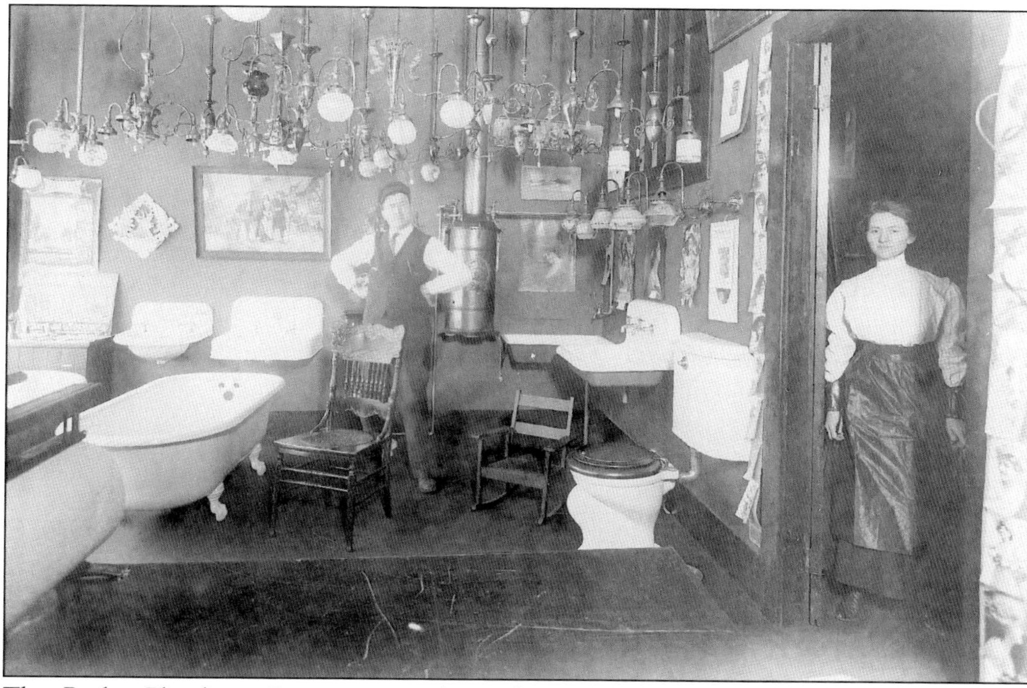

The Butler Plumbing Company was located at 545 Broadway. They sold the latest in "claw-footed" tubs and other fixtures. Note the new hot-water heater shown behind Mr. Butler. Ornate lighting fixtures are hanging from the ceiling display.

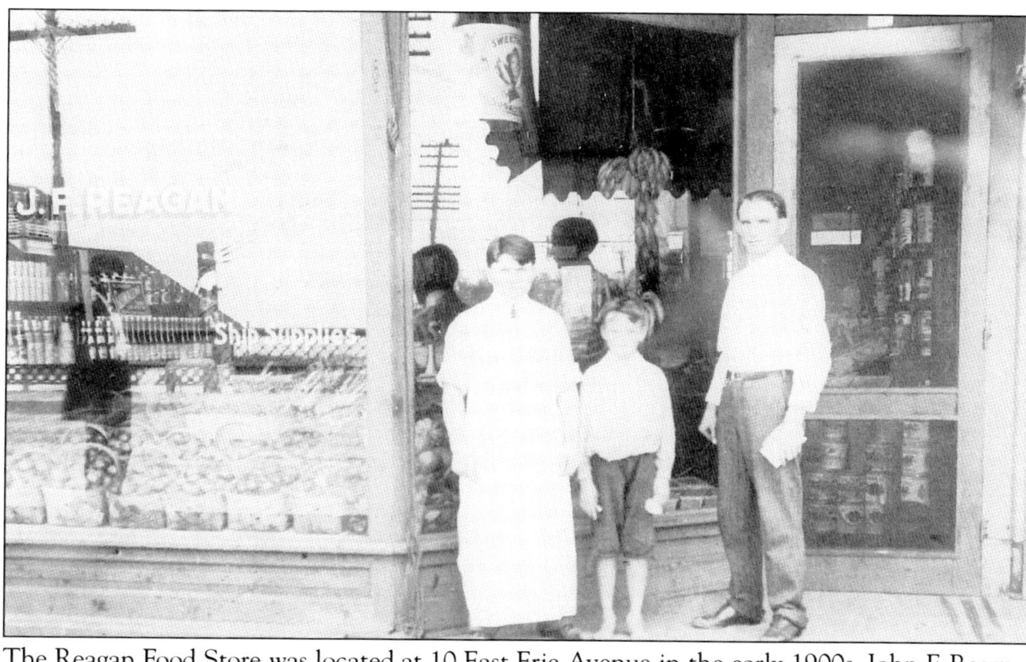

The Reagan Food Store was located at 10 East Erie Avenue in the early 1900s. John F. Reagan operated the store for the benefit of customers on the east side of town, but many people came from all over the town to deal at the store. The family business grew quickly when they began supplying the lake freighters of the Great Lake Commercial Shipping Fleet.

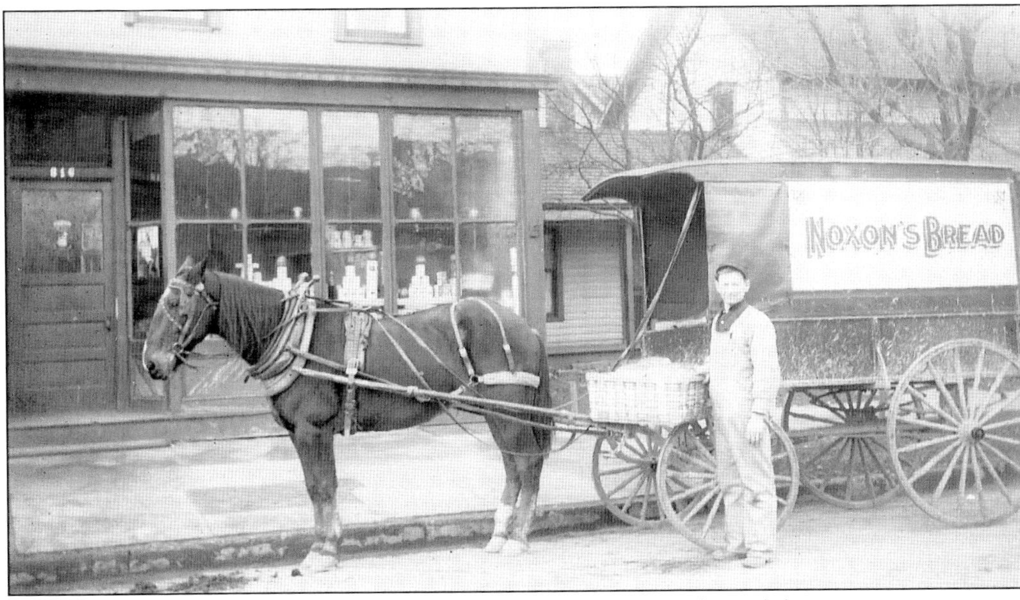

The small grocery store was the backbone of the town's food supply, and there were many around the community. Some merchants expanded to bring the store right to the local neighborhood. Noxon's Bread would deliver to your door. They often had established routes around town and would bring fresh produce to customers' homes.

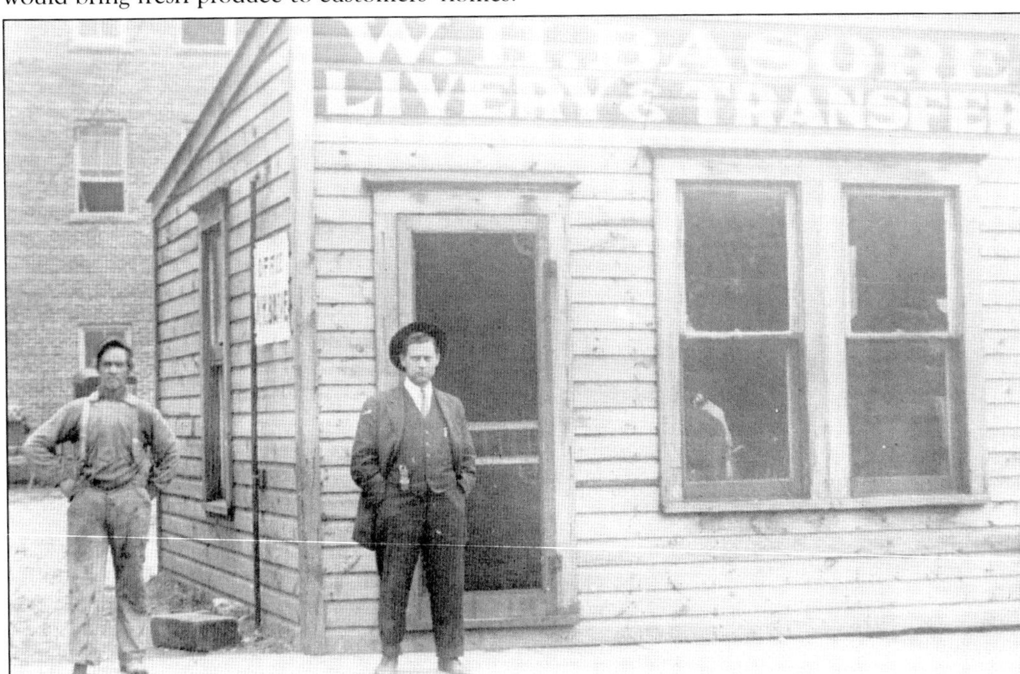

Today, it seems difficult to believe that the main means of transportation was the horse. Many people could not afford horses before the turn of the century, so when in need they would rent a horse from a place like Basore Livery and Transfer. Moving supplies and furniture was also their business, and in the early 1900s, the offices were located at 218 Washington Avenue. The company continued in business, with the use of trucks into the 1950s.

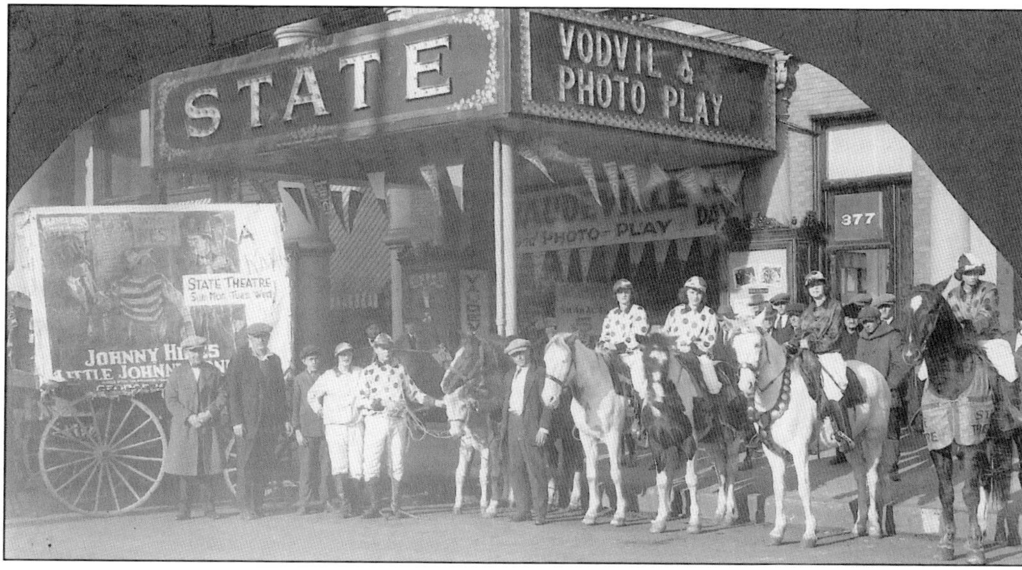

The Majestic Theater opened at 375 Broadway. In later years it was renamed the Opera House, and finally the State Theater. Above, notice the live performance that is to be on the stage. Below is one of the productions called "The Squaw Man." An eight-piece orchestra, directed by Phil Stephen, provided the music. The seating capacity was set at 1,350 people, which was quite a large theater for those days. Early productions were live on the stage. By the late 1920s, there were ten movie theaters located in Lorain.

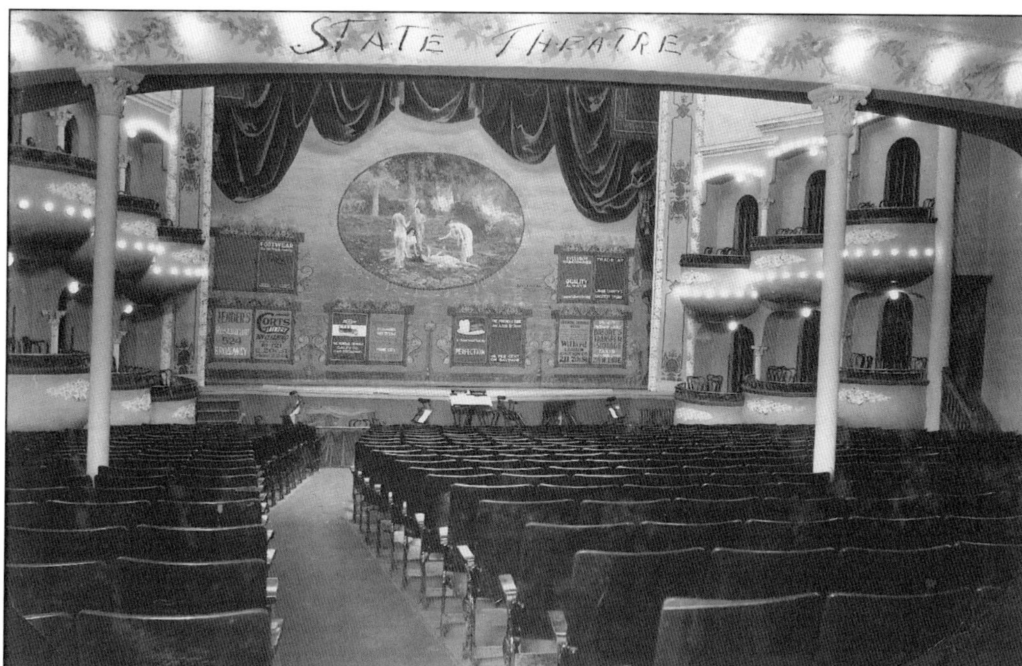

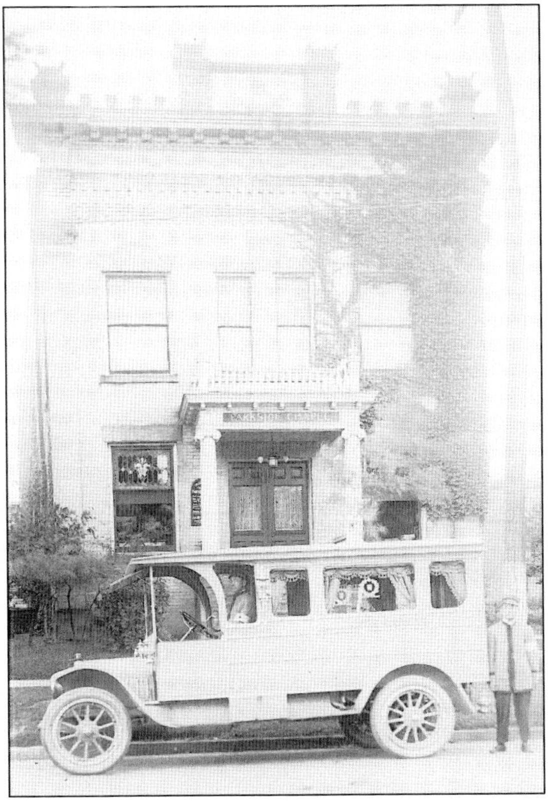

The Parkside Chapel was at 600 West Erie Avenue in 1904 and was operated by the Wickens Funeral Company. The motorized ambulance came complete with bed, hot water bottles, nurse's chair, and speaking tube to communicate with the driver. Later, the business moved to Broadway and then to 221 Fifth Street. The funeral company went out of business in the early 1940s.

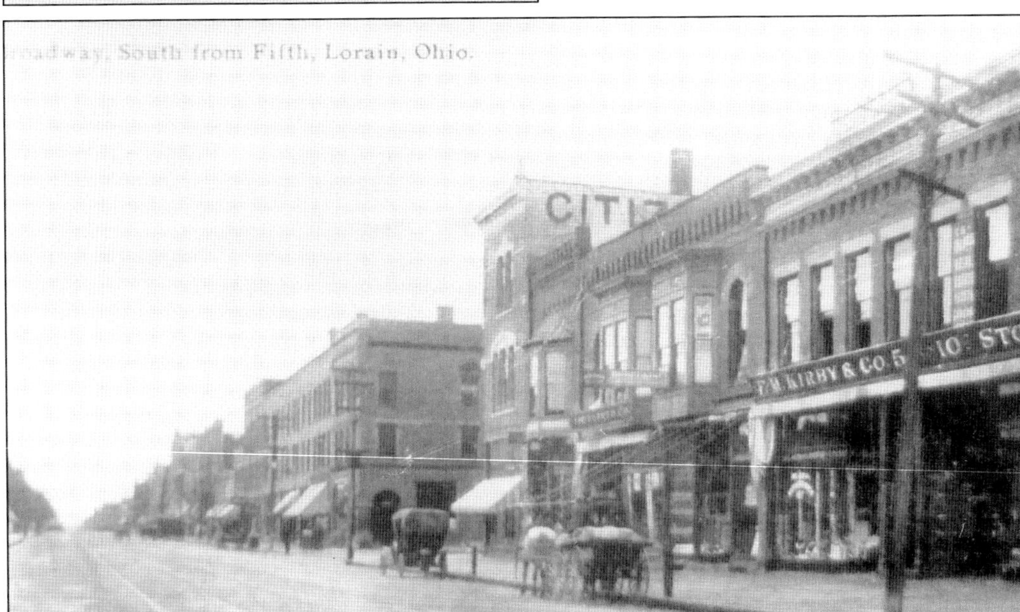

It seems difficult to imagine the business district of the town with mainly horse-drawn vehicles and perhaps just a car now and then. The five and ten cents stores really did only sell things for a nickel or a dime. At the corner of Broadway and Sixth Street is shown the Lorain Banking Company.

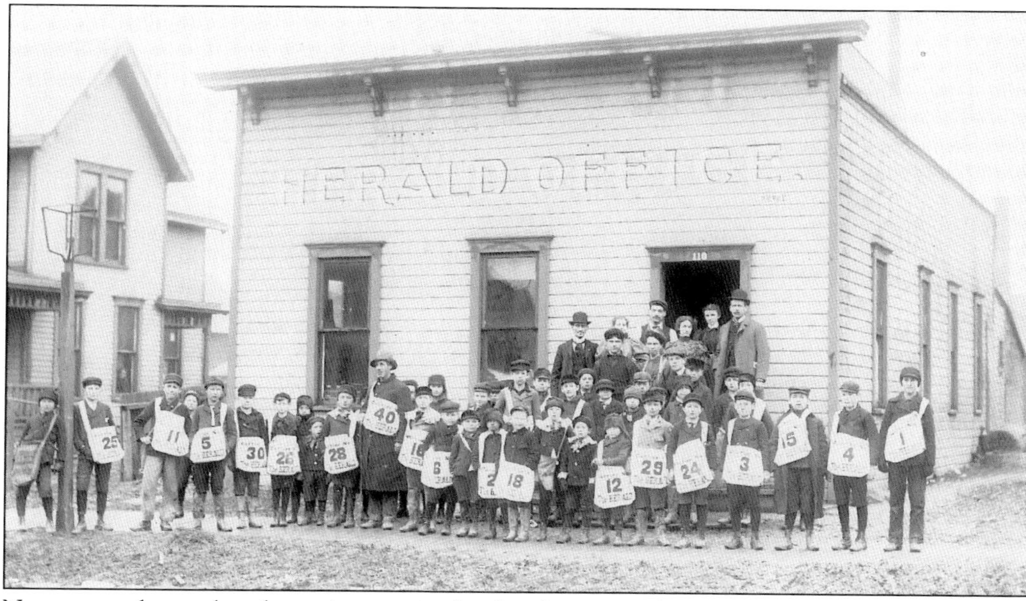

Newspapers have played a major part in the development of communication in the town. F.A. Rowley first published the *Weekly Times* on March 6, 1879. It was the first newspaper in the town. By 1894, the *Herald* opened a plant on Fourth Street and papers sold for 1¢ an issue. They had paper boys deliver the papers each day. The two papers merged into the *Times/Herald*. The *Lorain Journal* was founded in 1920 and purchased the *Times/Herald* in December of 1932.

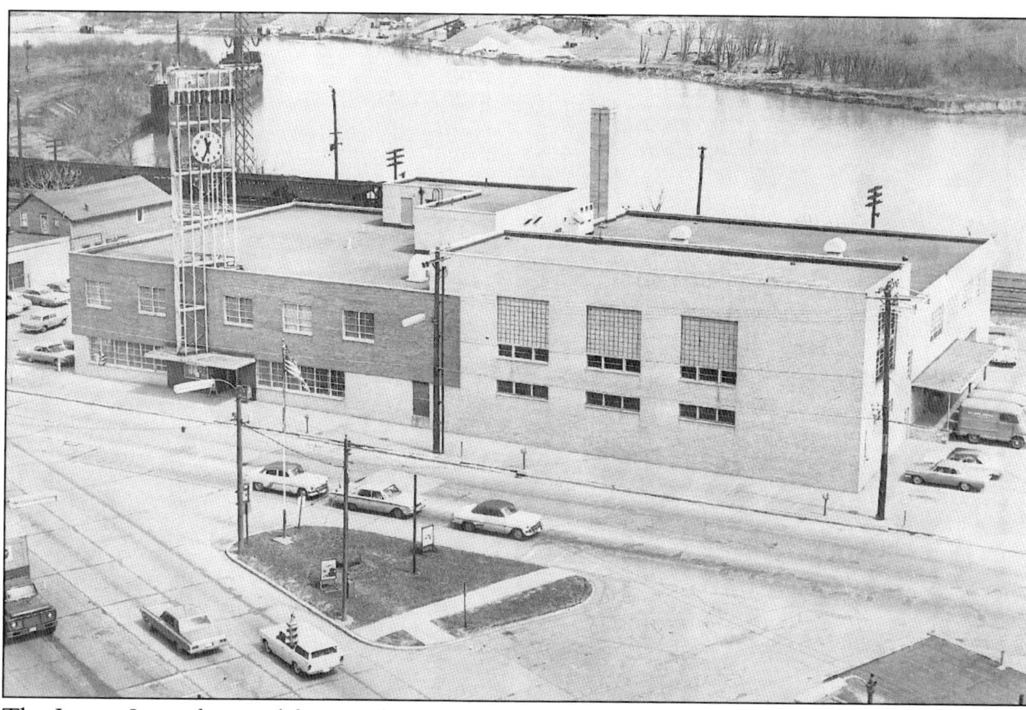

The *Lorain Journal* moved from its location on Seventh Street near Broadway to the new plant that was built at Broadway and Seventeenth Street in May of 1955. By 1990, it was decided to change the paper's publication to mornings, and it become the *Morning Journal.*

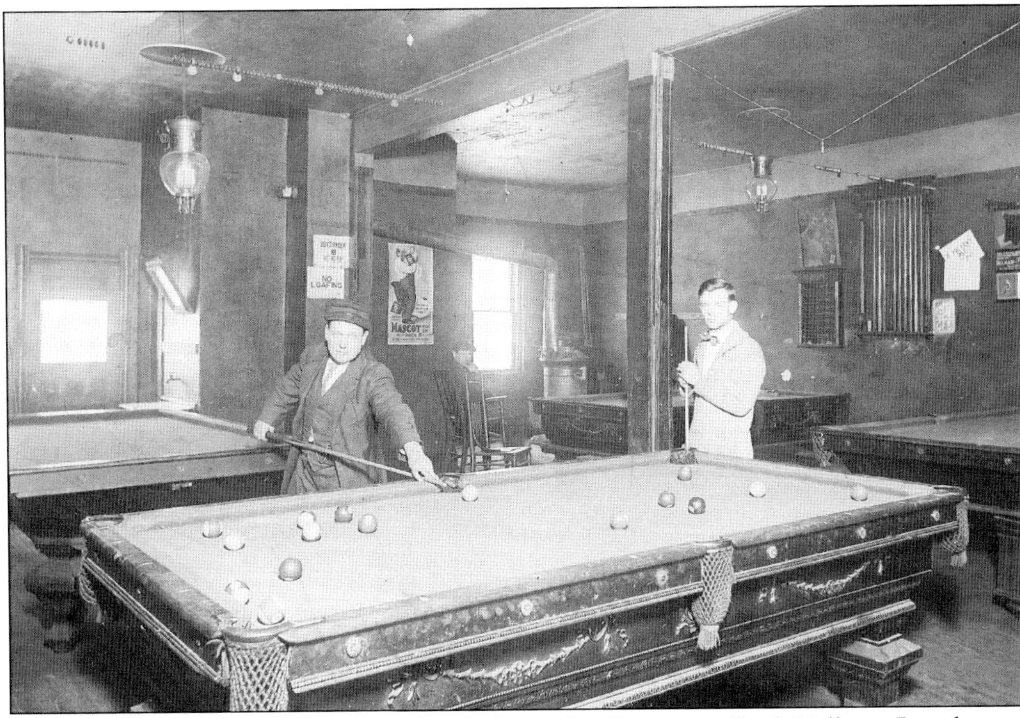

Recreation was available in the early 1910s at the Humiston Pool Hall on Broadway at Eighteenth Street. Later, Mr. Herbert Humiston ran the Central Cigar Store at 2035 Broadway. Pictured are Herbert and Harry, his son. The store is typical of the small businesses that were so successful in Lorain.

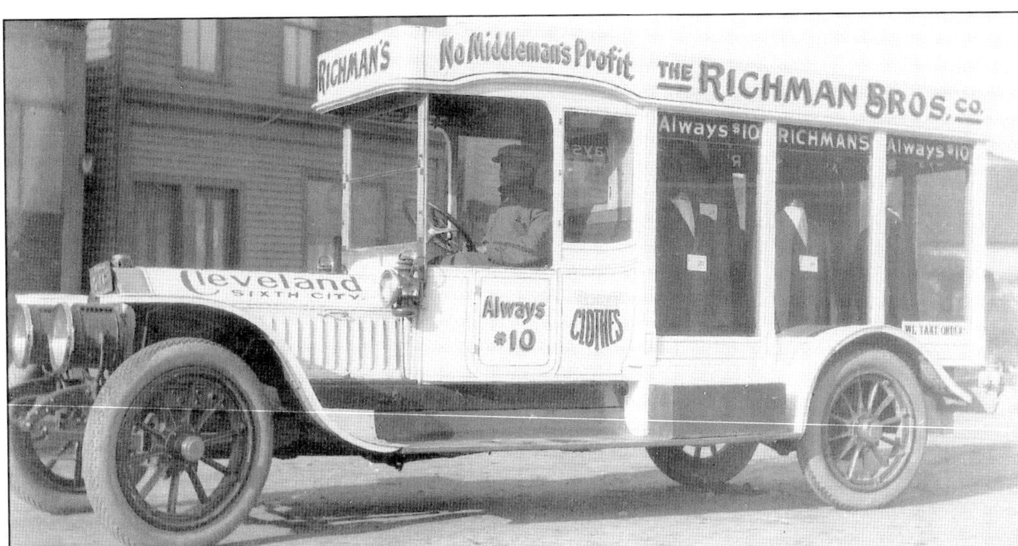

Richman Brother's Clothing Company was organized in Cleveland, Ohio. They sold quality suits for a low price and were so successful that they opened a retail store at 550 Broadway in Lorain. They also built a clothing manufacturing plant on Broadway, near the railroad tracks. This drive-up truck from the 1920s shows that suits were only $10, but that price came close to a week's wages for many.

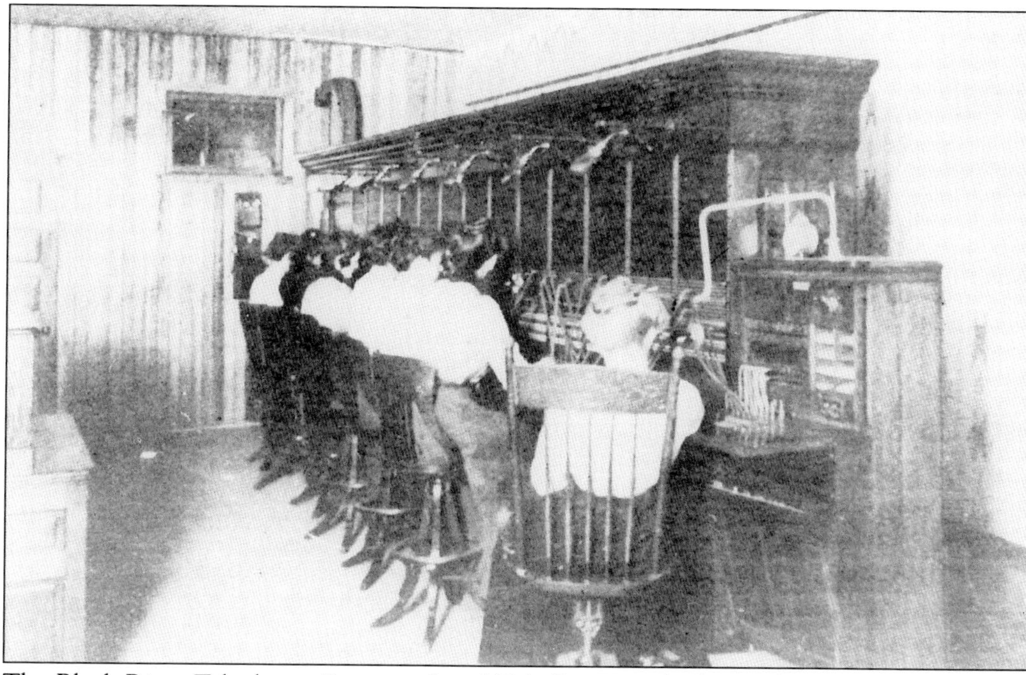

The Black River Telephone Co. started in 1894. Operators had to make all connections, and there was no long-distance service. The first telephone directory was printed on one page of paper in 1896. Phone numbers were all under 250. By 1917, automatic dialing phones started to replace switchboard operators. The name was changed to the Lorain Telephone Co. in 1929. In 1978 the company merged with Centel Corporation, and in 1993, Century Telephone bought Centel.

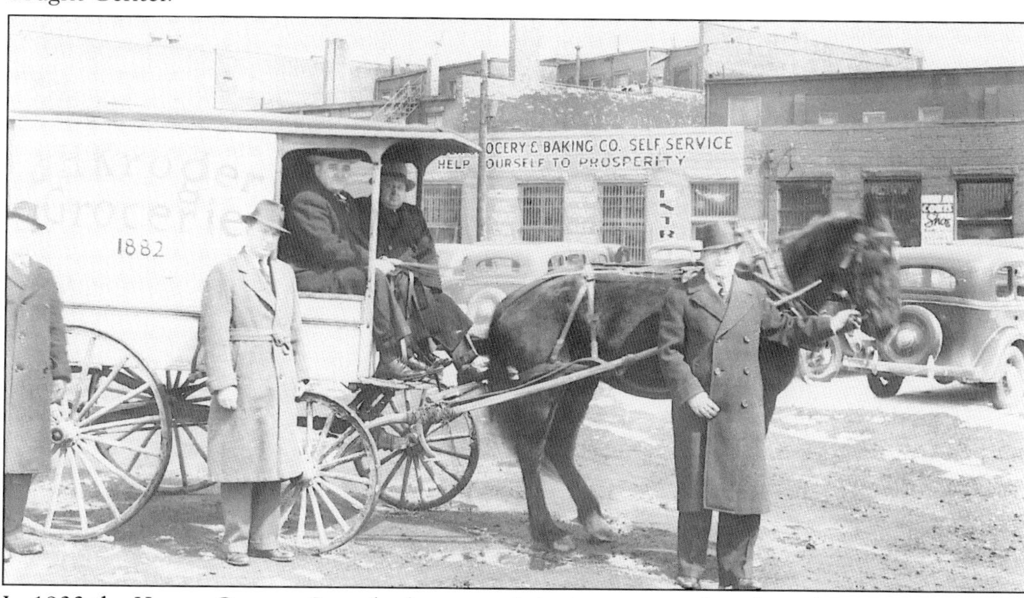

In 1933 the Kroger Grocery Store had preserved their wagon to show how deliveries were made in the 1880s. This scene is in back of the Kroger store that was on Broadway in downtown Lorain. The emphasis in those days was to have quite a few stores spread around town within walking distance for people.

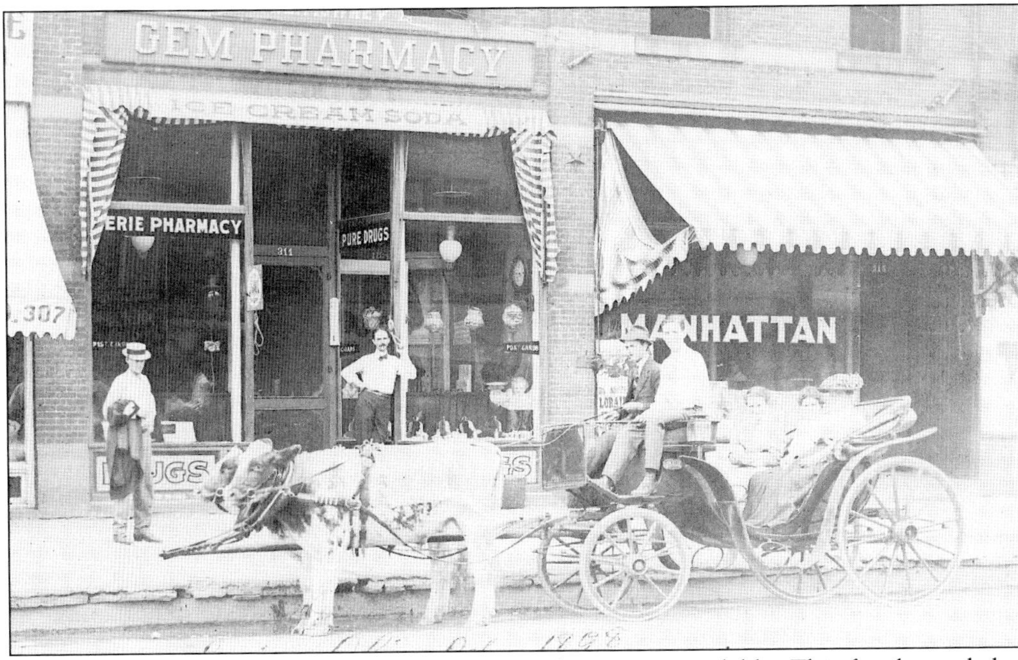

If you do not have a horse to get to town, use whatever is available. This family used their cows or oxen to bring them to market. Around 1898, the Manhattan Market was doing a good business on Broadway. A careful look at the picture shows that the sidewalks were made of wood and the road was not paved.

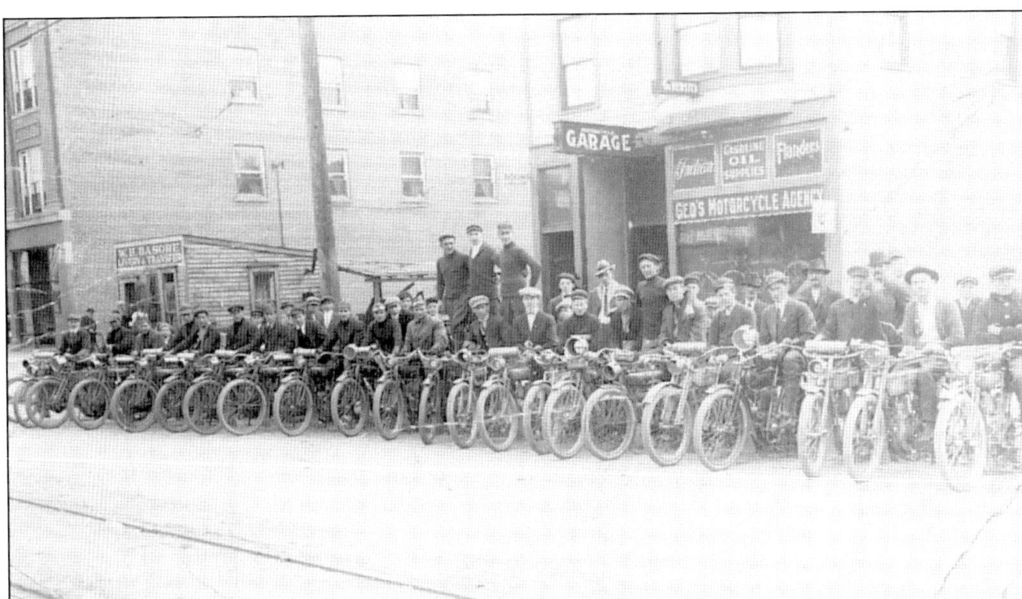

The George Williams Garage specialized in motorcycles. His garage was at 301 West Erie Avenue. It looks like the club will have a "roaring" time on this day in 1914 as they head for the open road. Motorcycles were often used for racing here in Lorain. They could be seen with the trail of dust behind them at the track. Motorcycles were also used for touring and just riding around town.

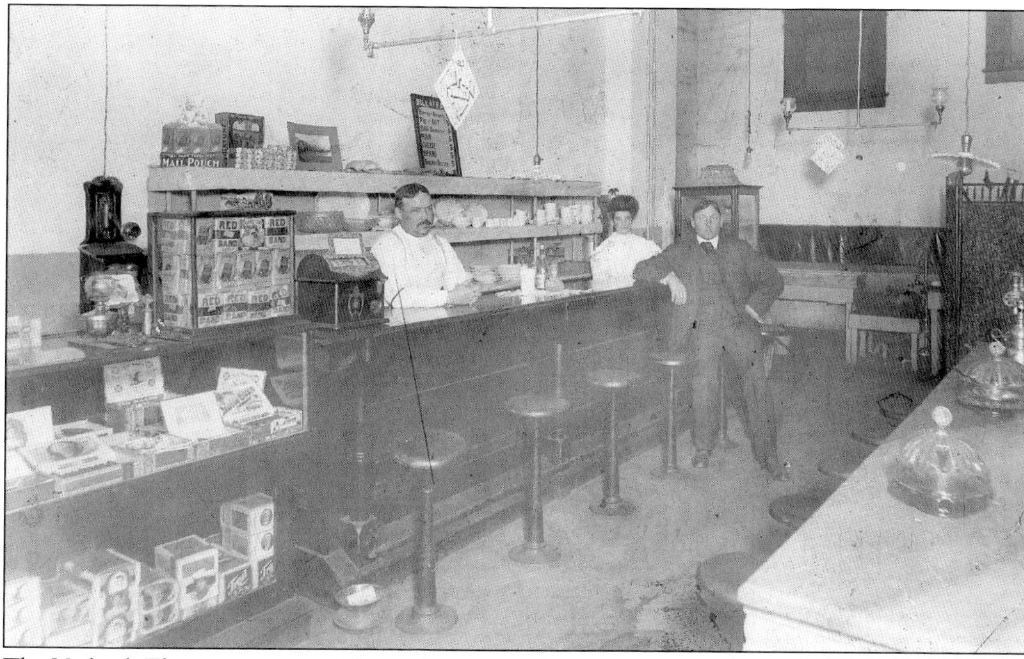

The Verbeck Theater was one of the early centers of entertainment. George H. Verbeck authorized construction in August of 1901. Within 30 days, King & Ashbolt dug the basement. Burgett Brothers built the foundation. The ground floor had 484 seats, and there were two balconies. It opened December 24, 1901, and was quite a grand place for Lorain. The candy store pictured here was in the basement and staffed by Howard and Tina Stone with John A. Stone, customer.

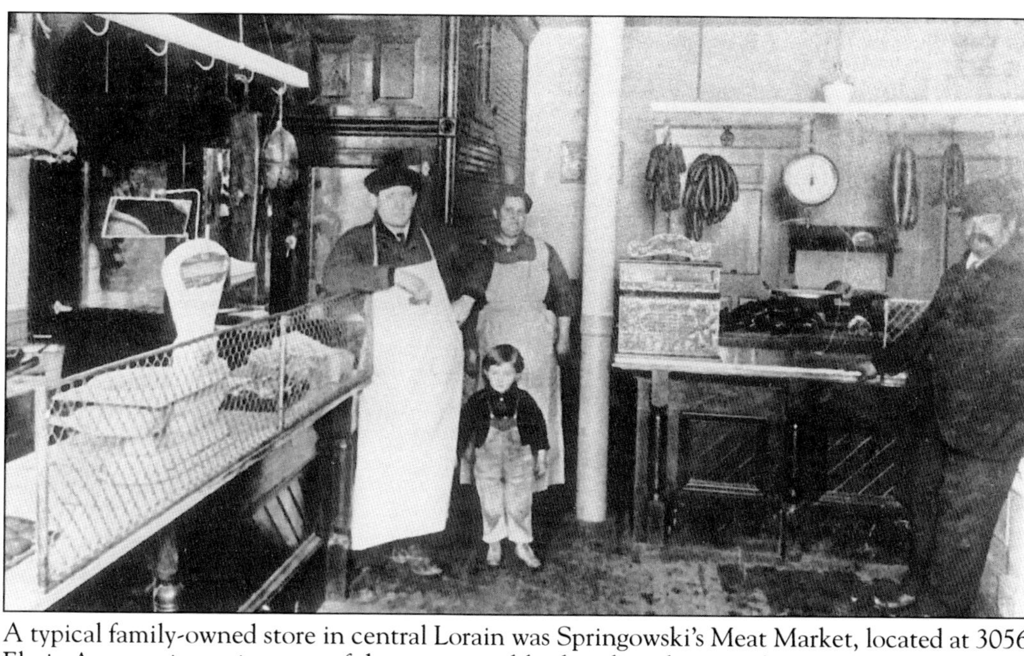

A typical family-owned store in central Lorain was Springowski's Meat Market, located at 3056 Elyria Avenue; it was just one of the many neighborhood markets. In this 1917 picture is owner Ignatius Springowski, his wife Martha, and their son, Walter. An unidentified customer waits to be served.

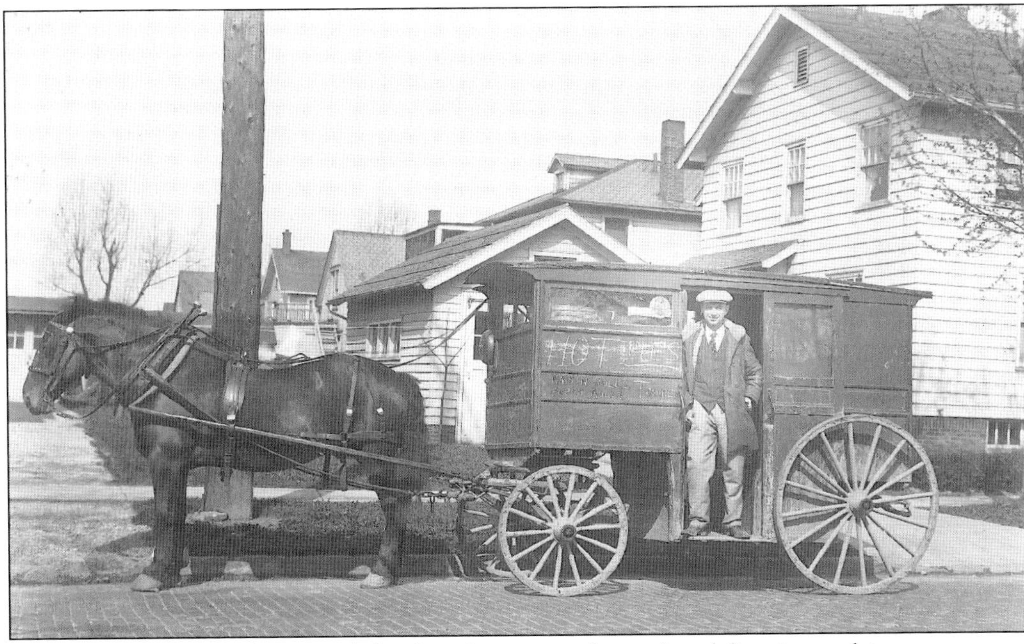

Mr. William Grall is shown with his bread wagon as he makes deliveries on his route around town. Hot pies and warm bread were brought to the people's homes. Mr. Grall became mayor of Lorain in the early 1930s and later was the Lorain County Sheriff.

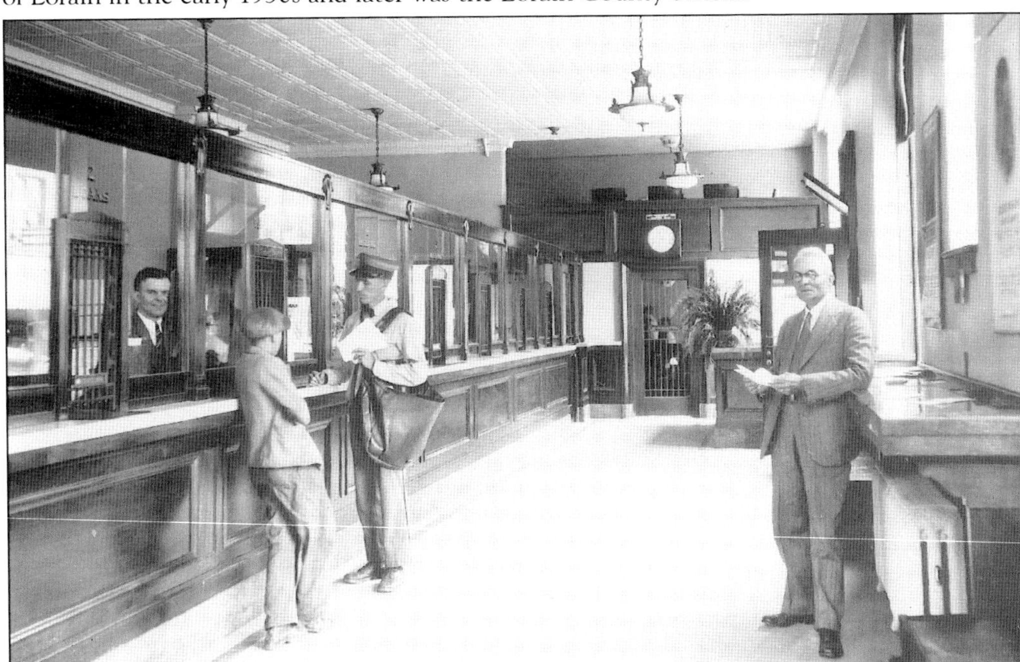

Many banks were formed in the town. One was the Lorain Banking Co. at the southwest corner of Sixth and Broadway. Future Mayor Harry VanWagnen is the teller, and Charles Irish (at the right counter) was executive vice-president of the bank. Notice the typical décor: the marble counter, the teller's protection with bulletproof glass, and cage windows and doors. Later came the open and friendly look.

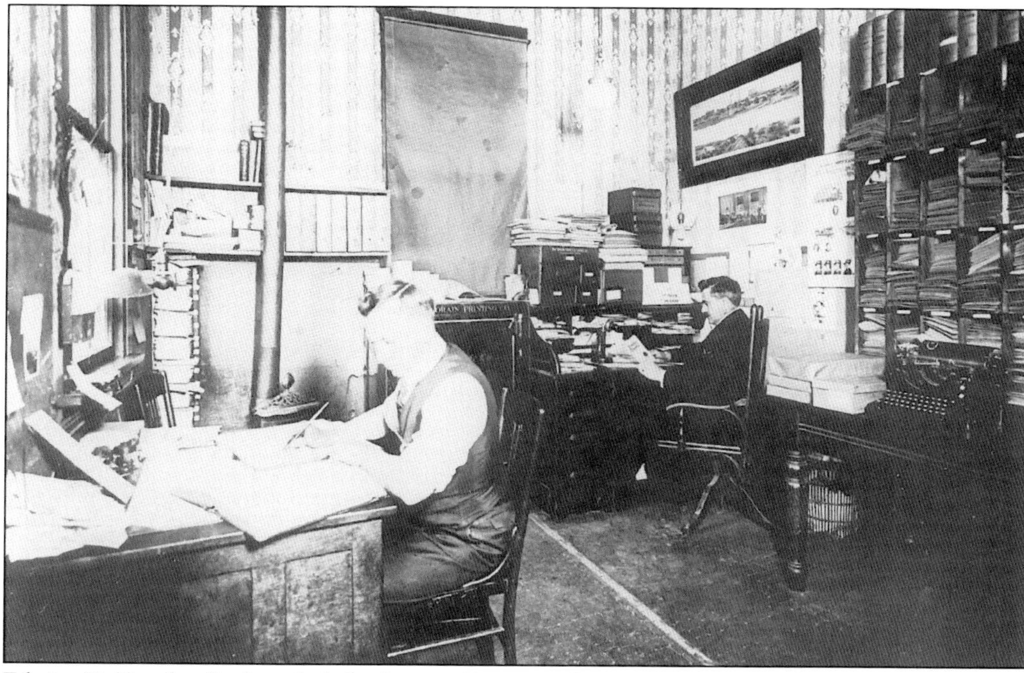

Edwin G. Koethe Sr. founded the Lorain Printing Company in 1905. The first shop was in a small building on Sixth Street. Later, the company moved to 219 Fourth Street, where it did all varieties of printing for many years. A new and greatly enlarged plant was built in 1954 at 1310 Colorado Avenue with many modern innovations.

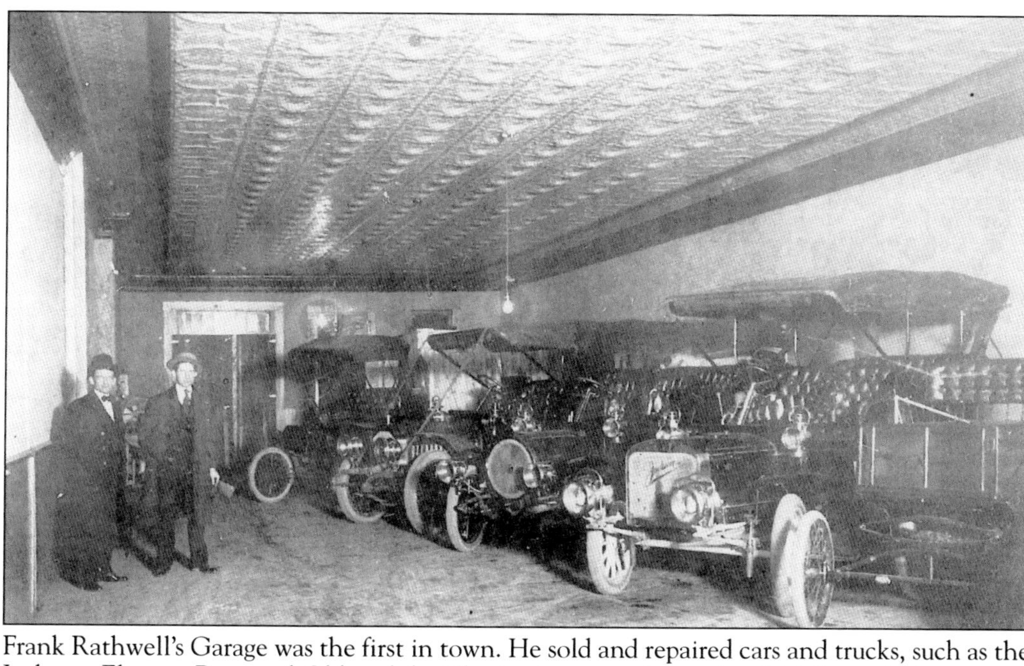

Frank Rathwell's Garage was the first in town. He sold and repaired cars and trucks, such as the Jackson, Elmore, Reo, and Oldsmobile. The business was located at 213 Seventh Street, just west of the town's newspaper building. Later, Mr. Rathwell sold Dodge cars for many years after surviving the Depression.

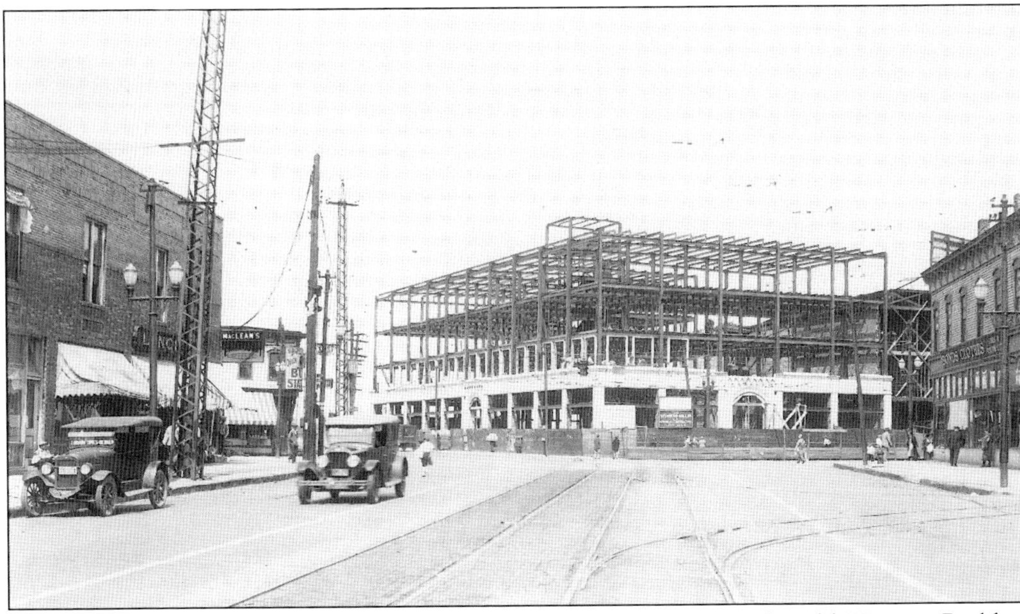

After the tornado of 1924 destroyed much of the downtown area, the old Wagner Building was torn down at the corner of Erie Avenue and Broadway by 1925. A new structure, called the Broadway Building, was constructed on the site of the original Reid House Hotel and the Wagner Building.

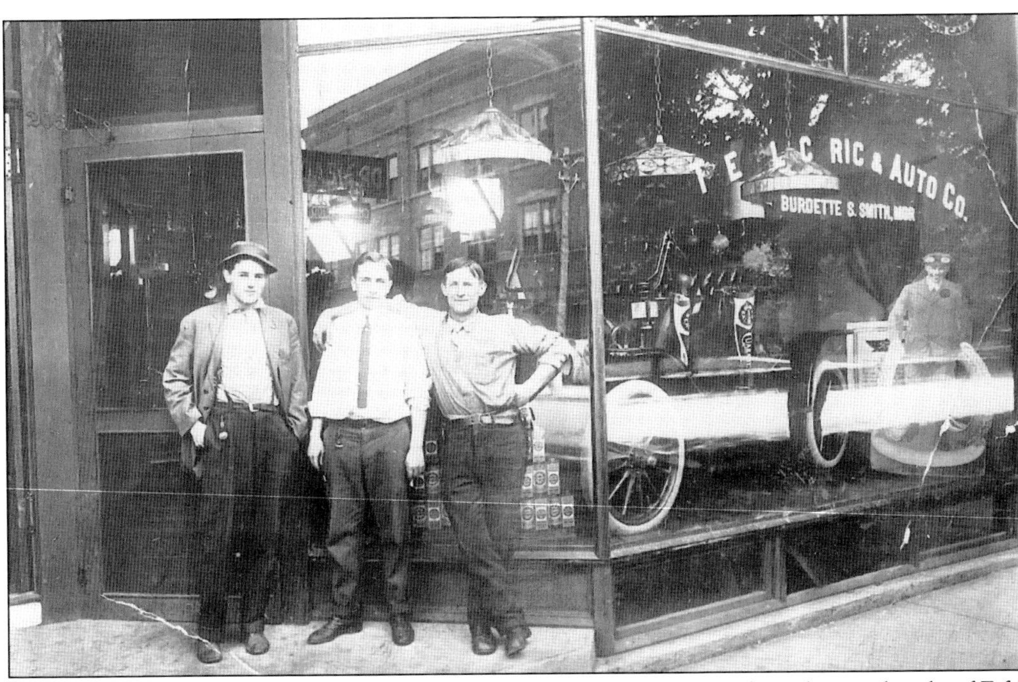

The Electric and Auto Company was a new business that was located on the south side of Fifth Street, just west of Broadway. Burdette S. Smith was the manager. Gasoline and electric cars competed for quite a few years before the gasoline motor was developed enough to beat out the competition.

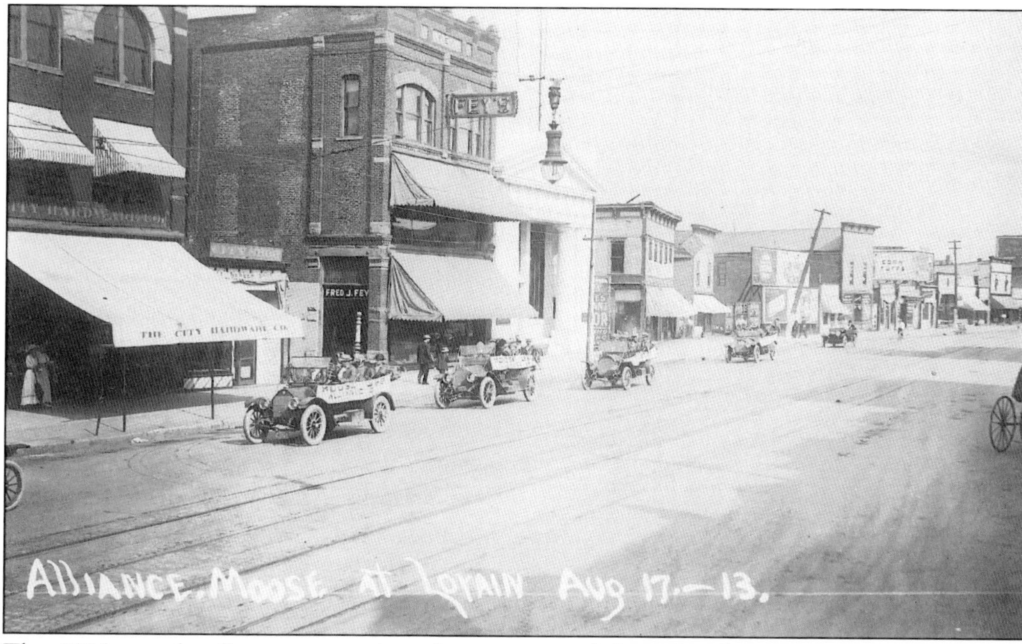

The 1913 parade of cars was to introduce new candidates for the Moose Lodge in Lorain. The picture shows Broadway, near Fifth Street. The National Bank of Commerce is the white building with pillars. It later became the Lorain National Bank. The building to the left of it, in the 400 block, served as the YMCA building for a few years.

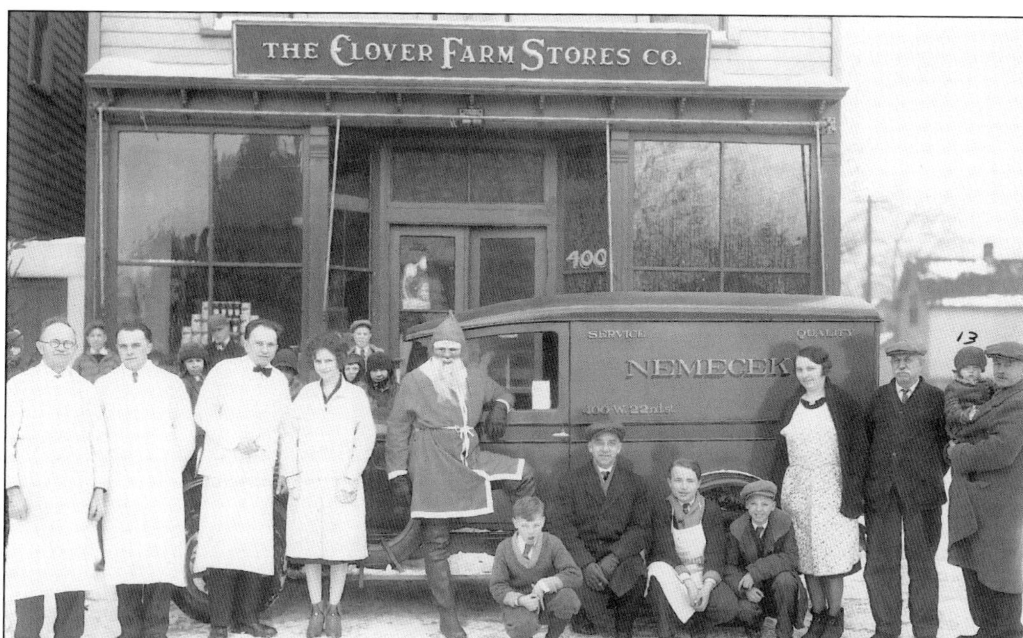

The Joseph Nemecek & Sons Grocery Store even had Santa visit them around the 1930s. At their store on Reid Avenue and Twenty-Second Street, they had a five-pound bag of flour for 29¢, two cans of beets for 19¢, pork loin roast for 15¢ a pound, and a Spang's Bakery butter ring for 15¢. Eating was good in those days.

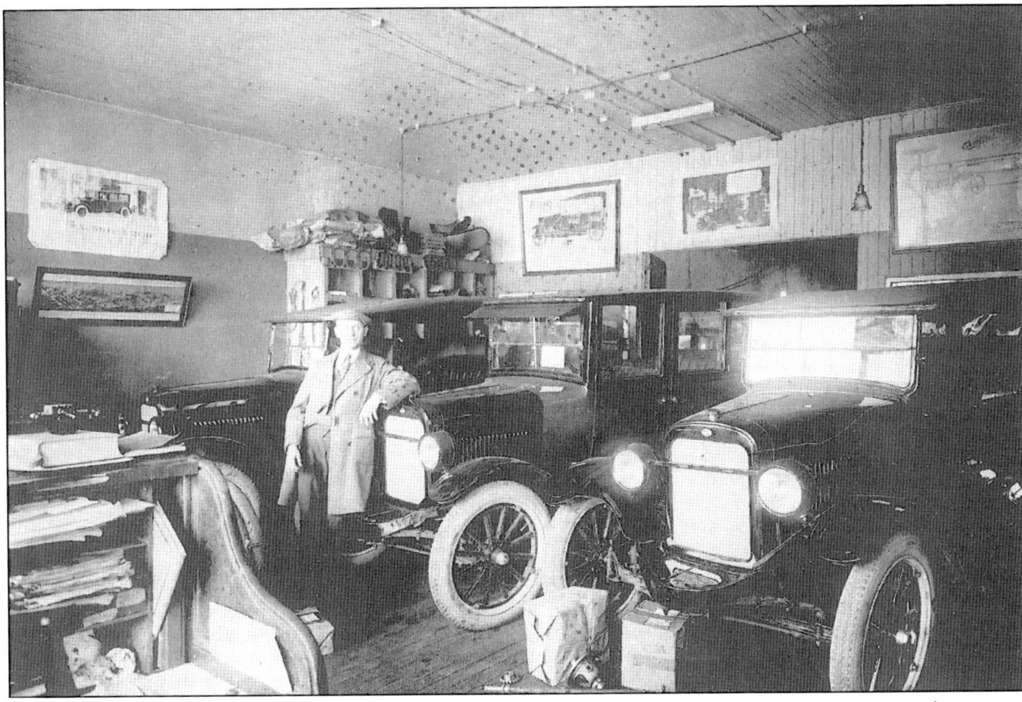

In 1917 Mr. Kilgore left his job as an engineer on the B & O and moved to Lorain. The center of commerce was on North Broadway. Kilgore opened Kilgore Auto Sales in the early 1920s, where he sold Willis-Overland cars. In 1924, just two months before the tornado hit Lorain and destroyed many of the buildings on North Broadway, he moved the agency to Broadway and Twenty-third Street. When Willis-Overland went out of business during the Depression, he became an Oldsmobile dealer until his retirement in 1952. Fred Haff is the salesman in the picture, and his brother, Oscar Haff, was the chief mechanic.

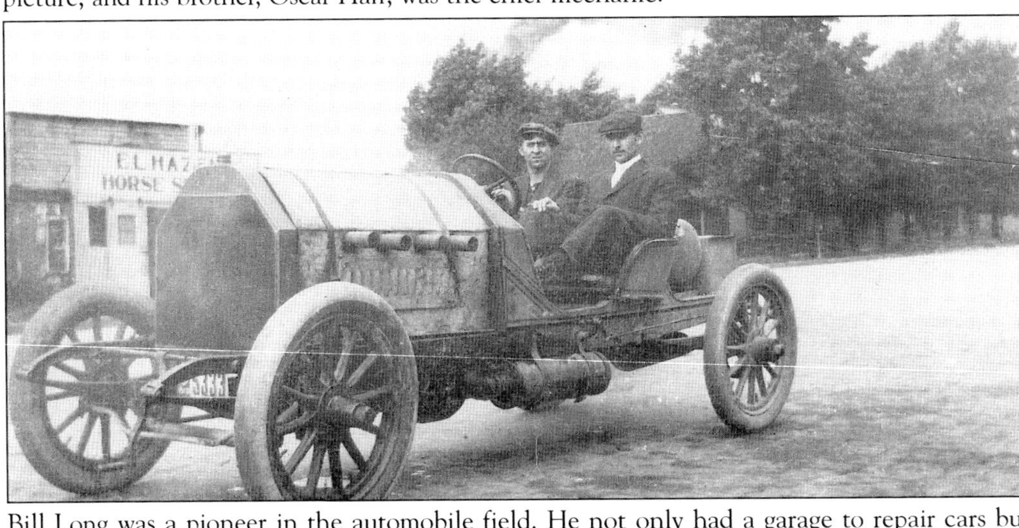

Bill Long was a pioneer in the automobile field. He not only had a garage to repair cars but also built his own racing cars. This is a picture of the "Green Hornet" he built for racing on the track just north of the railway line and Leavitt Road. The track is now referred to as the Kings Woods. Notice the horseshoe business in the background. Mr. Long also started one of the first airports in the town.

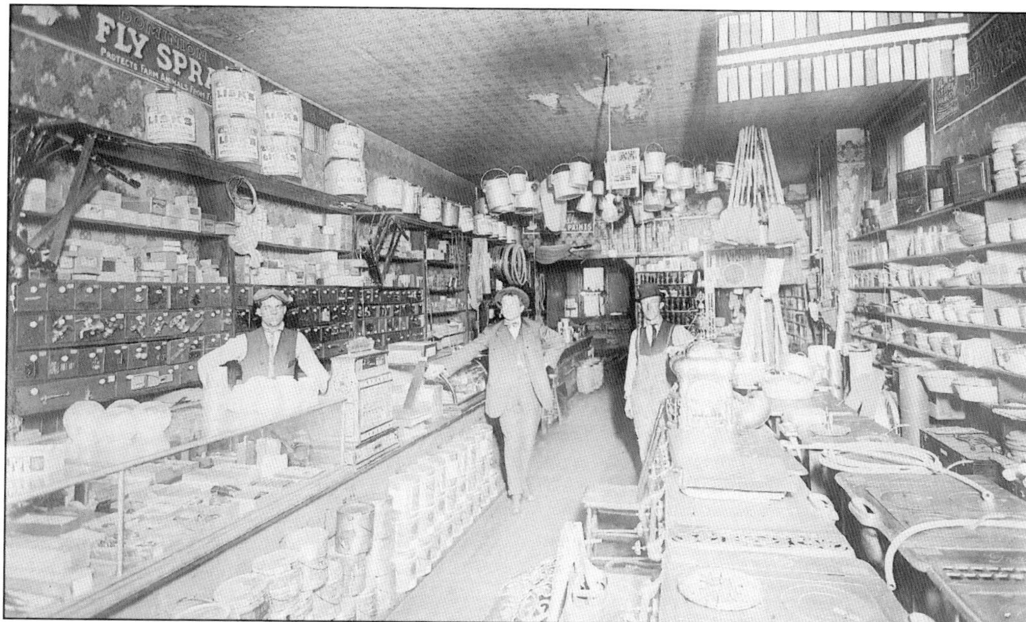

The Geiger Hardware Store shows a typical business in 1914. The clerk would always wait on you and get the items you wanted. Most items were behind the counters, and customers received personal attention in the stores. Hardware stores were almost as numerous as grocery stores, and most of them were local.

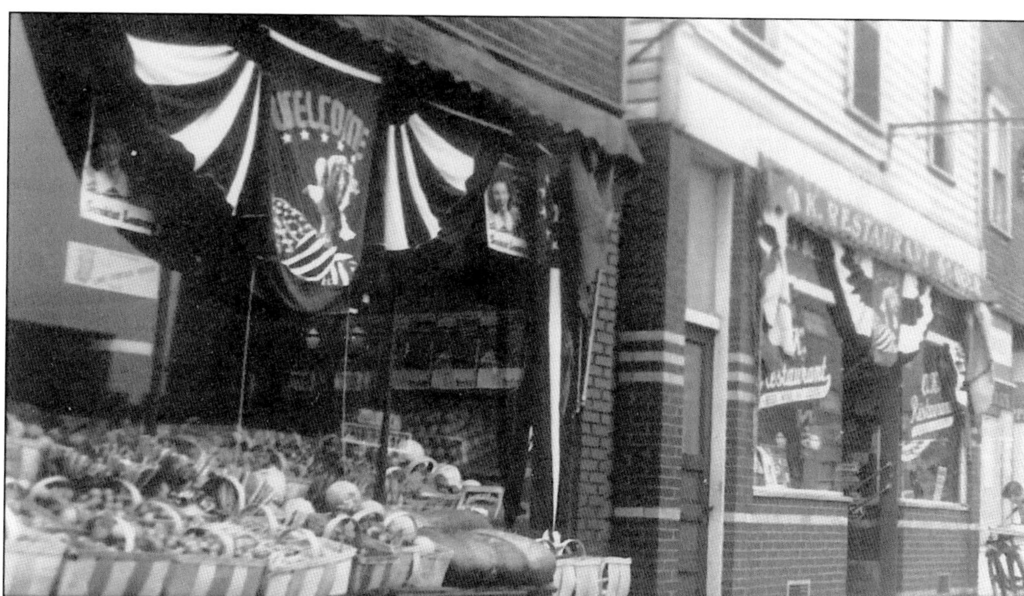

Fazio's Market on Broadway, between Twelfth and Thirteenth Streets, shows a typical grocery store with bulk produce out on the street. You could select some produce, or take an entire basket to the clerk inside. Stealing was not common; everyone in this section of town knew each other, so no one would never get away with it.

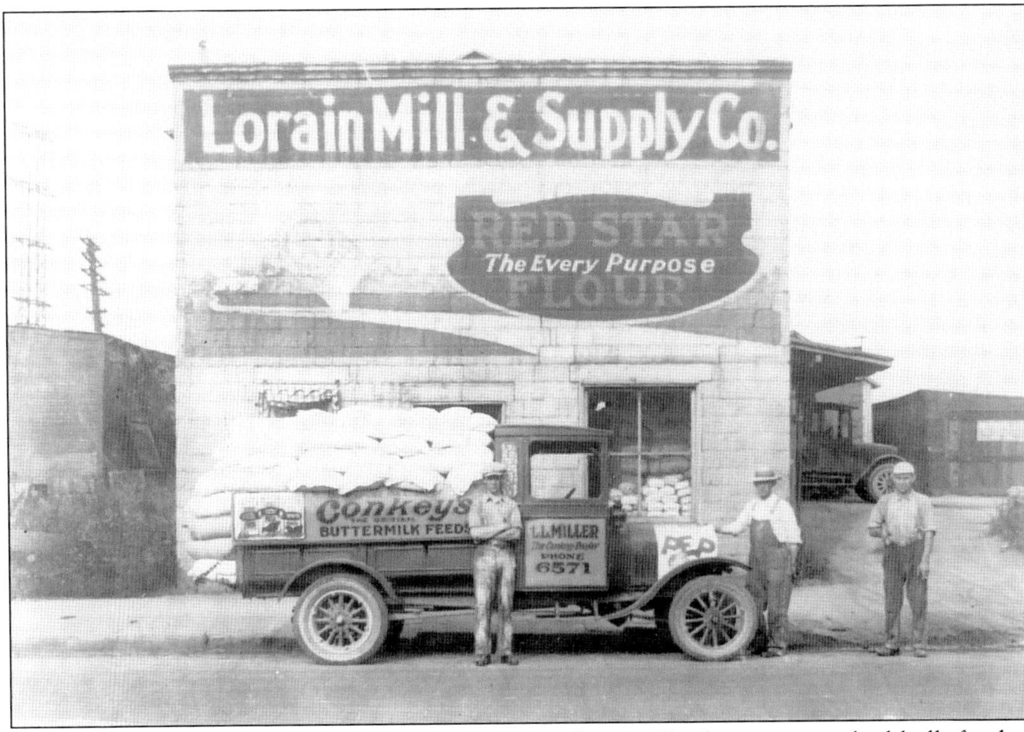

Lloyd Miller was the owner of Lorain Mill & Supply Co. The business supplied bulk food to stores, farms, and bakeries. Sometimes the entire building was filled with bags of grain and flour. Fire was an ever-present threat, and eventually, the building did burn down.

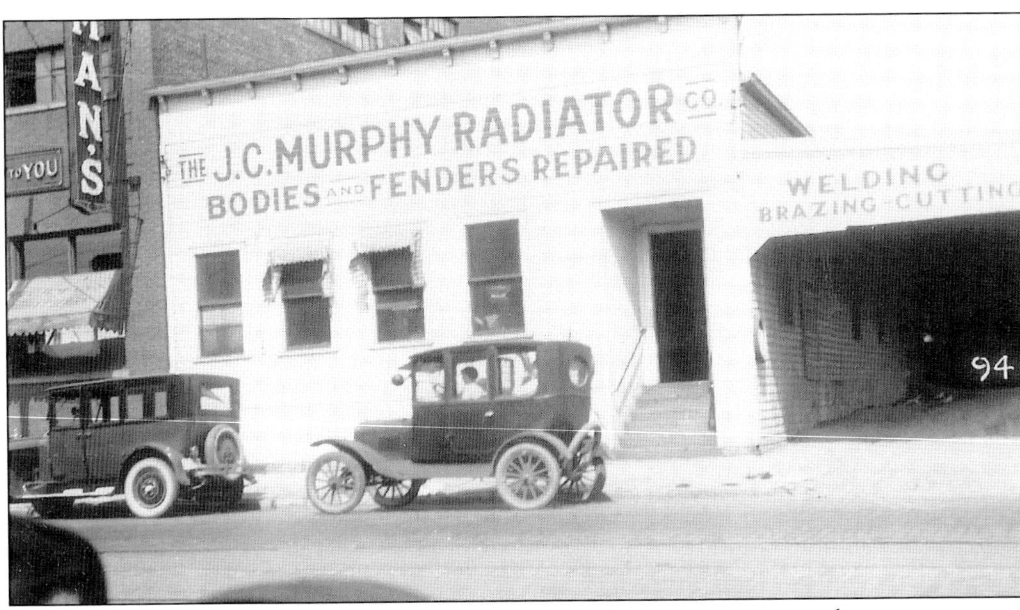

When cars first came to town, there were no stop signs. If you came upon another car at a corner, you would just turn into the other street to avoid it and drive around the block. Sometimes you met the same car at the next corner. When accidents happened, you took your car to a repair shop like J.C. Murphy's, which was located at Broadway and Twelfth Street.

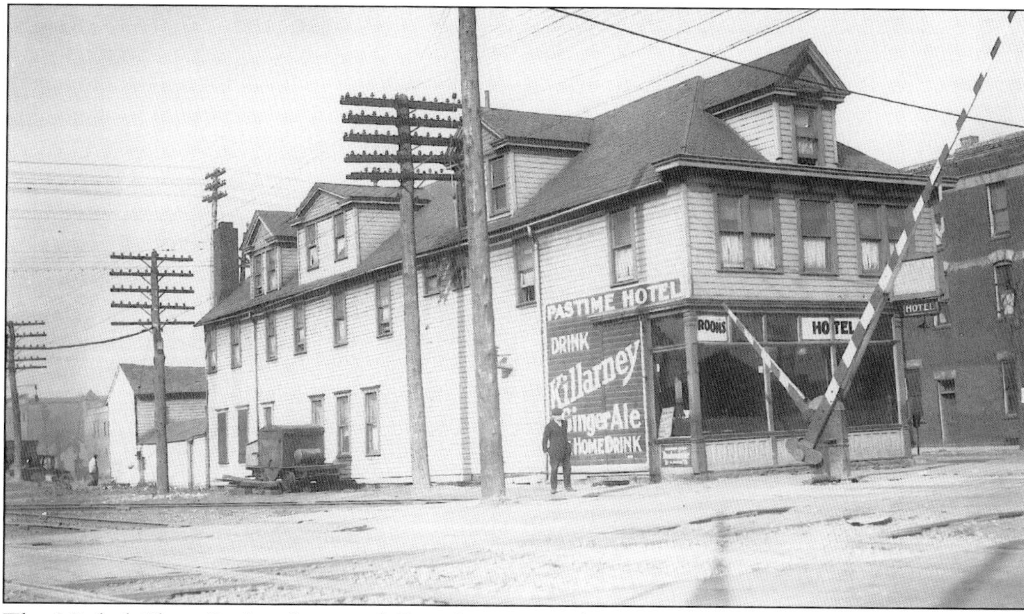

The Nickel Plate Railroad crossed Broadway near the railroad station. This view is looking northwest, where the Lorain Street Railway crossed the Nickel Plate tracks. The Pastime Hotel was almost across from the railroad station.

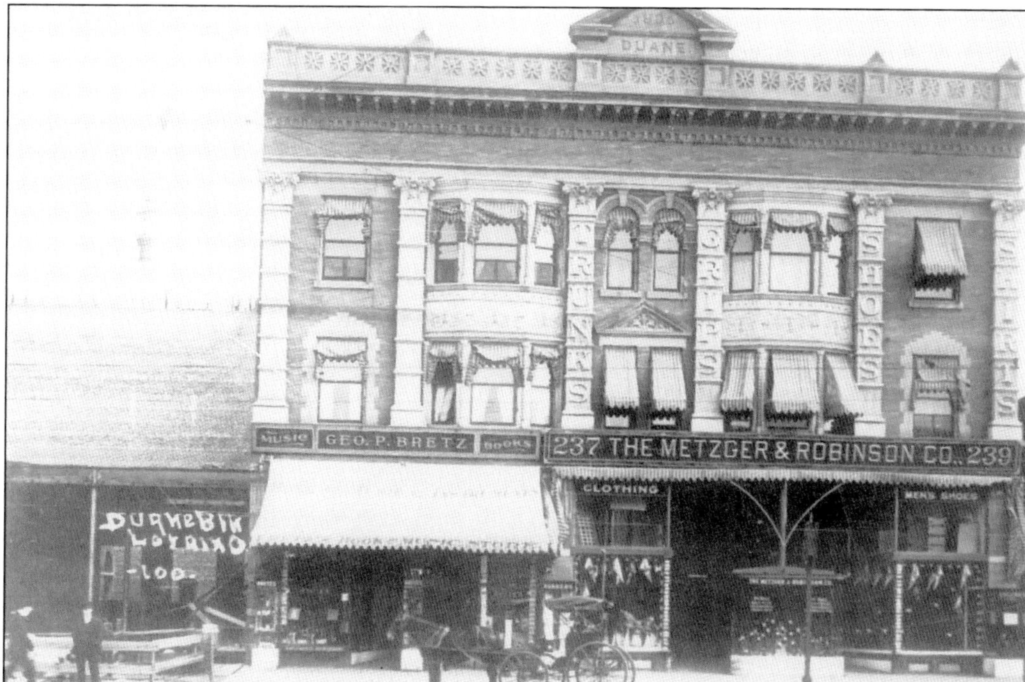

The Duane Building was one of the leading commercial blocks in town. George Bretz had a bookstore on one side. Mr. Bretz later became mayor of Lorain in 1938, and during his administration a tunnel was dug under Black River to supply the east side with its utilities. On the right of the building is the Metzger & Robinson Co. They sold quality clothing and furnishings. Later, the Cleveland Trust Company established offices in the building to the left.

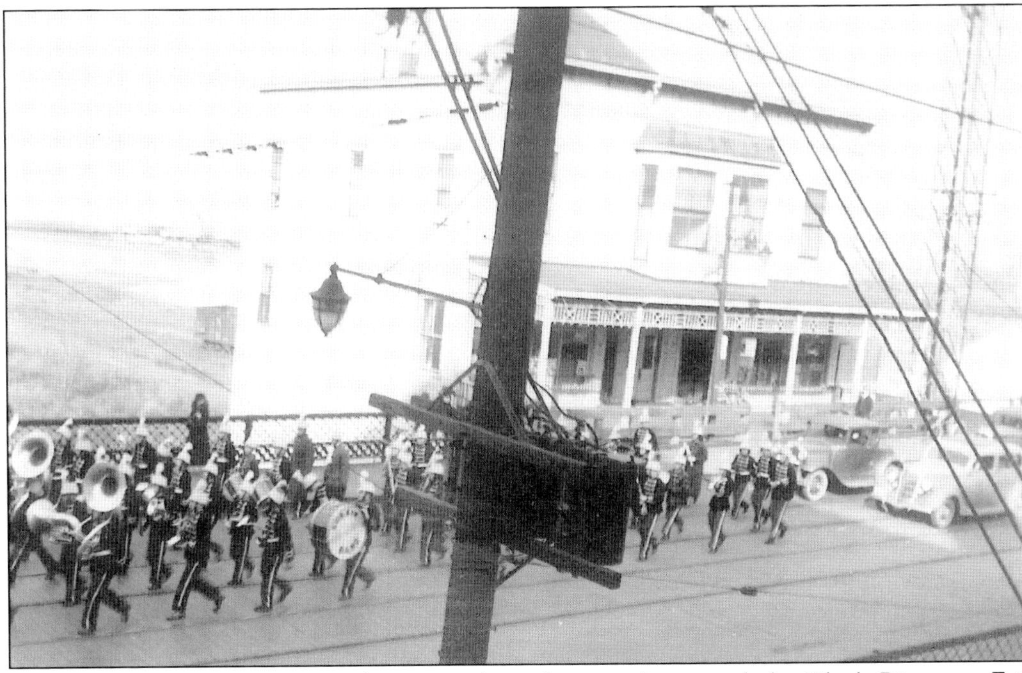

The Swamp Lily Hotel was in business when this parade crossed the Black River on Erie Avenue Bridge. While much swamp land was nearby, the hotel was named for the flower. Its location was just north and across the street from the Broadway Building, at the corner of Erie Avenue and Broadway.

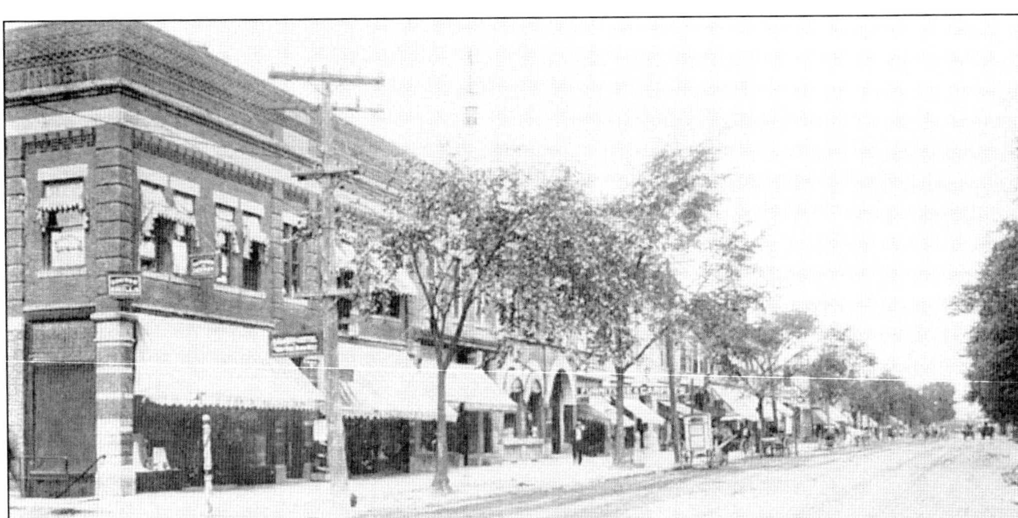

This is a view of the corner at Kent Street (Twentieth Street) and Penfield Avenue (Broadway) looking north. Notice the horse-drawn vehicles and the fact that the street is not paved. St. Joseph's Hospital is just to the left of the picture. It is worth noting that, in 1907, many of the streets in Lorain were renamed.

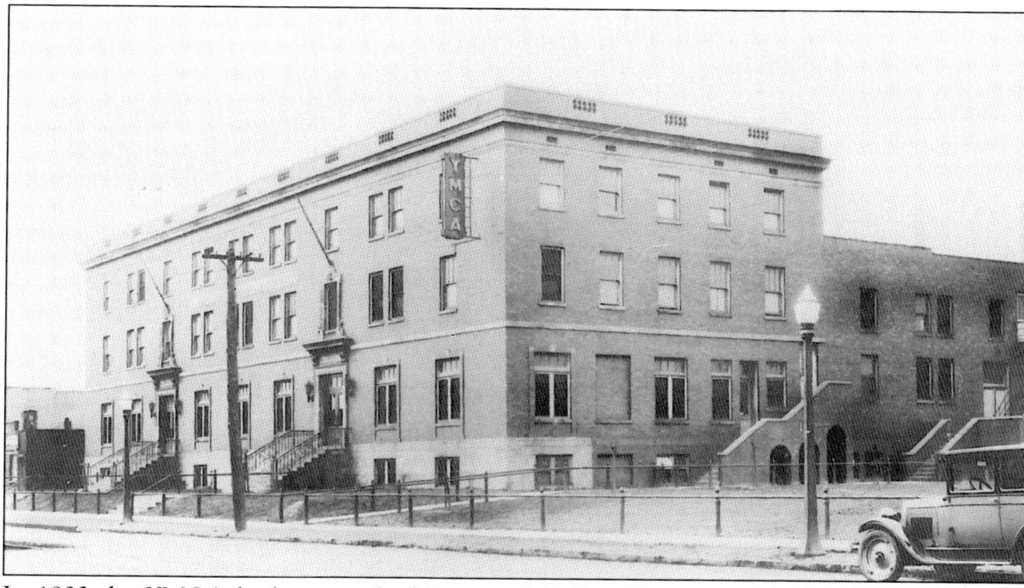

In 1923 the YMCA built a new building at 1769 East Twenty-Eighth Street to replace the structure built in 1899 on the same location. A north-end branch was built on Broadway at Fifth Street in 1904, but it closed in 1908. A new YMCA is now located on Tower Boulevard.

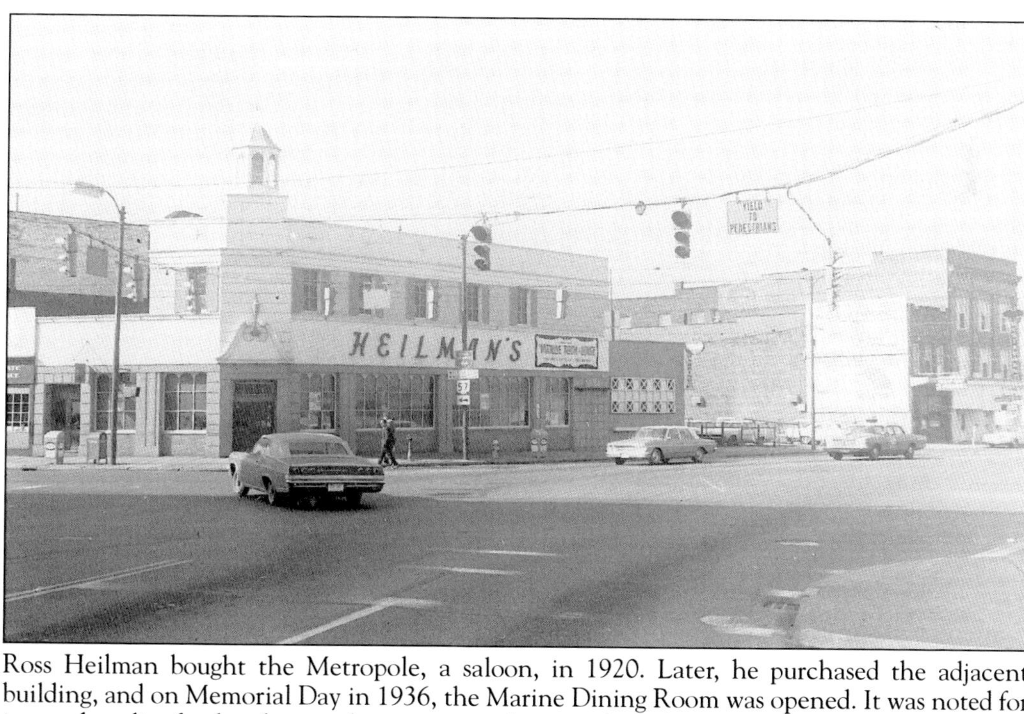

Ross Heilman bought the Metropole, a saloon, in 1920. Later, he purchased the adjacent building, and on Memorial Day in 1936, the Marine Dining Room was opened. It was noted for its good quality food and most pleasant atmosphere, and was located at the southwest corner of Broadway and Erie Avenue. He later opened a branch in Florida.

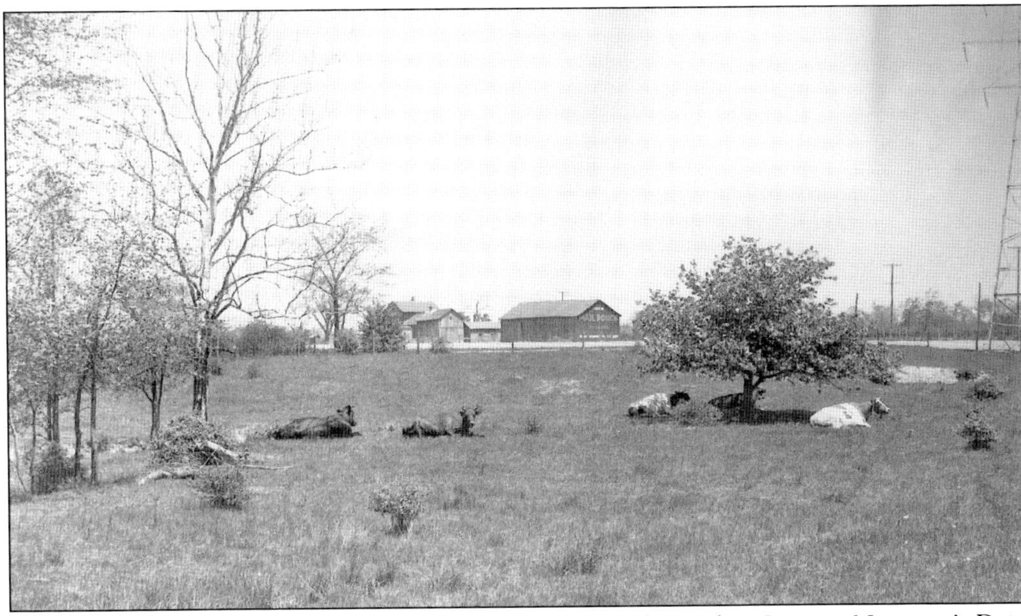

This picture is from 1932, when there were nine dairies located in Lorain. Newman's Dairy Farm was one of them. It was situated on the northwest corner of Oberlin Avenue and Meister Road. It seems difficult to believe that cows once grazed there. This farm was later turned into an airport and then into a commercial and housing development.

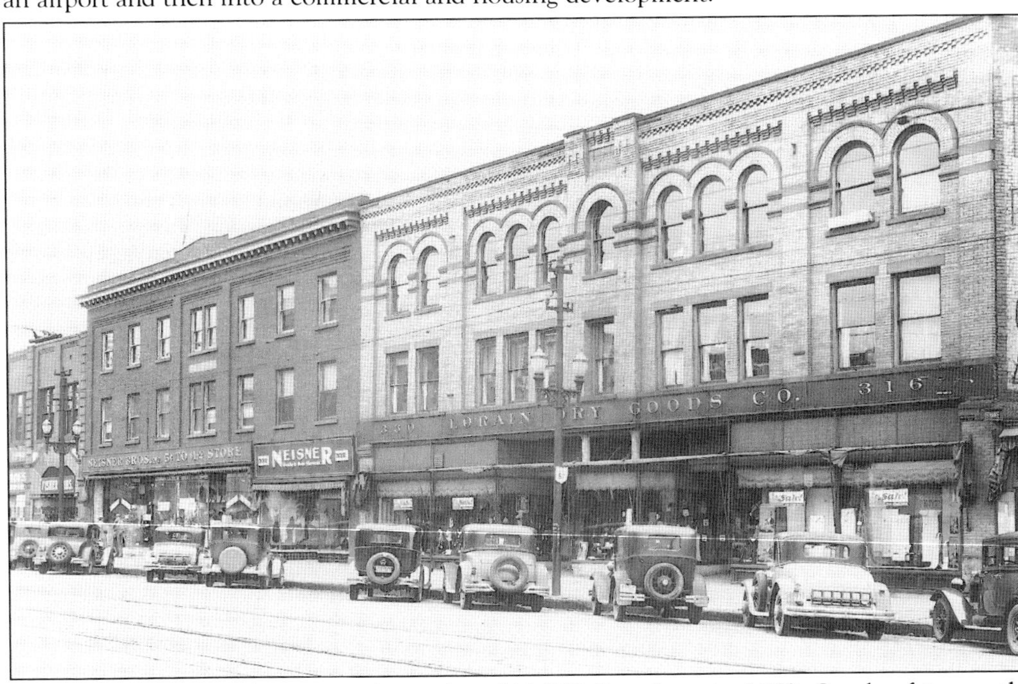

The Lorain Dry Goods Co. was located at 316-330 Broadway in 1933. South of it was the Neisner Dime Store. Later, Neisner's moved into the Lorain Dry Goods building, and when they closed, a Fisher's Grocery Store was in business there for years. Notice the tracks on Broadway. The streetcar tracks were removed in 1939, when buses came to town, and Broadway was repaved.

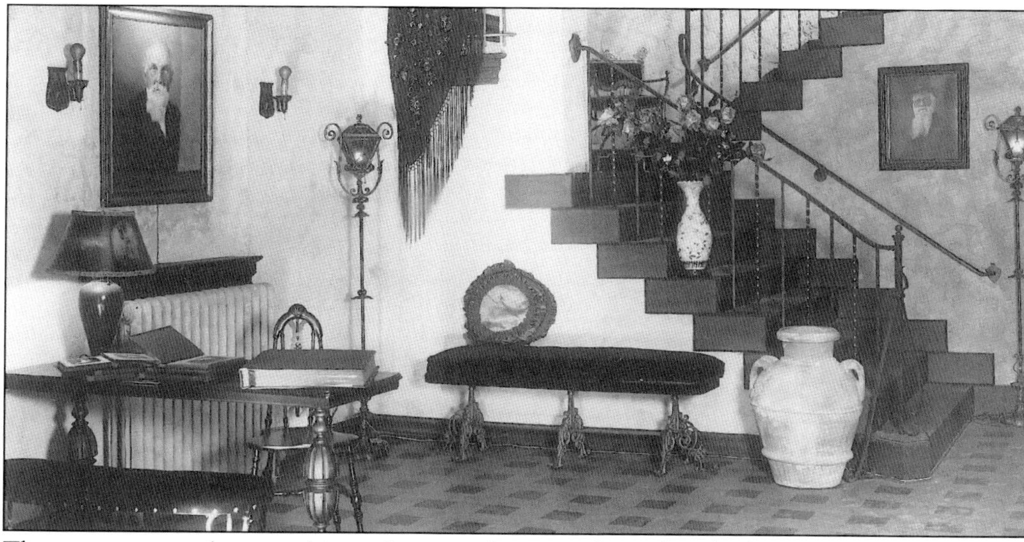

There were many photographic studios over the years. Started in the late 1800s, Leiter's was one of the earliest and provided many historical pictures as well as portrait work. His book, *Leiter's Souvenirs of Lorain, Ohio*, was very popular. Later, Michael's Studio at Seventh and Broadway, and Rudy Moc Studios at 1939 Broadway were two of the best-known photographers. Rudy Moc was also known for his pictures of the Lorain tornado of 1924 and for the book of pictures he published.

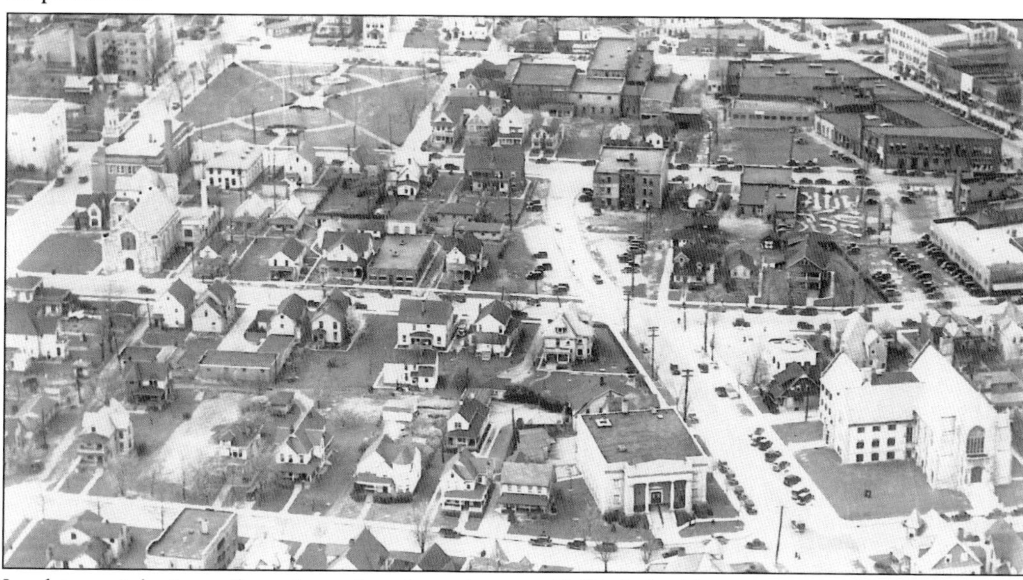

In this aerial view of northern Lorain, taken in 1937, Lake Erie is just to the north. Black River is to the right (off the picture), with the Broadway Building at the top right and stores to the south. The two churches at the bottom right are the First Methodist Church and the Emmanuel Evangelical Church, separated by Reid Avenue, which was named for the pioneer Reid family. The Moore House, now home of the Black River Historical Society, is in the center. The house at the extreme left center was the home of the Porters, who owned a hotel on Broadway and Tenth Street called the Porter House. Across the street are the Christian Temple, Congregational church, Masonic Temple, and Antlers Hotel. City Hall is across from the Washington Avenue Park.

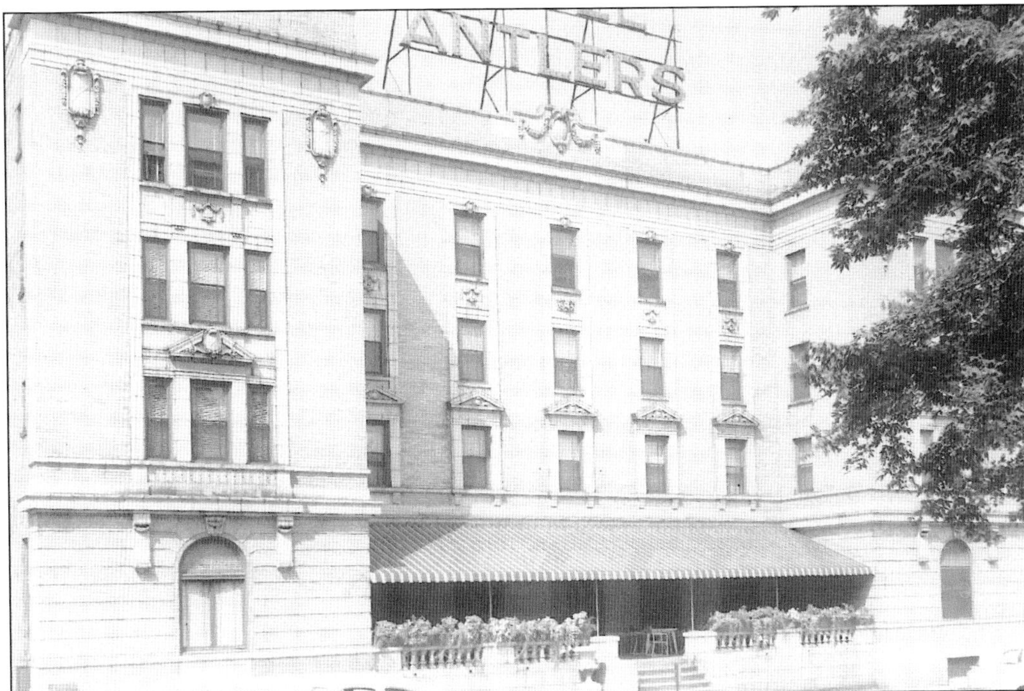

The Antlers Hotel was built in 1922 by the Fraternal Order of Elks. The hotel was very successful through the 1950s, when it fell into disrepair and was finally abandoned in the early 1970s. In 1984 Jon Veard bought the building, rehabilitated it and turned it into 34 luxury apartments, a restaurant, and offices. The building is on the National Registry of historic buildings.

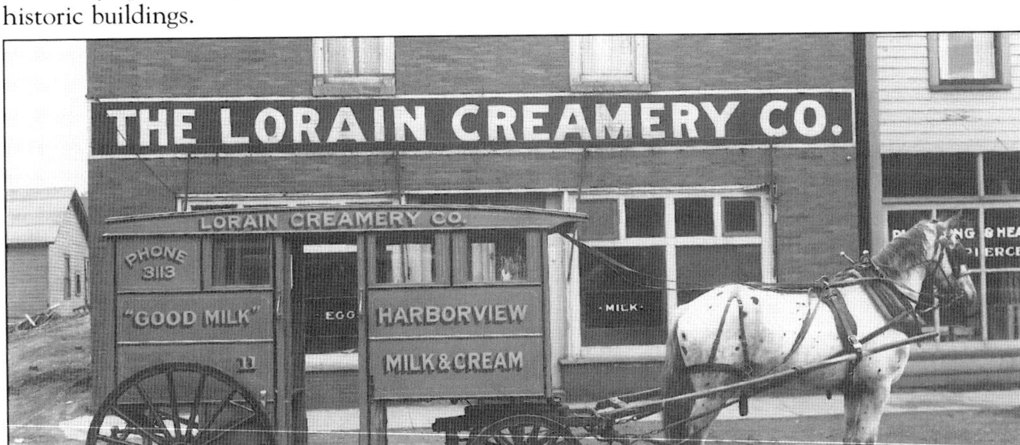

Milk used to be delivered to the house every other day by horse-drawn wagons. Originally the only refrigeration was by ice in the icebox, thus people could not buy very far ahead because of spoilage. This Lorain Creamery wagon was one of the last to be in service. It was a metal wagon although earlier models were made of wood. The wagon was horse-drawn and the milkman would take glass milk bottles (not cartons) with him for three or four houses. The horse would know the route as well as the driver and would meet the man at the end of the block.

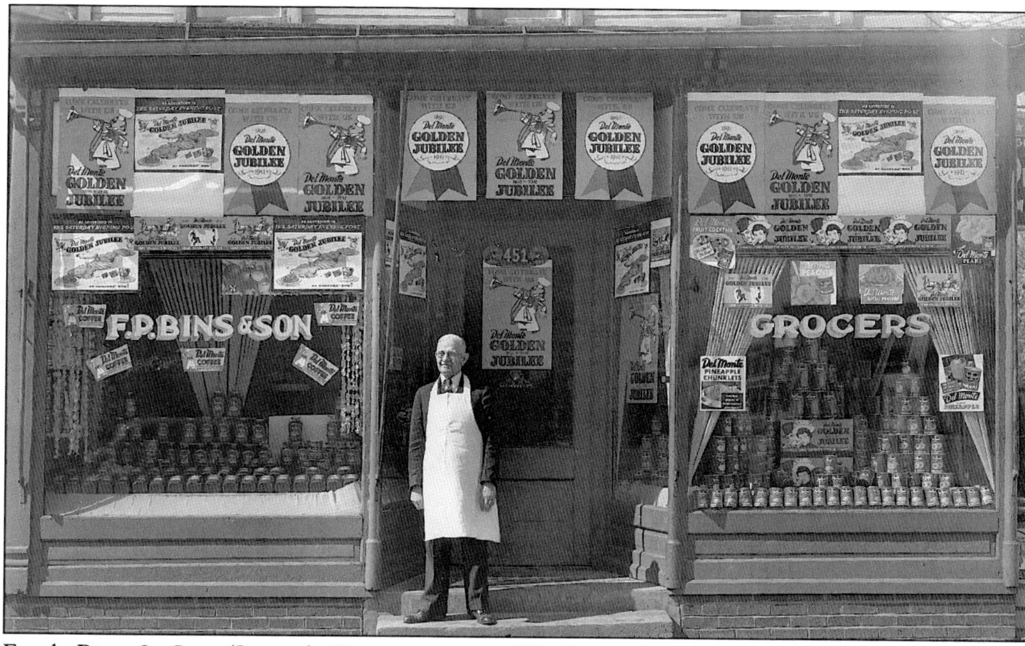

Frank Bins & Son (Jimmy) Grocers was at 451 East Erie Avenue, as shown in this 1941 picture. The Bins ran a quality grocery on the east side. They bought cheese in large wheels and let it continue to age in the basement before they would sell it at the peak of its fine taste. Bins is an example of the many small grocery stores that were within walking distance for a neighborhood.

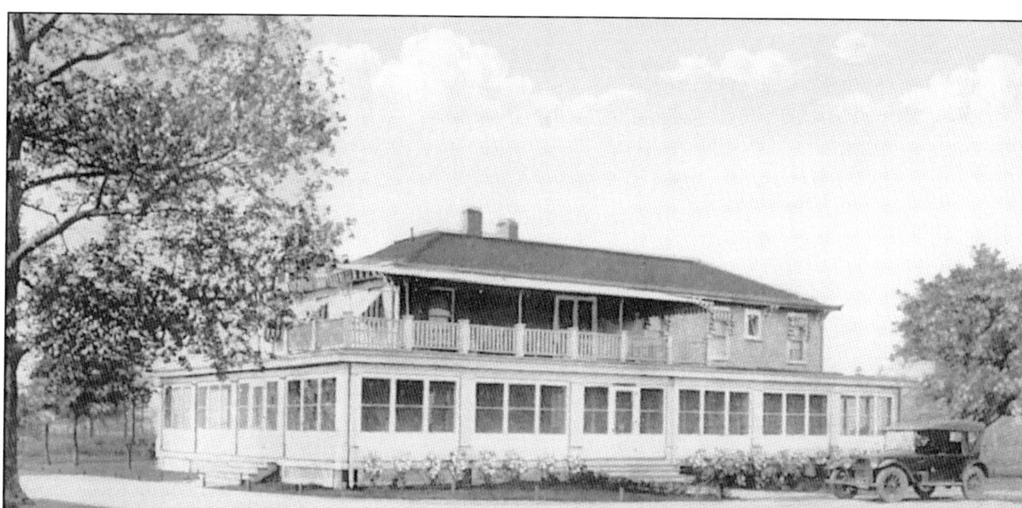

The Lorain Country Club was one of the centers for entertainment and golf in the town. The building was near the undercut for the railroad, west of Leavitt Road. The course itself is where the present-day Sherwood Allotment of homes is located. The building was not used after the early 1940s and was destroyed by fire in 1954.

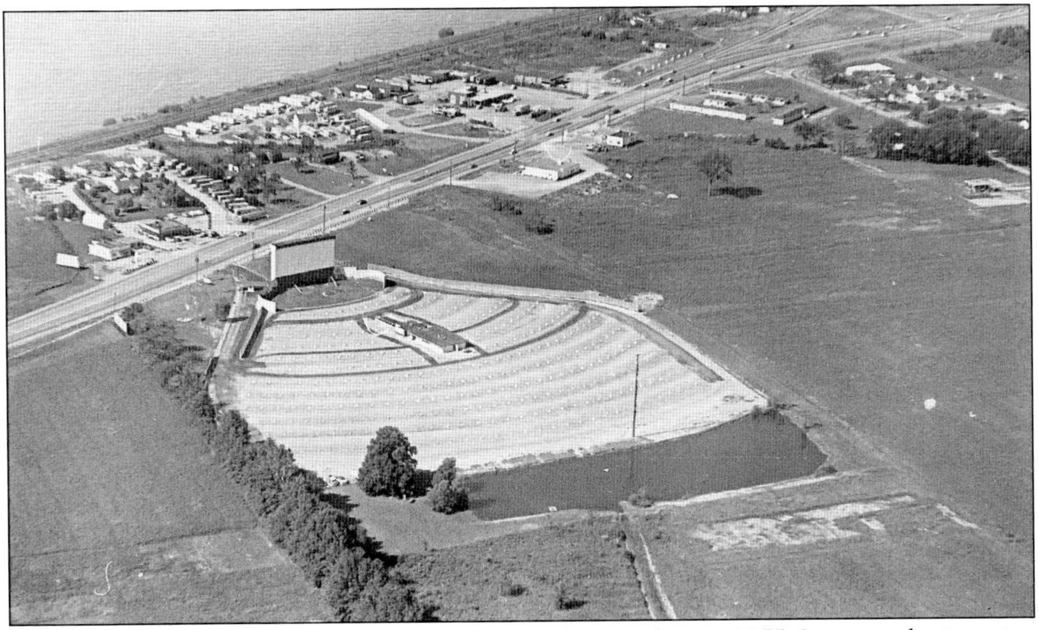

The Lorain Drive-In Theater is shown in this aerial view taken in 1955. It was at the junction of Route Six and Twenty-First Street. Also in this view is Lake Erie at the top, the old Blahay Trucking Co., A&W Restaurant, and Ed's Place Motel.

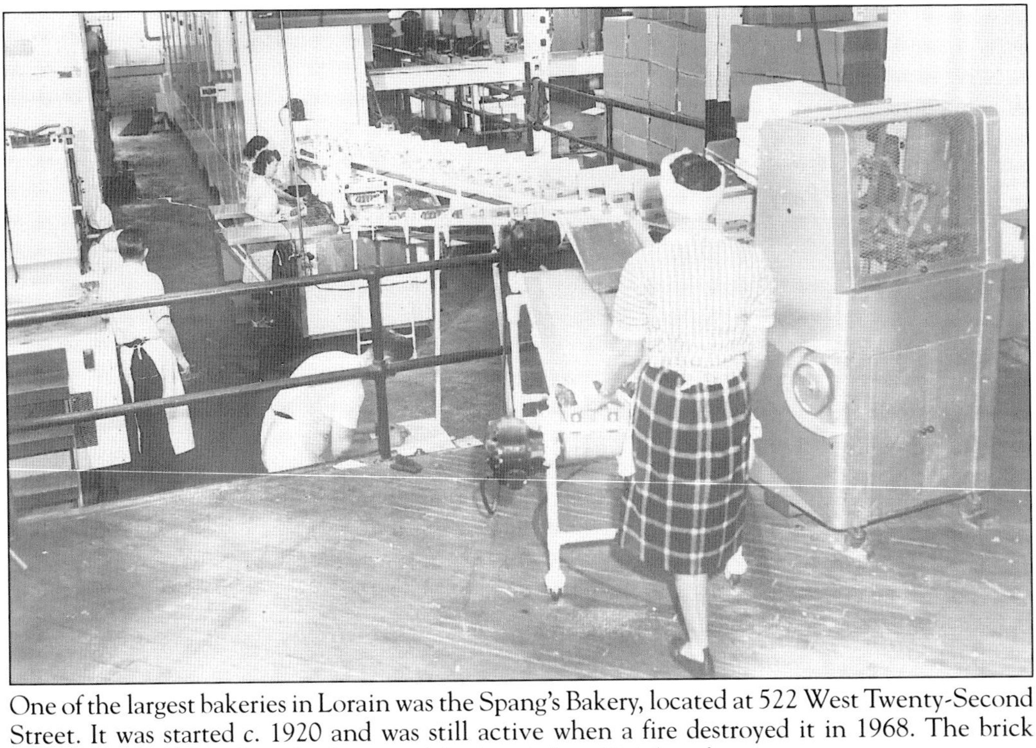

One of the largest bakeries in Lorain was the Spang's Bakery, located at 522 West Twenty-Second Street. It was started *c.* 1920 and was still active when a fire destroyed it in 1968. The brick ruins of the building furnished material for Lorain's artificial reef.

Lorain Auto Parts was a major supplier for garages and home mechanics in the Lorain area. Lewis Conn and William Scutt were partners for a while, and then Conn bought the business. For three generations either he, his son, Wayne, or his grandson, George, operated it until it was sold in December 1998. The business was moved many times.

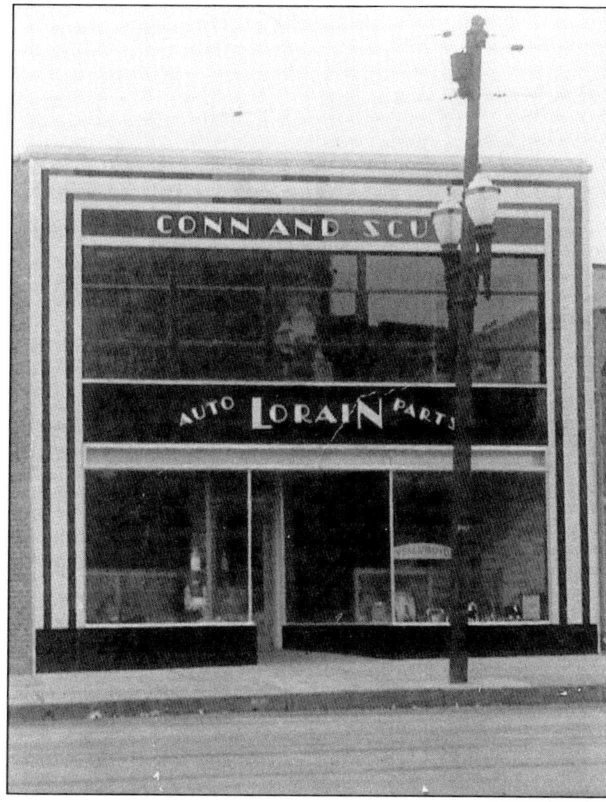

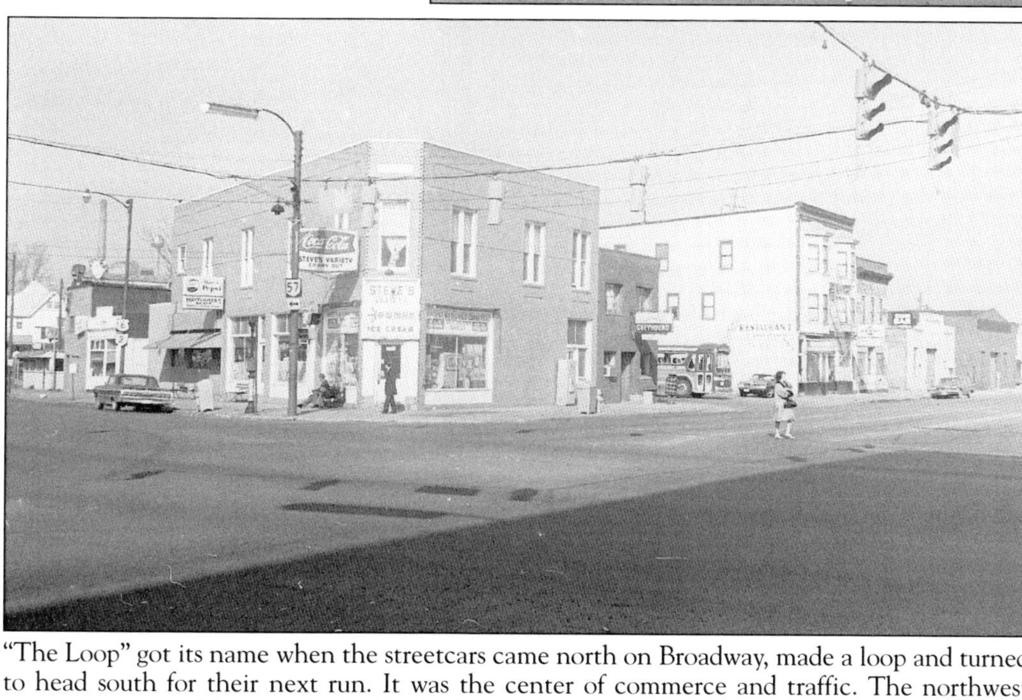

"The Loop" got its name when the streetcars came north on Broadway, made a loop and turned to head south for their next run. It was the center of commerce and traffic. The northwest corner, as pictured here in the 1960s, had many businesses, including the bus station. In 1973 this entire area was leveled and a new City Hall and police station were erected.

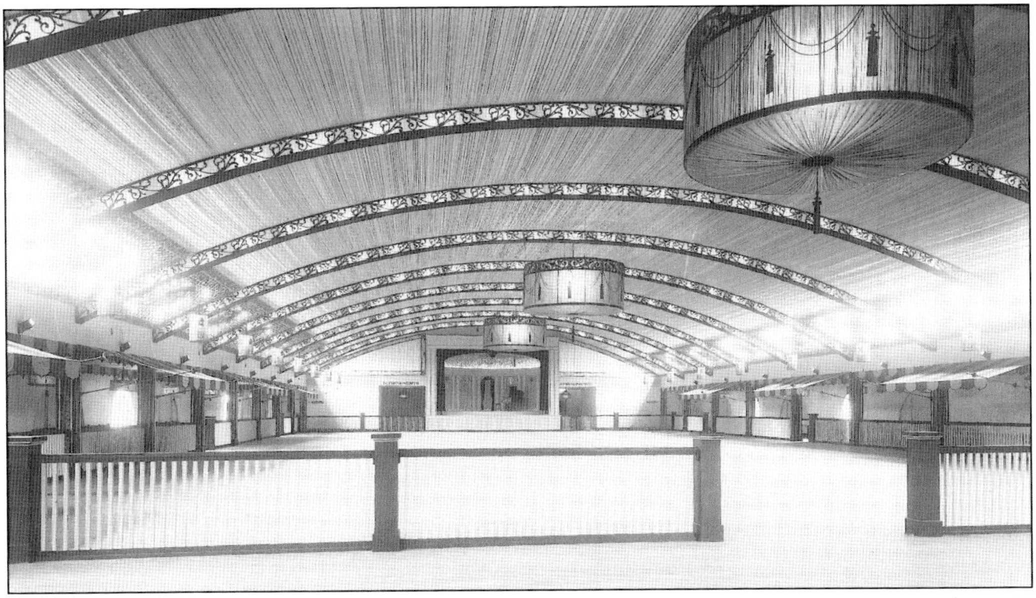

West of the city limits was the location of the Coliseum. The Lorain Moose Lodge Number 552 built it in 1926 at a cost of $115,000. The building served as a center for skating, dances, and entertainment for many years. The structure burned down the night of May 5, 1952.

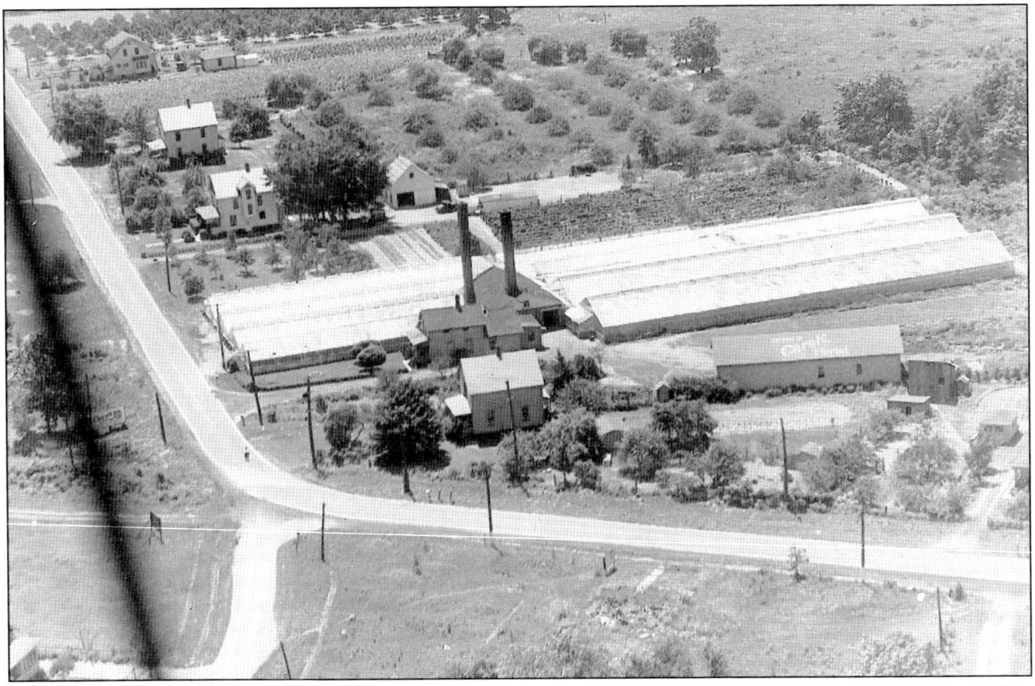

Carek Florist has been a popular source of flowers in time of need and appreciation. This picture shows the home, power plant, greenhouse, and business buildings c. 1910 at "Penfield Junction," near Clearview School. Frank Carek started the business by peddling flowers in Lorain from a horse-drawn cart. The Carek family worked at the greenhouse or at their meat market on Thirty-First Street and Broadway.

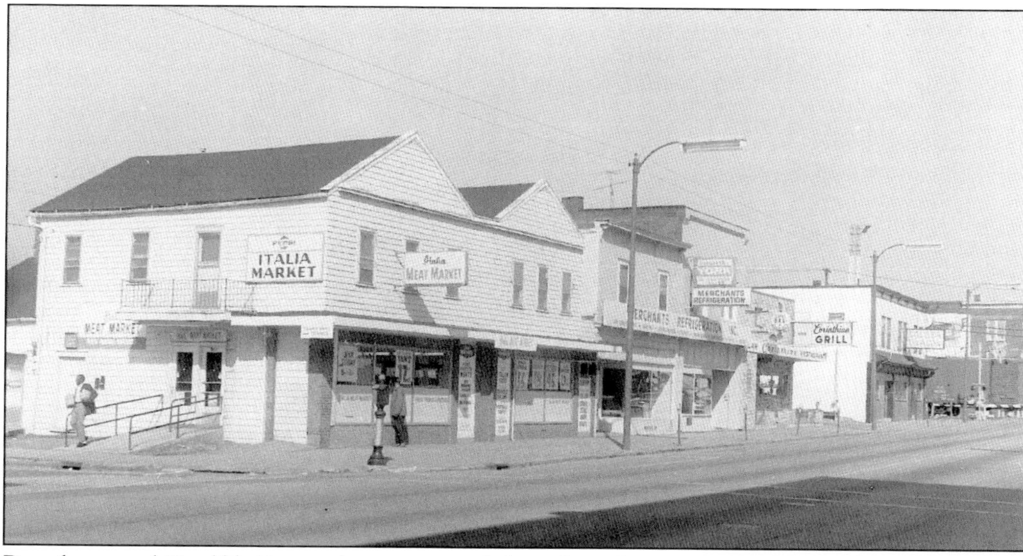

Broadway and Twelfth Street shows some of the ethnic businesses in town. The Italia Market was famous for its foods from Italy. The Corinthian Grill (Greek food), and the Golden Dragon (Chinese food) were very popular places to eat.

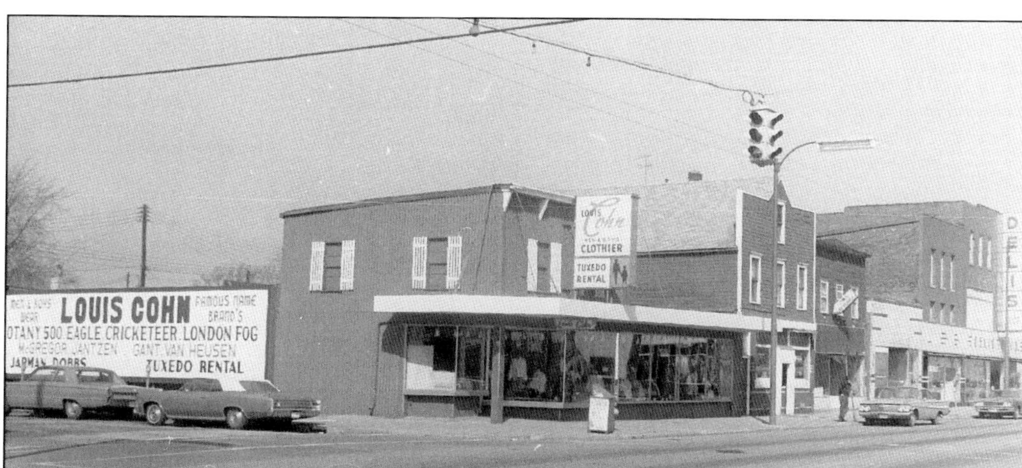

Central Lorain's business district is shown in this photograph. Louis Cohn was a clothing store that was popular with the men in town. Just down the street was one of the very successful furniture stores run by the Delis Brothers.

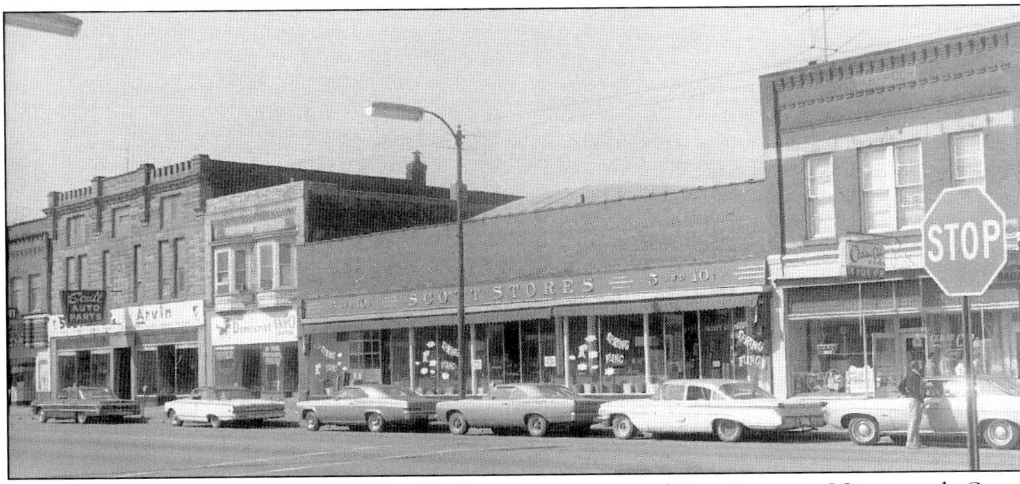

Scott's Dime Store was another popular business in central Lorain, near Nineteenth Street on Broadway. Further south was Scutt's Auto Parts store. These stores were popular during the mid-1900s.

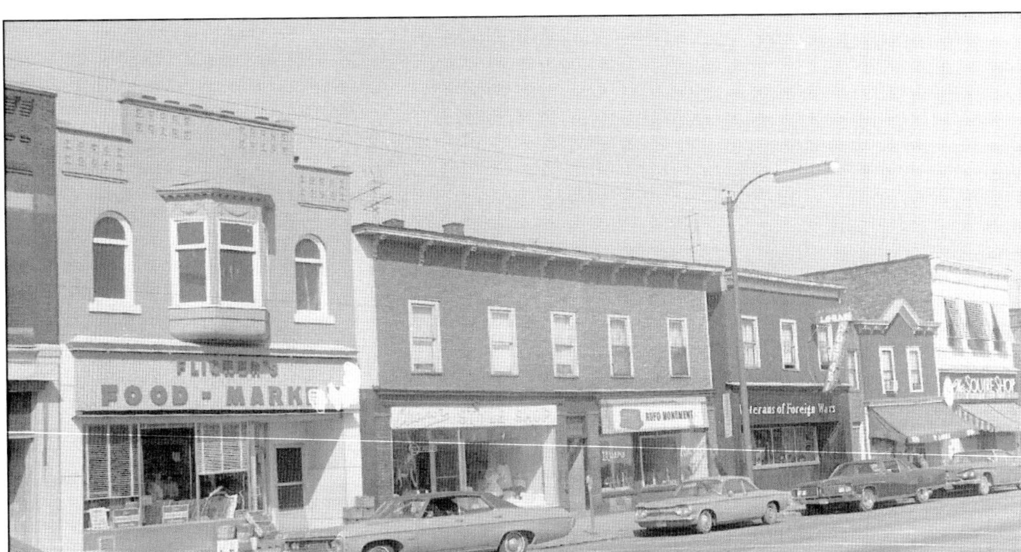

Fligner's Food Market, one of Central Lorain's most popular stores, is shown in this picture from the 1960s. The store became so successful that it moved north of this site to 1846 Broadway in order to expanded its facilities. The store still remains a major independently-owned food store in the Lorain economy, and plans have been made for more expansion.

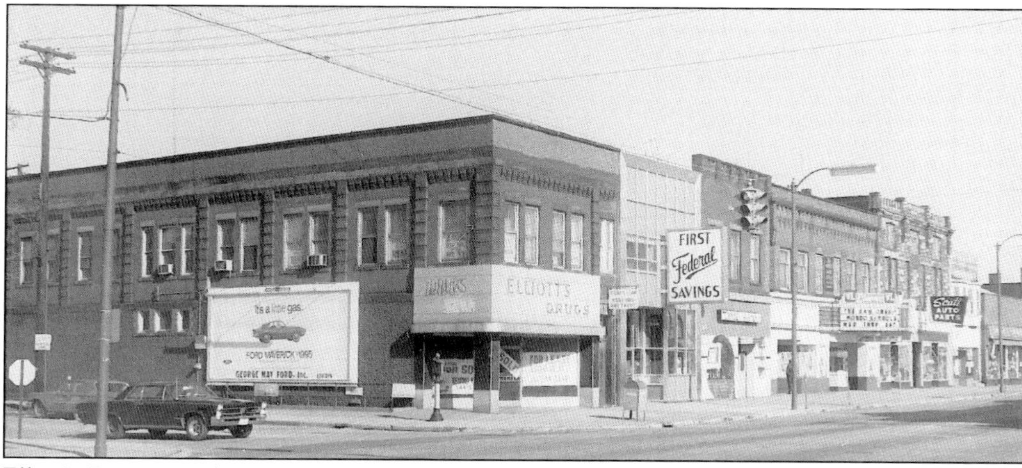

Elliot's Drugs was located at the corner of Twentieth Street and Broadway. It went out of business in the 1960s and a bookstore moved in. The original First Federal Savings and Loan began operation here. Later, a new building was built on Oberlin Avenue and this office became a branch. The movie marquee shown is from the Dreamland Theater, which was one of many in Lorain in that era. Today, very few are in existence, as most people go to the movies at the malls.

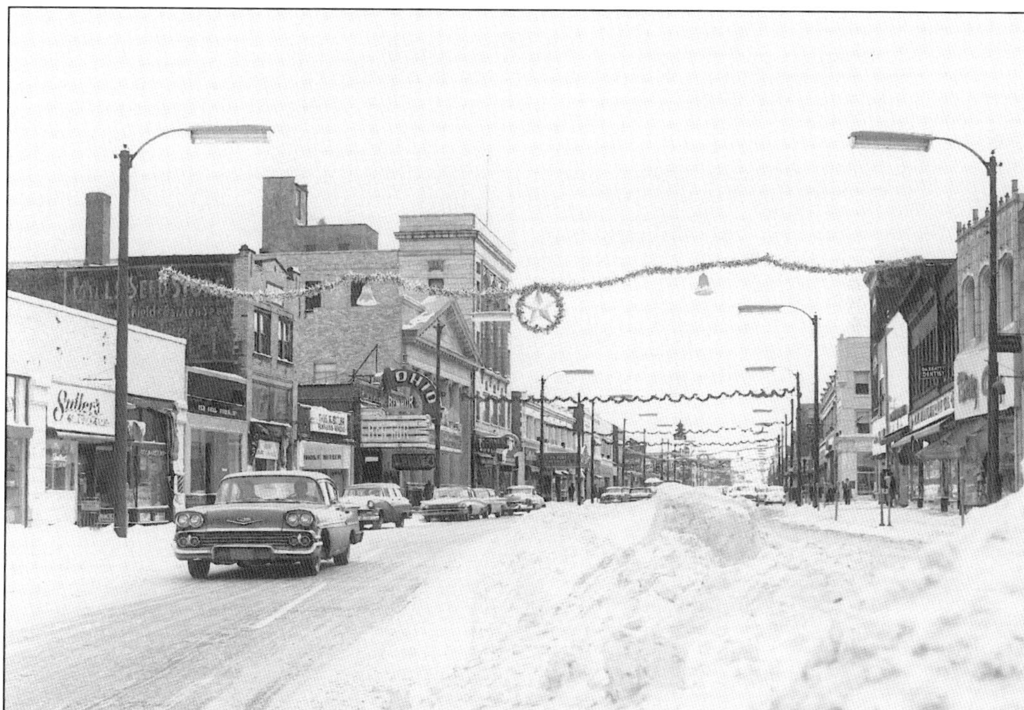

This view is of downtown Lorain in the winter of 1958, looking south toward Sixth Street. Heavy snows provided the scene, but also pictured are many businesses. Sutter's Sandwich Shop was a favorite stop. The Ohio Theater and the Palace Theater can be seen at the intersection. They were two of the three downtown movie houses. The Tivoli was farther south and across the street. The Betty Gay Ladies Clothing, the F.W. Woolworth, and Tom McAn's Shoes were on the right.

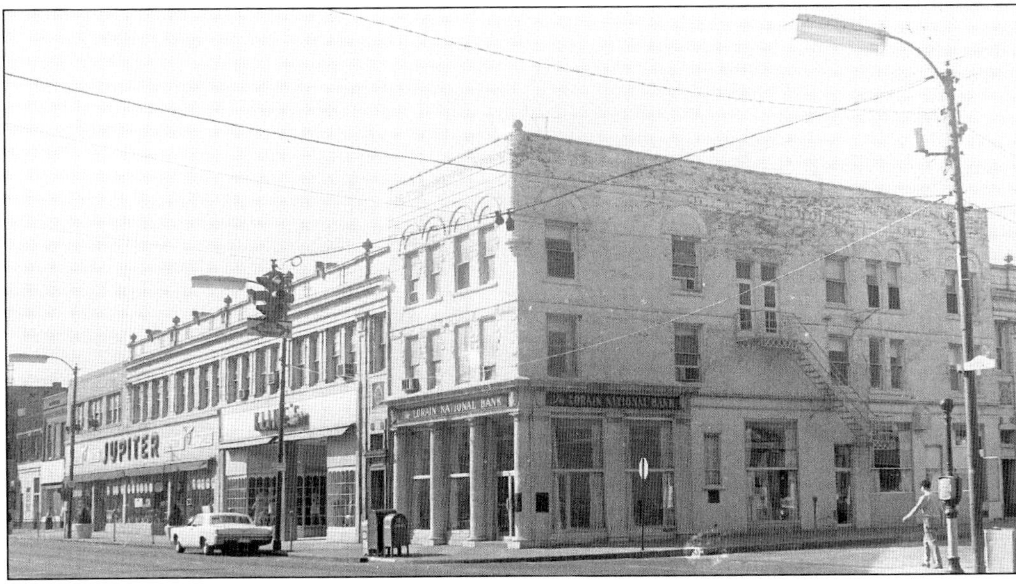

The corner of Sixth and Broadway shows the Lorain Banking Co. building that later joined with the National Bank of Commerce to become the Lorain National Bank. The next business is Kline's Department Store. The Lorain branch was the first in a system that eventually included 38 outlets. For 17 years the store was located at 710 Broadway; it then moved to 610 Broadway. Ben Weintraub was the manager and was very active in civic affairs. The Jupiter Department Store was located next door.

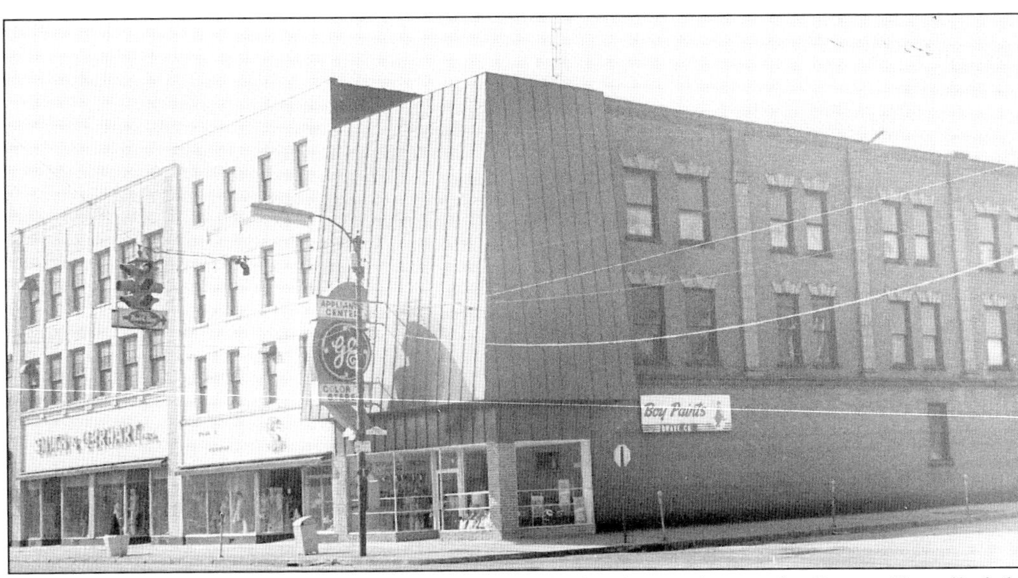

Smith and Gerhart Department Store was one of the leaders in dry goods. Originally called the Boston Store, they put their own names on the front when it became the largest shop in Lorain. The business continued until 1980. Rakich and Rakich, a fashionable men's clothing store, and some law offices have recently taken over.

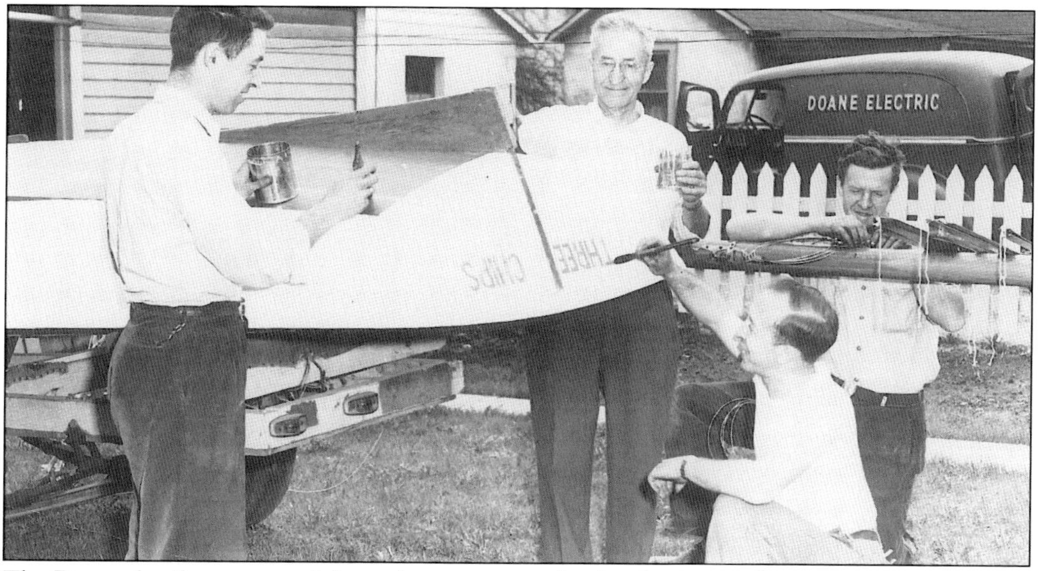

The Doane family was one of the early pioneers in the development of Lorain. They owned and operated Doane Electric Co. Aside from the business, the family has long been interested in boating on Lake Erie. In this 1954 picture are Roger, Carl (father), Bob, and Neil Doane. They loved to sail and won many races on the lake.

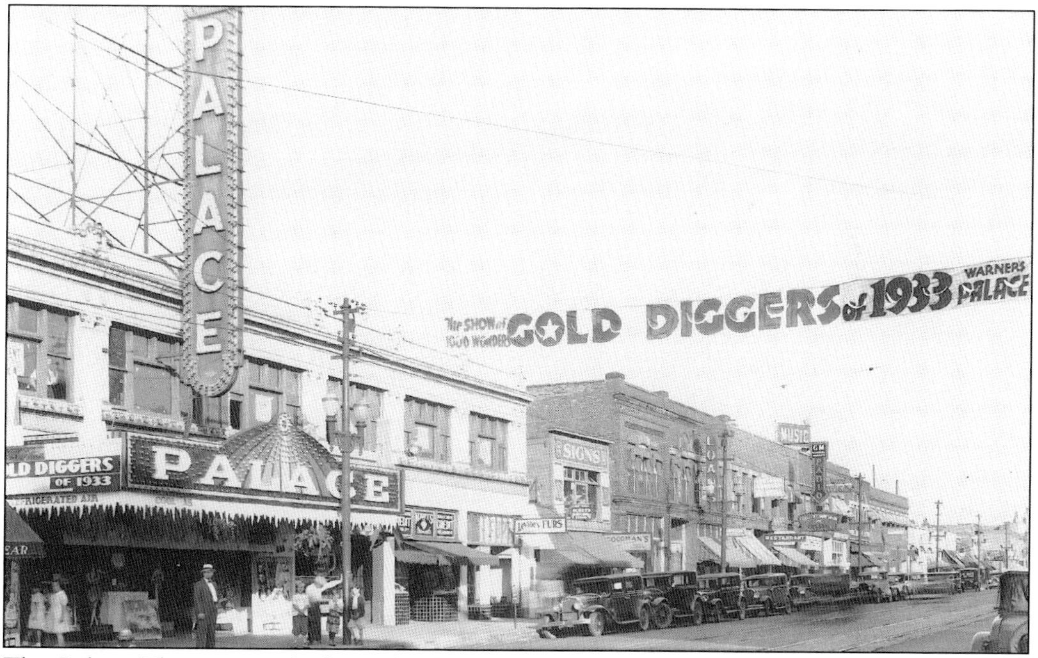

The Palace Theater was built in the late 1920s, after the tornado hit Lorain in 1924. At the time, it was one of the largest theaters showing movies and presenting stage productions between Cleveland and Toledo. The Wurlitzer organ provided music for the silent films that were shown. This picture shows the Palace Theater in 1933, although later it had fewer customers and went into disrepair. The restoration became a project for the Civic Department of the Lakeland Women's Club. After many years of hard labor and fund drives, it opened as the Civic Center and is on the National Historic Registry.

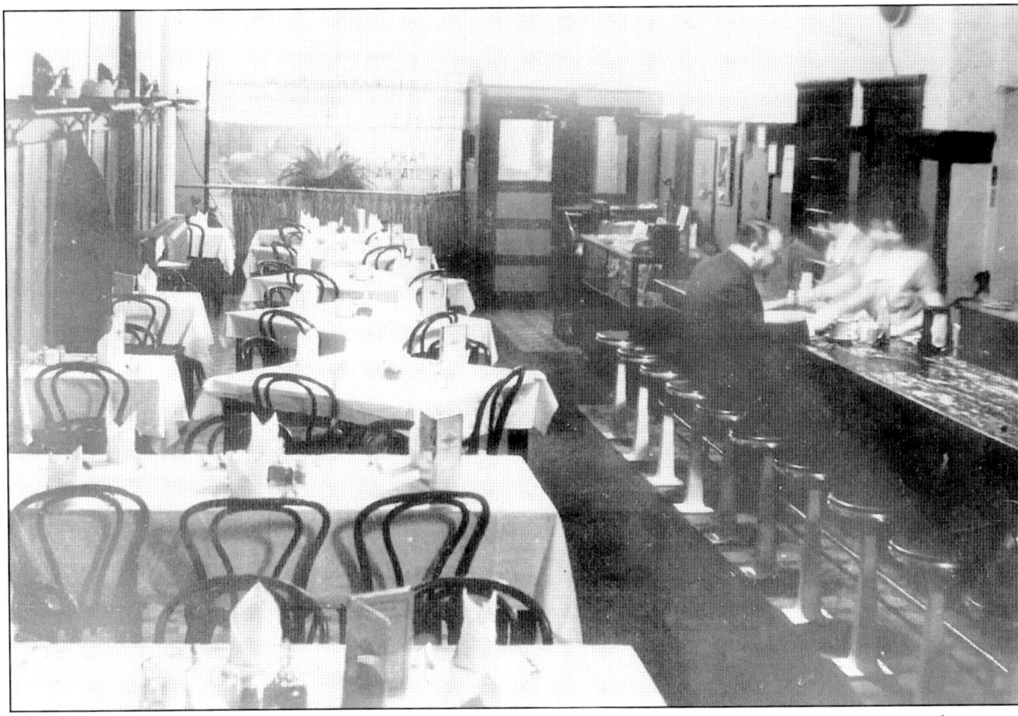

The Park Restaurant started in 1924 at 211 West Erie Avenue. It built a reputation for good-quality meals. Fred Davidson and Harold Brogan operated the restaurant 24 hours a day. There were accommodations for 60 people. The restaurant was finally sold to Heilman's.

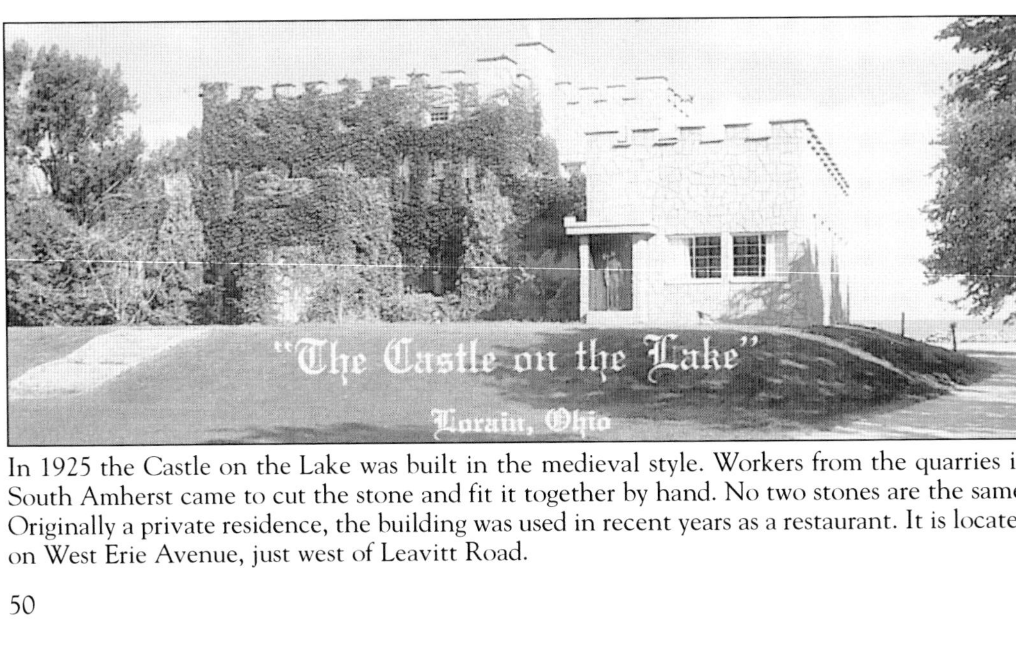

In 1925 the Castle on the Lake was built in the medieval style. Workers from the quarries in South Amherst came to cut the stone and fit it together by hand. No two stones are the same. Originally a private residence, the building was used in recent years as a restaurant. It is located on West Erie Avenue, just west of Leavitt Road.

Three

Our Community

Parades, Celebrations, Hospitals, Churches, and Disasters

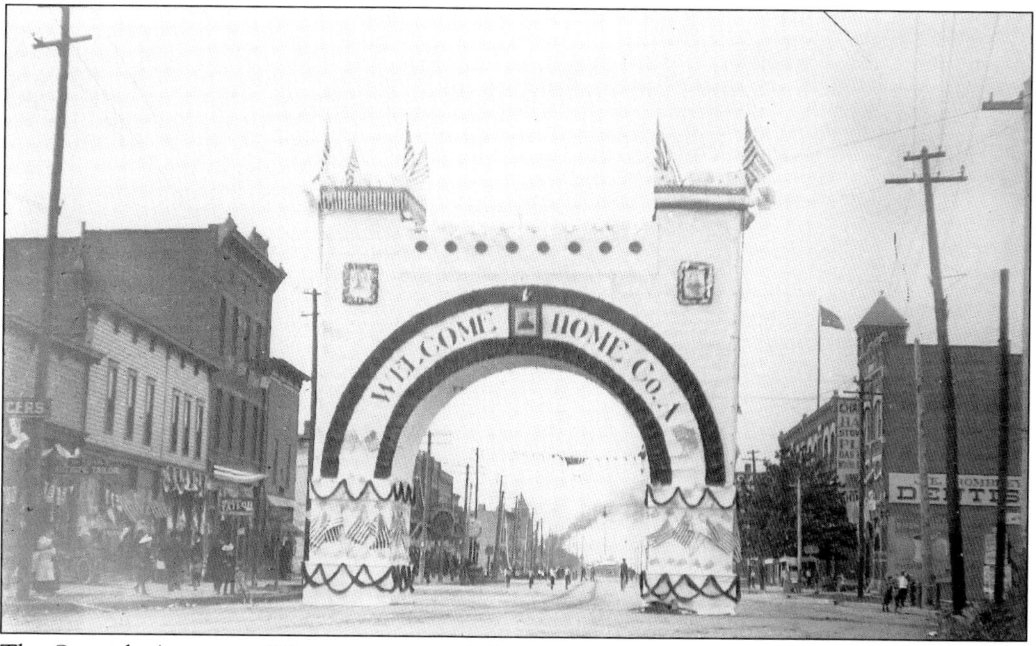

The Spanish-American War was over, and the troops were just coming home in 1898. Cuba was free and the United States had won the Philippines. This scene is located on Broadway, between Fifth and Sixth Streets, looking north to Lake Erie. Company A was the unit into which many Lorainites enlisted for the short war.

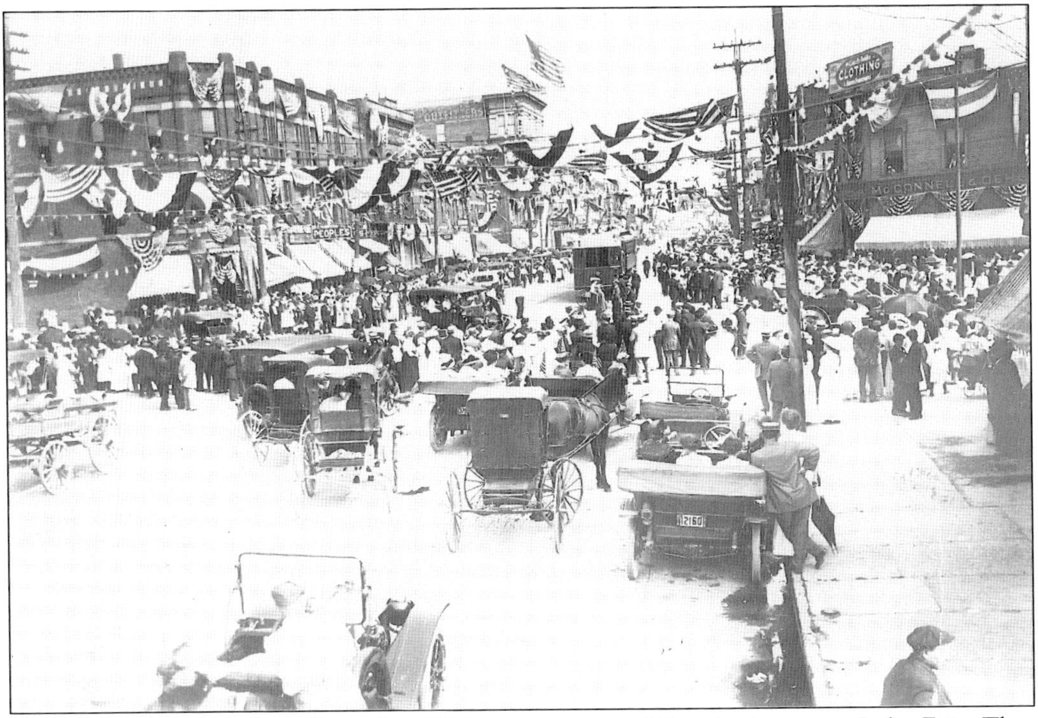

In 1913 Lorain helped celebrate the 100th anniversary of Perry's victory on Lake Erie. That victory caused the British to withdraw from the American West, and eventually resulted in the Northwest Territory being part of the United States. This picture is looking south on Broadway, with Erie Avenue cutting across the picture. Note that a few people had automobiles, but most got around by horse and buggy.

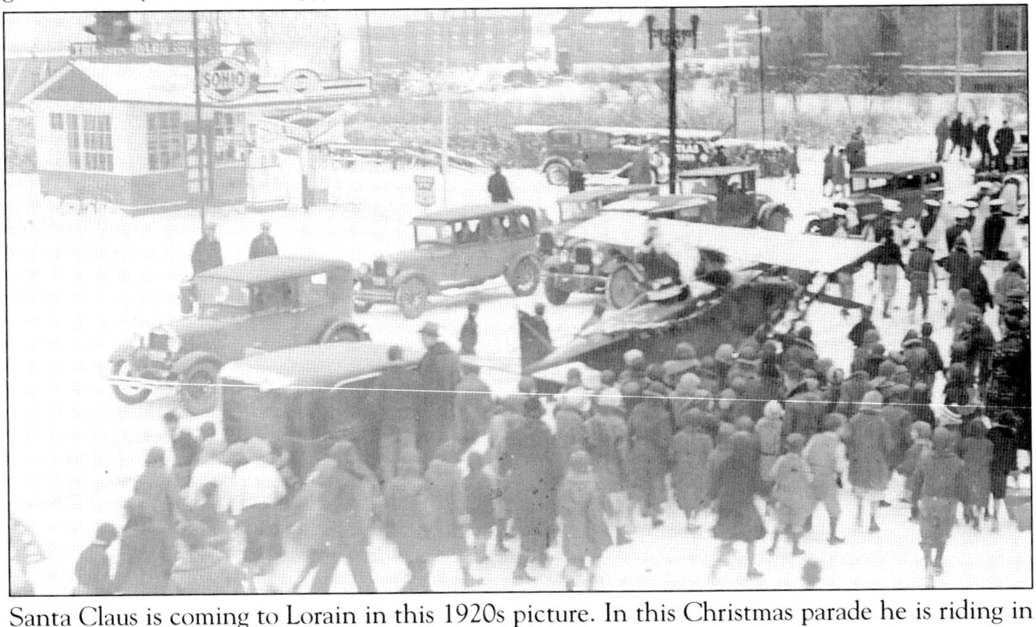

Santa Claus is coming to Lorain in this 1920s picture. In this Christmas parade he is riding in the airplane and waving to the crowd. The large building in the background is the post office on Broadway at Ninth Street. A "modern" gas station is shown on the left.

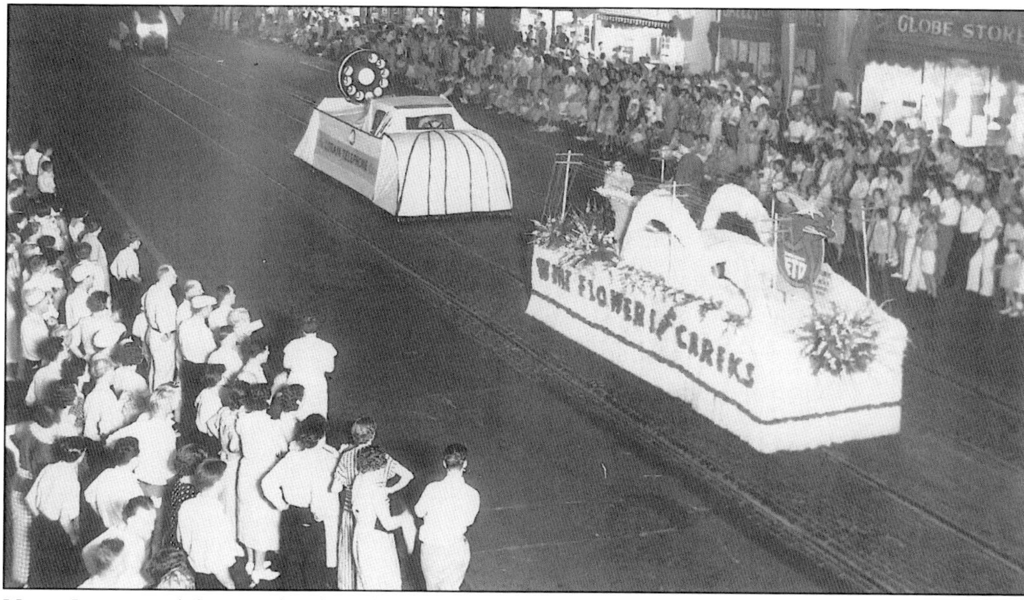

Here, Lorain celebrates the founding of the city. The Centennial Grand Parade was held on Friday, July 20, 1934. There was a week of public events, including the Illuminated Marine Parade, Horseshoe Pitching Exhibition, and the Historical Night program. This photograph shows the west side of Broadway, between Fifth and Sixth Streets. J. Ford Thompson was the President and Director of the Lorain Celebration Association.

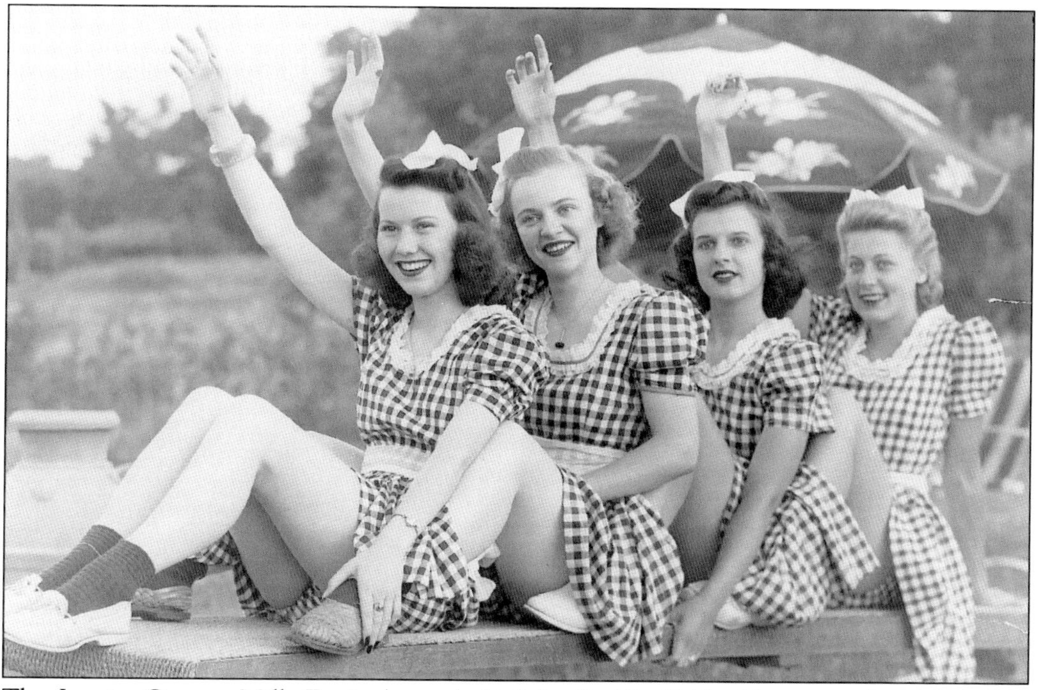

The Lorain County Milk Festival was held July 11–13, 1941. Above are four of the 50 "Gingham Girls" from the festival. They are Isabelle Smithheisler, Florence Lumsden, Joan Slavina and Shirley Firestone, all of whom are residents of Lorain. One event was a night show on the beach, with the announcement of the healthiest boy and girl in the county.

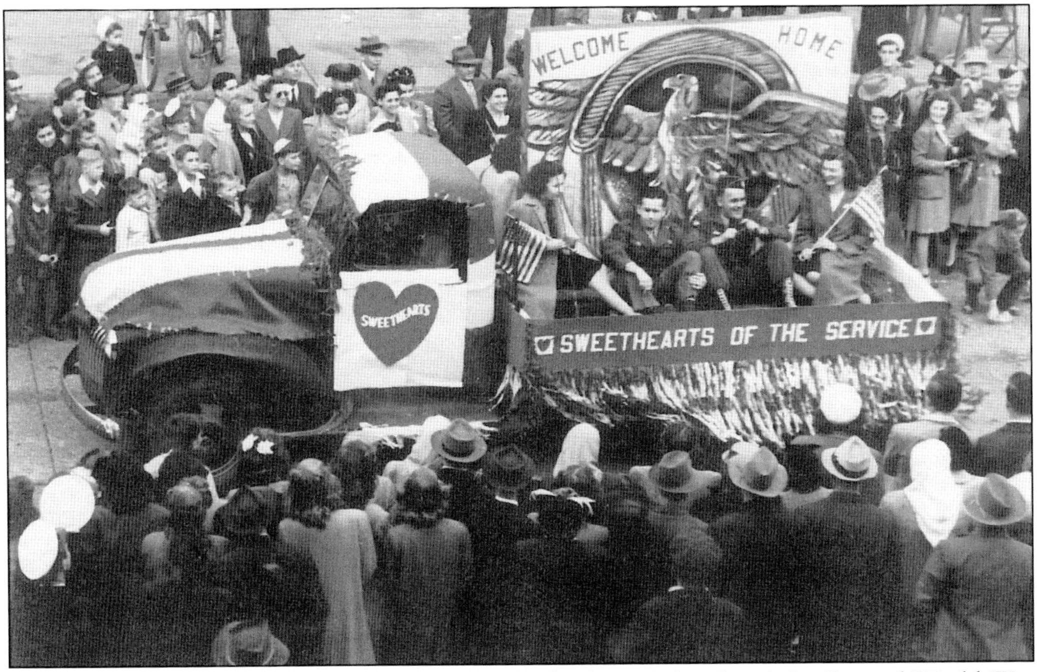

The news came in August 1945 that the Japanese had surrendered and the Second World War was at an end. Within a short time, Lorain had a huge parade to celebrate that victory and the coming of peace. Pictured is one of the many floats that were put together as the armed forces started coming home.

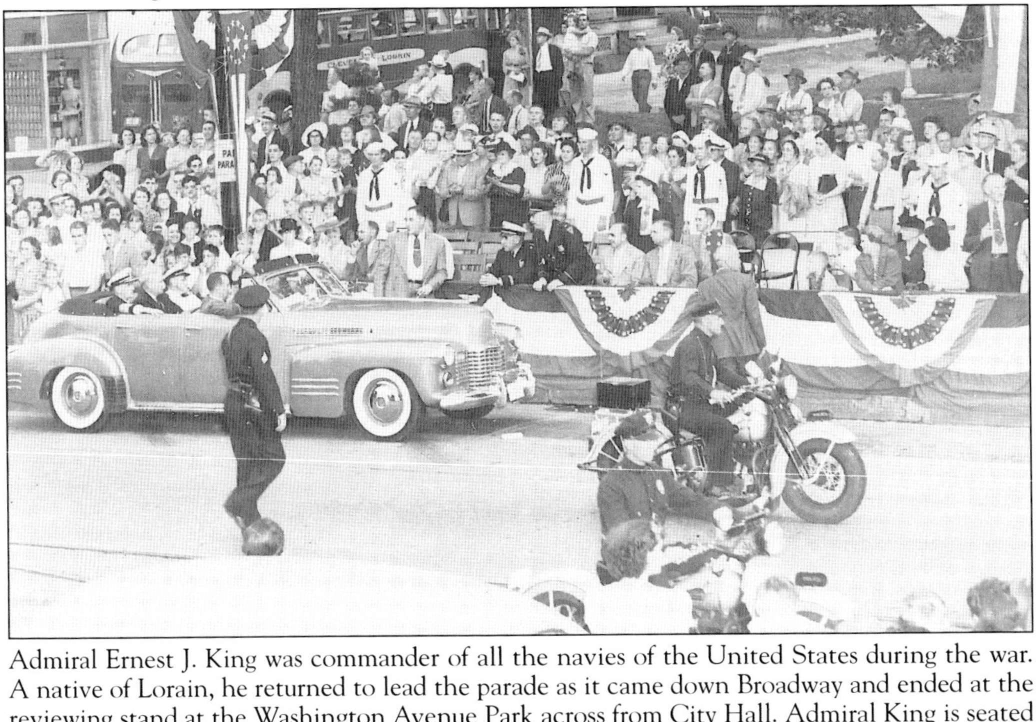

Admiral Ernest J. King was commander of all the navies of the United States during the war. A native of Lorain, he returned to lead the parade as it came down Broadway and ended at the reviewing stand at the Washington Avenue Park across from City Hall. Admiral King is seated in the back of the Cadillac convertible, with Ohio Gov. John W. Bricker next to him.

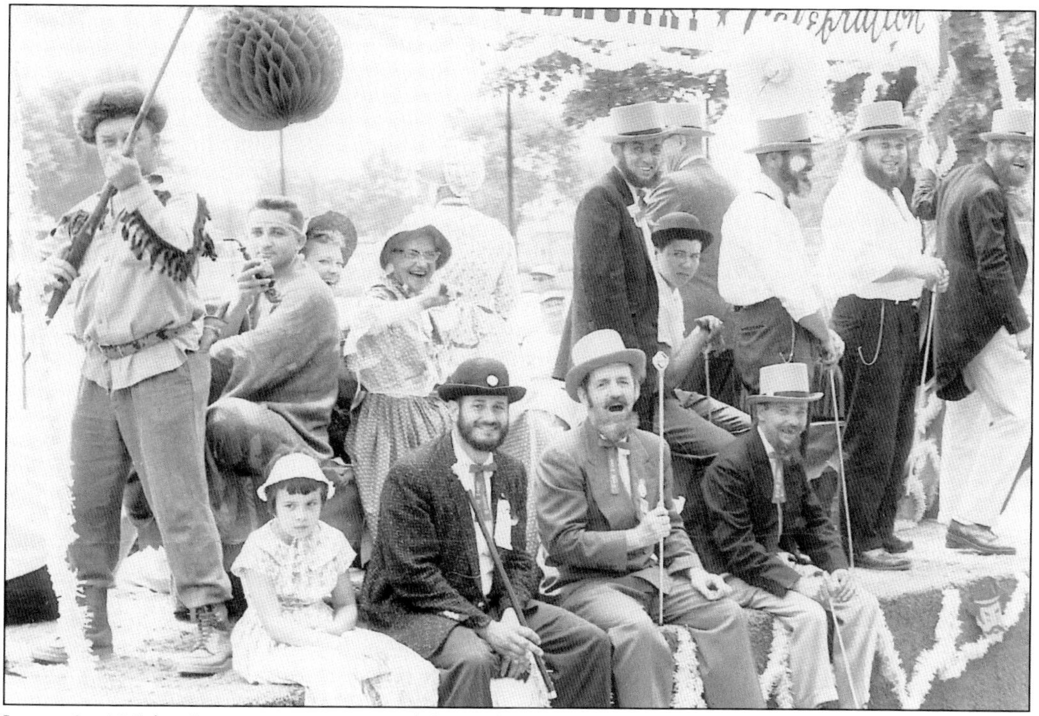

Lorain's 125th Anniversary was celebrated in 1959. The celebration was sponsored by the Lorain Civic Memorial Association and was a ten-day celebration that included a pageant called "This Is Lorain." This float carried "Brothers of the Brush" and "Sesquibelles" in the parade.

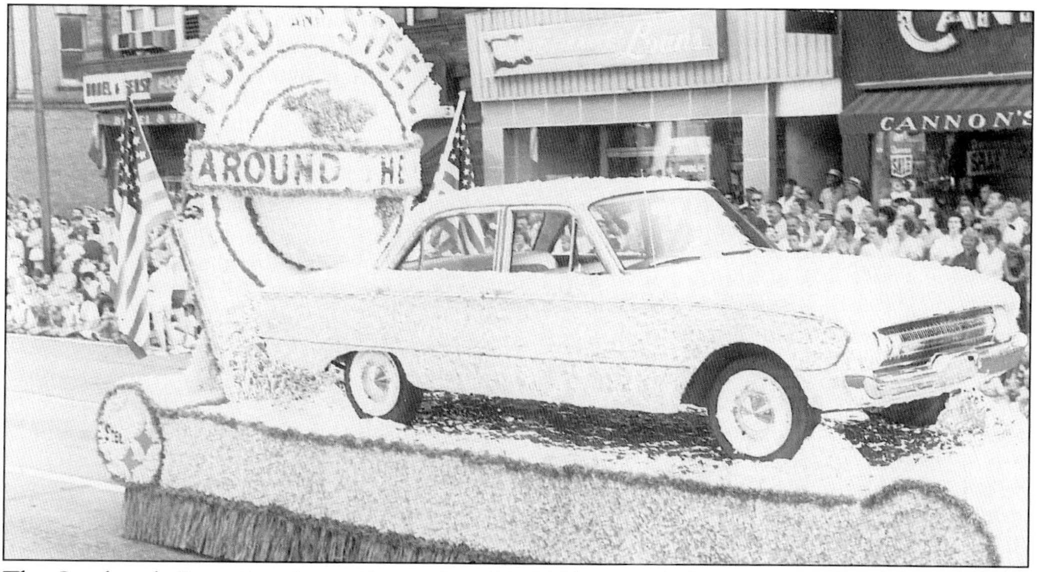

The Steelmark Days Parade on September 22, 1965, started the activities for the next three days of celebration. The purpose was to call attention to Lorain's importance as a steel center and the contribution of its steelworkers from the National Tube Plant. It also dramatized Broadway as a merchandising center. The float depicts a Ford Falcon car manufactured at the Lorain Ford Assembly Plant.

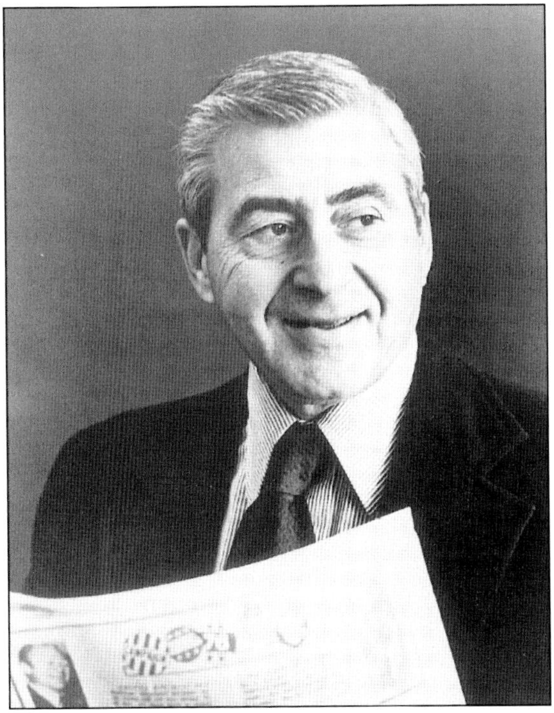

Recognizing the rich ethnic heritage of Lorain, Irving Leibowitz, editor of *The Lorain Journal*, established the International Festival in 1967. It was to be a yearly, week-long celebration of the customs, traditions, foods, and dress of Lorain's more than 55 nationalities. This first International Parade had 80 units in it, and over 15,000 people watched. The first queen was Irene Kychun, who represented the Ukrainian nationality. The tradition continues. (Photograph courtesy of *The Morning Journal*.)

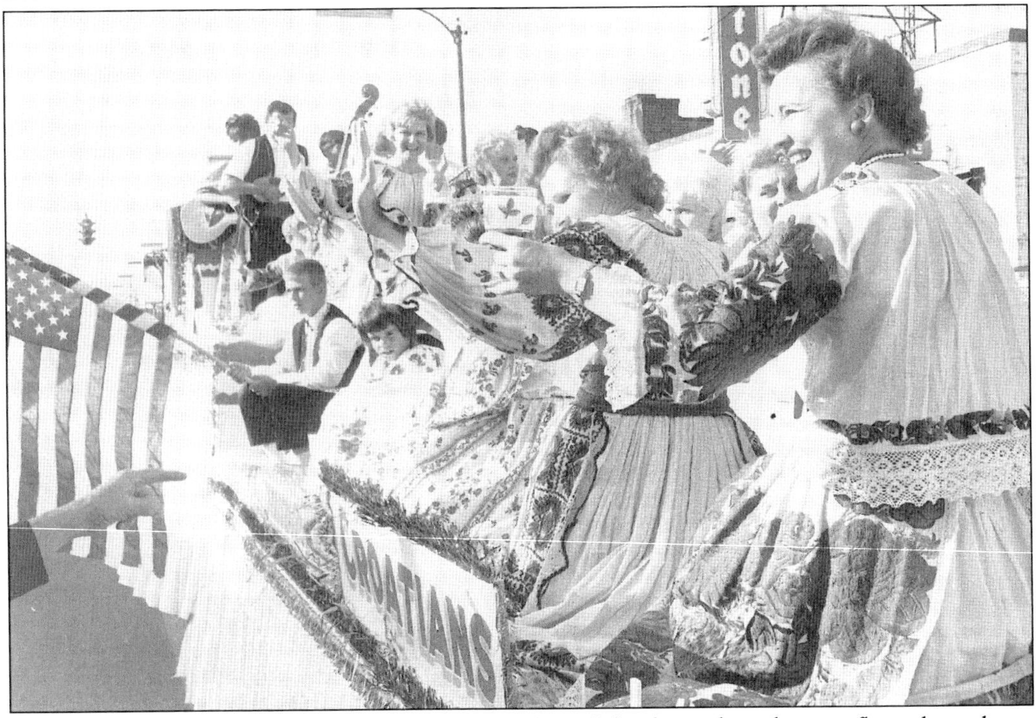

The International Parade was one of the highlights of the festival, and many floats have been in the parades over the years. Many nationalities had their own float. Pictured is one such float, representing the Croatians in a parade held in the late 1960s or early 1970s. Each nationality was dressed in their elaborate native costumes and made a very colorful display.

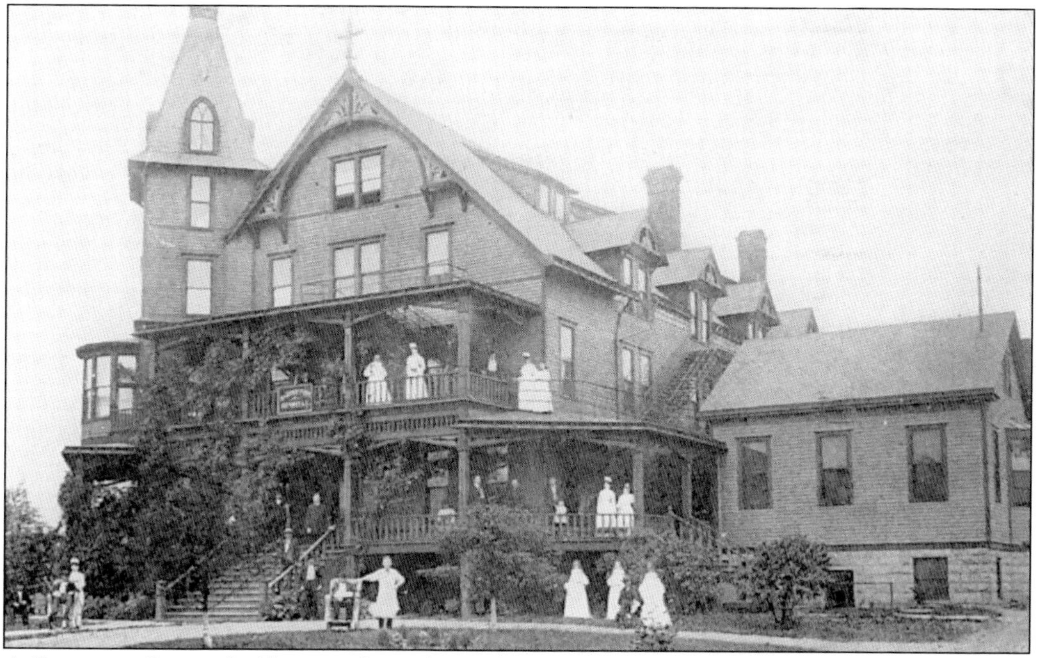

A Devonian Spring (sulfur water) was located at Twentieth Street and Broadway in the 1890s. The building above was a hotel where guests stayed while they went across the street for the sulfur water baths, which it was said, had curative powers. When the spring gave out in 1892, the Reverend Father Joseph Bihn acquired the building and established the Sisters of St. Francis Orphan Asylum. The building became St. Joseph's Hospital on January 1, 1903.

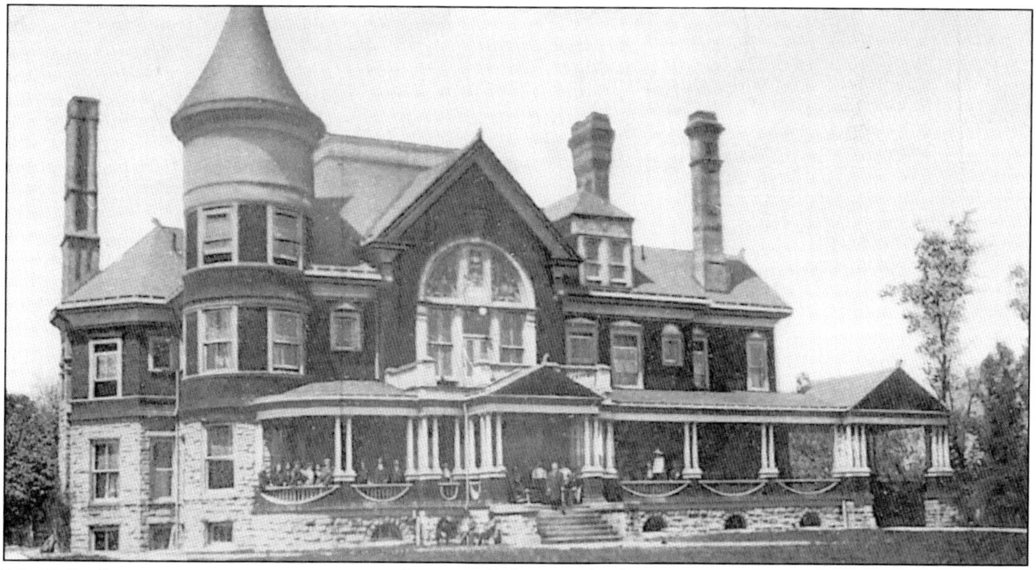

Mr. Moxham was an executive in charge of the steel plant in Lorain. He and his wife built a large home at 1980 East Thirty-Second Street. When he decided to accept a job in Nova Scotia, his wife refused to move unless he took all the beautiful furnishings, paneling, and decor with them. He agreed. The home was later converted to the American Carlsbad Sanitarium, and was used for many years as a health spa until it was torn down.

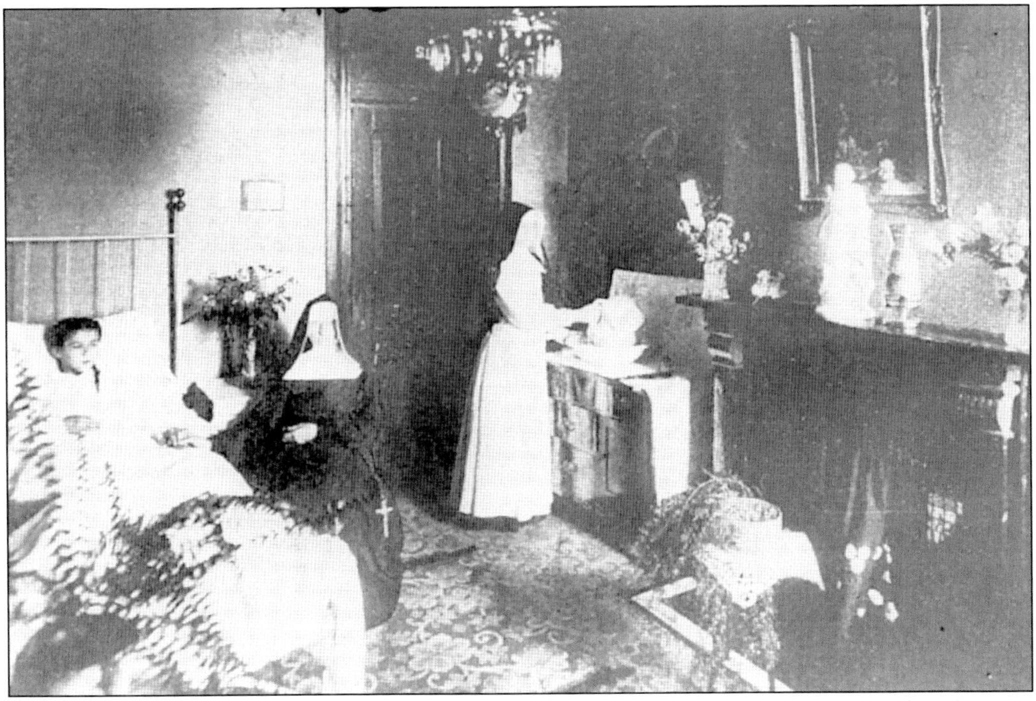

St. Joseph's Hospital was the first hospital in Lorain. Previously, serious cases had to be sent to Cleveland for treatment. Shown here is the elaborate room for private patients. Doctors Brown, Cowley, Cox, Crawford, Frederick, Carver, Gilbert, McGarvey, Monosmith, Robinson, Thompson, VanTilburg, and Wheatley were the first to staff the hospital. Dr. Wheatley was chief of staff in 1903.

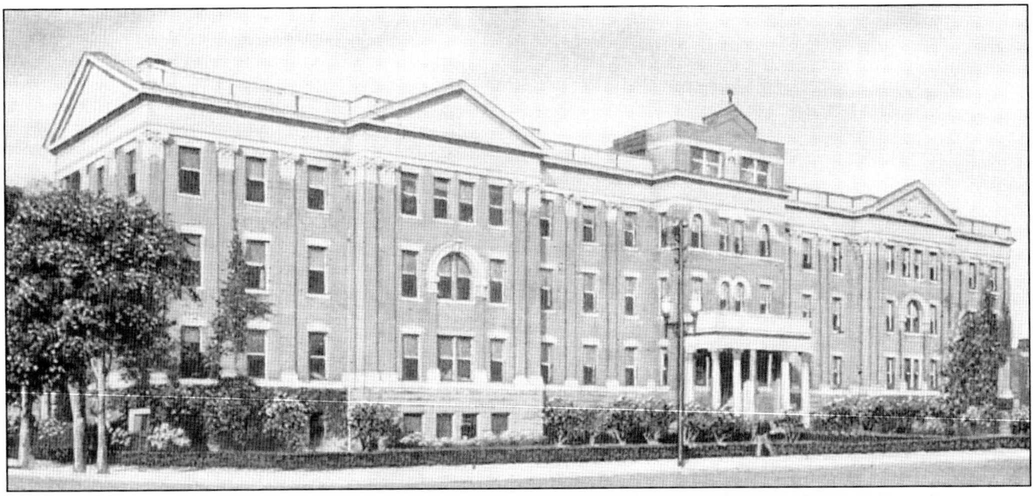

As the city grew, there was a need for a greatly expanded hospital. The former hotel was not enough. A new brick building was constructed next door, and both the hotel and building were used for a while. Many expansions became necessary. The original hotel was torn down and, eventually, the hospital expanded along the entire block between Twentieth and Twenty-first Streets on Broadway. A school for registered nurses was built south of the main building on Twenty-first Street. After WW II, it became a school for licensed practical nursing. As more space was needed, construction continued, expanding the hospital to Reid Avenue.

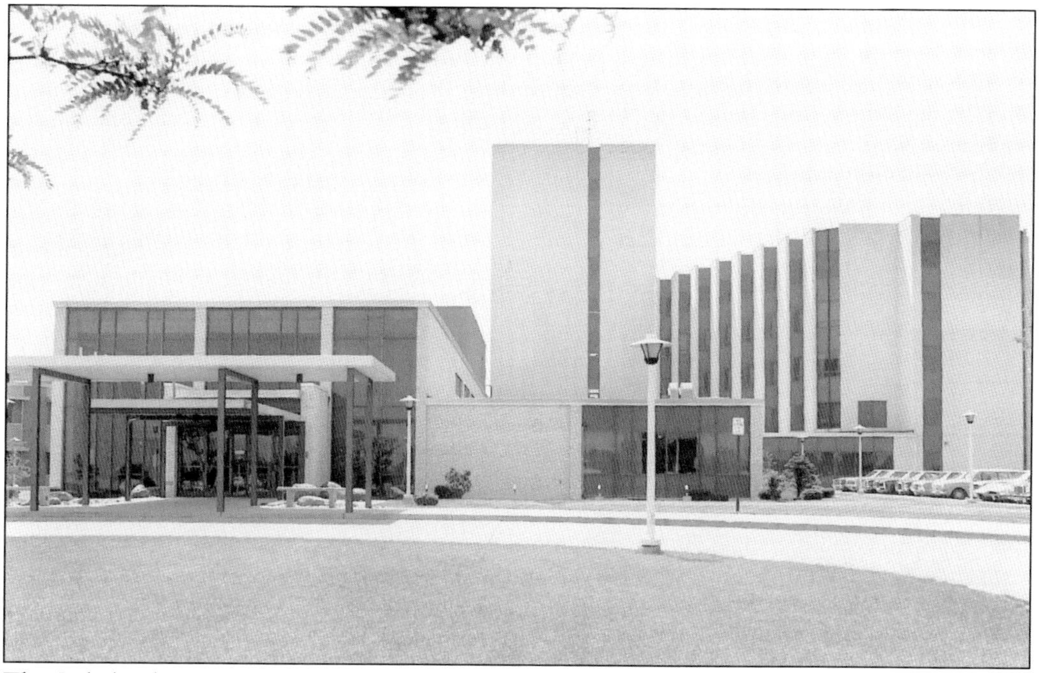

The Lakeland Women's Club thought Lorain needed a second hospital, and in 1957, they started fund-raising. A bond issue was put on the ballot and passed. The original building was dedicated May 3, 1964. The Lorain Community Hospital grew, and in 1994, St. Joseph Hospital and Community Hospital merged into Community Health Partners in western Lorain.

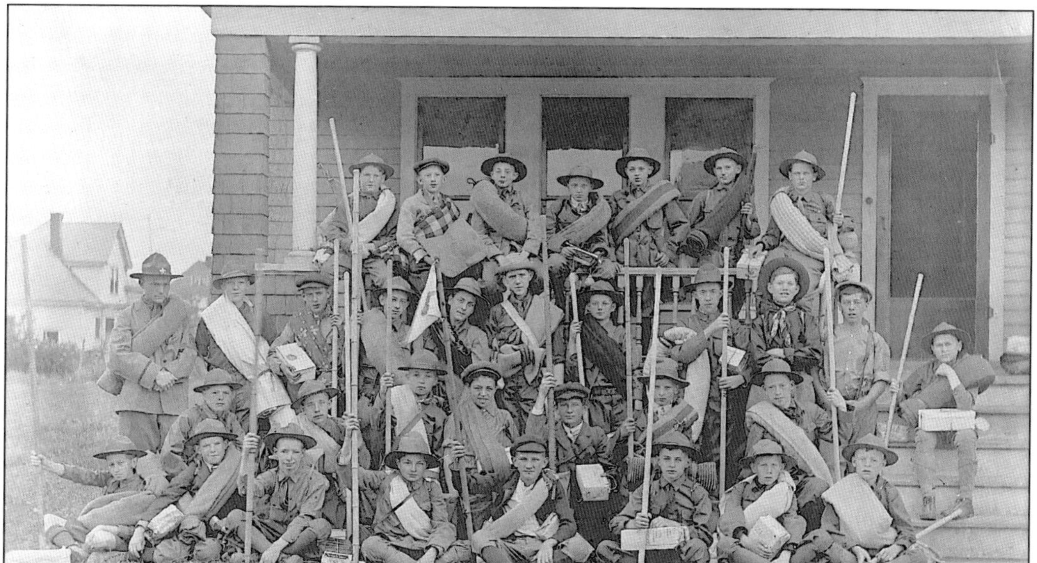

The Boy Scouts organization came to Lorain and many boys enjoyed the activities. In the picture above, Lorain Troop Number Four, the boys are ready to start their latest project, which was a hike to Columbus, Ohio, and back. The first evening found them at Wellington Fair Grounds, where they slept around a fire, with two boys rotating fire duty during the night. Thirty-one boys made this trip in 1914. The scoutmaster was Raymond Sullivan and Lewis Goodell was the assistant. Bill James is in the front row, second from the right.

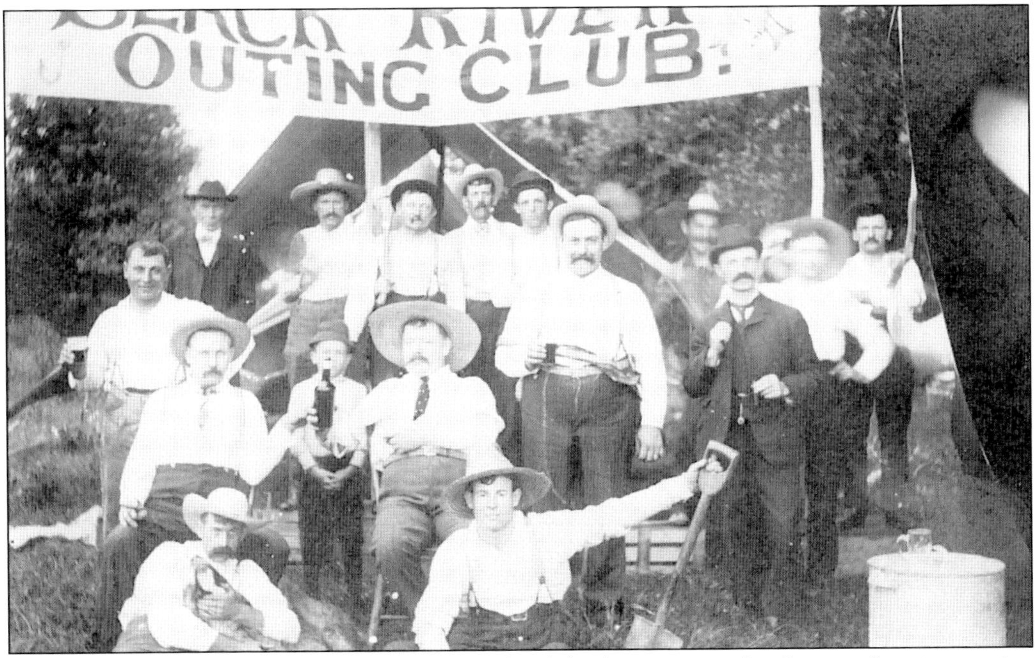

The Black River Outing Club is one of the early clubs that organized in Lorain. It is interesting that in 1921–1926, there were nine clubs in Lorain. They included the Cosmos Club at 651 Broadway, Eagles at 573 Broadway, Elks at 444 Broadway, Mercury Club at 3052 Vine Avenue, Moose at 1112 West Erie Avenue, Slovak Gymnastic Union at 3009 Broadway, United Polish Club at 332 West Fourteenth Street, and the German Club House at East Twenty-ninth Street and Apple Avenue.

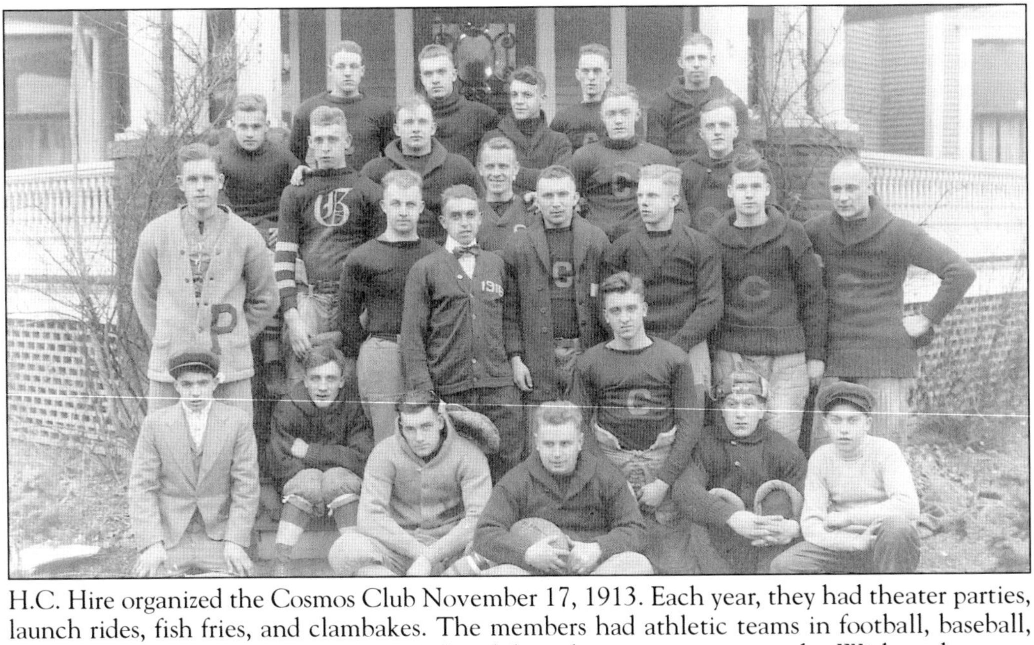

H.C. Hire organized the Cosmos Club November 17, 1913. Each year, they had theater parties, launch rides, fish fries, and clambakes. The members had athletic teams in football, baseball, basketball, and bowling. In June 1916 the club took up its quarters in the Wickens home at Fifth and Hamilton.

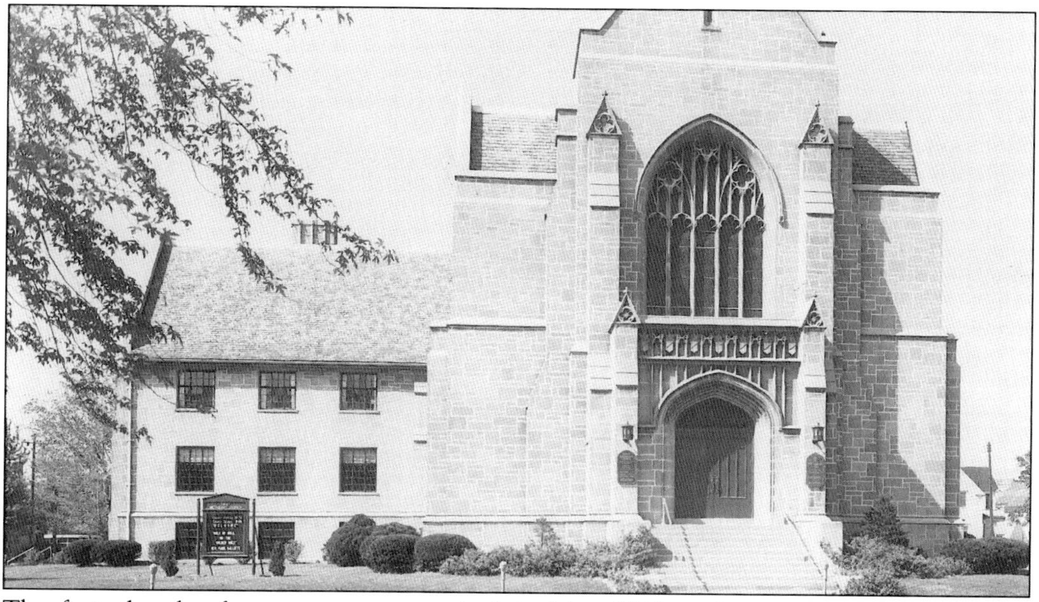

The first church of any sort was organized in May 1839, and services were held in the schoolhouse. It started as a Presbyterian church, but later some of the members became Congregationalists. The German farmers founded the Emanuel Evangelical Church in 1851 and built the first church, which is still in existence. A Methodist preacher came and formed the First United Methodist Church in 1856. The churches grew and prospered at what is now the corner of Sixth Street and Reid Avenue.

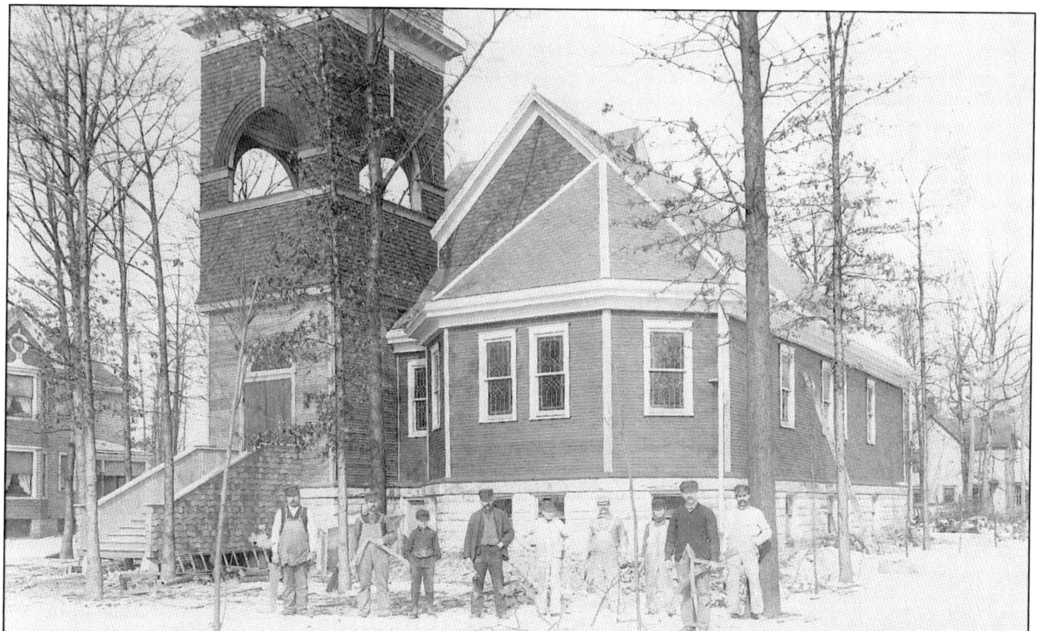

By 1904 the Grace Methodist Episcopal Church had a new minister, Rev. H.D. Fleming. The church was originally known as the South Lorain Methodist Church. Later, its name was changed to the Thirteenth Avenue M.E. Church. In 1907 the city renumbered all the east-west streets, and that changed this church's address to East Thirty-first Street.

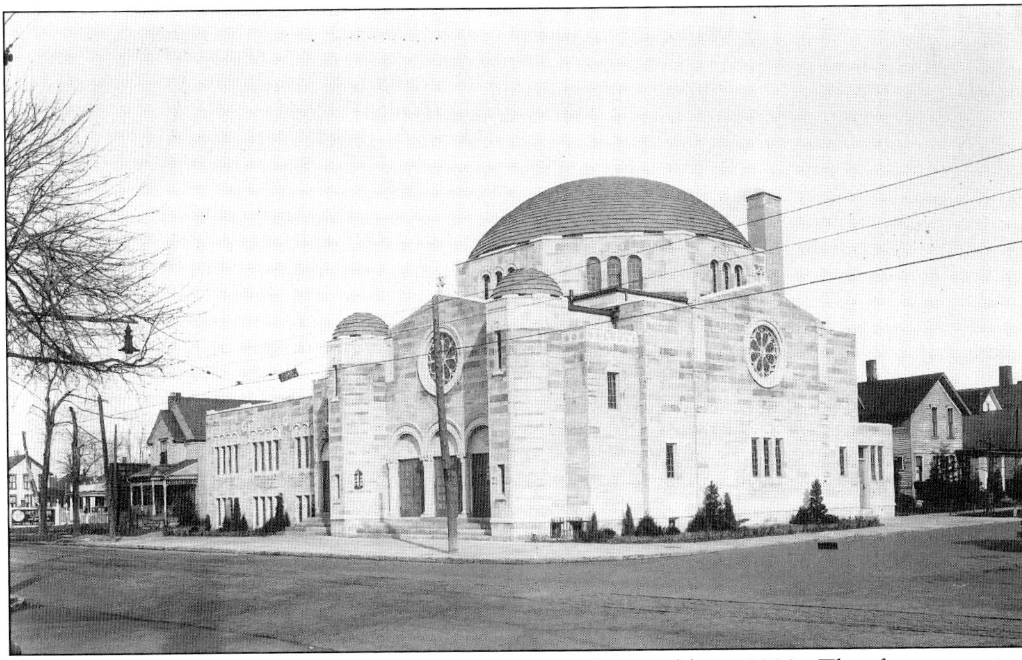

The first Jewish child born in Lorain came into the world in 1890. The first organized Synagogue was in 1901. This picture shows the Agudath B'nai Israel Synagogue, which was located on Reid Avenue and Ninth Street. The building was completed and dedicated in June 1932. The congregation later moved to a new facility at Meister Road and Pole Avenue. The building now houses the New Bethel Primitive Baptist Church.

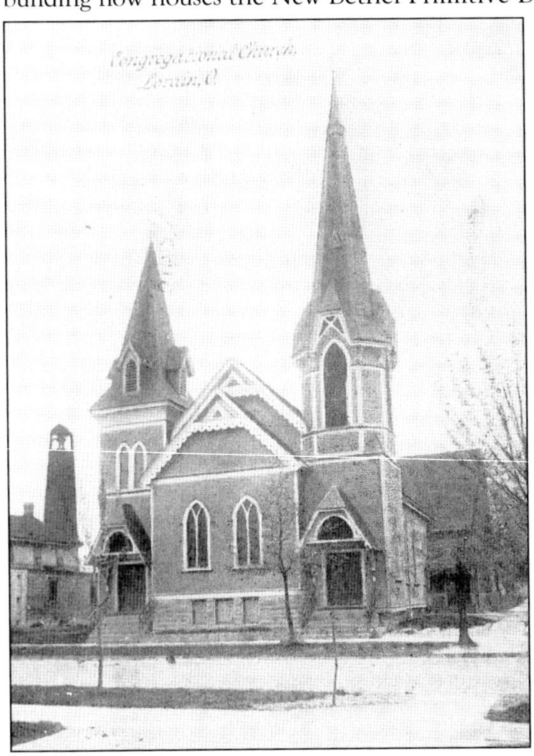

In 1836 a Congregational Sunday School was started by Mrs. William Jones in her home. The Jones's lived in what was the old City Hall on West Erie Avenue. The building of the first Congregational church started with nine people who laid the corner stone in 1872 at the corner of Washington Avenue and Fourth Street. That wooden structure was used until the 1924 tornado blew it down. A greatly enlarged, new brick building was dedicated in 1926. Notice the fire station on the left with the tower that was used to dry the hoses.

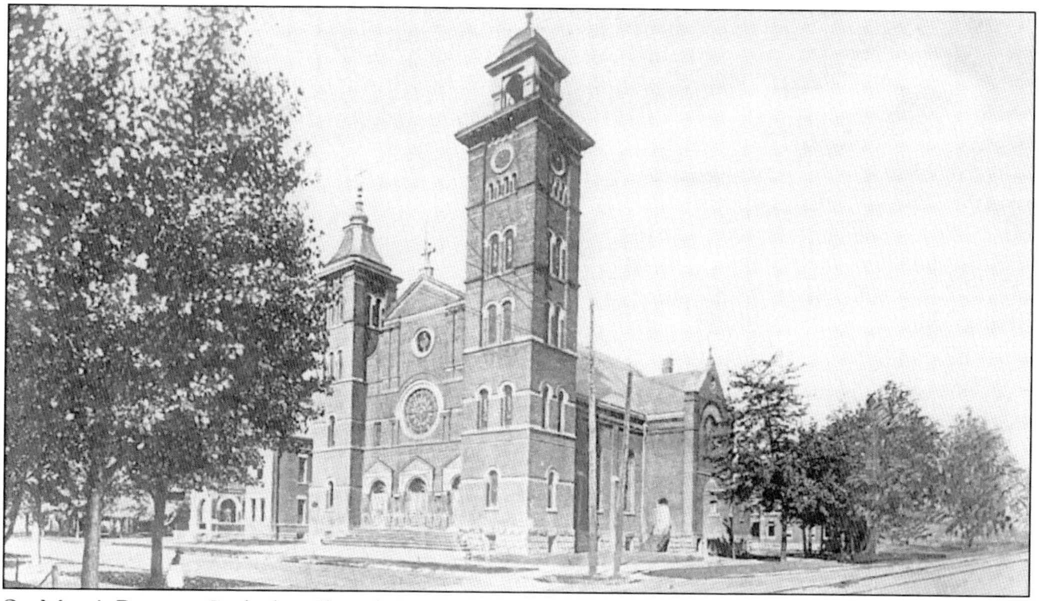

St. Mary's Roman Catholic Church began in 1873, and the wooden structure was dedicated in 1880. In 1886 a school with 127 pupils opened, and two years later, they were housed in a new brick building. In 1895 a fire caused the church to burn and the brick structure shown above was constructed. When the tornado hit in 1924, the brick structure was damaged and a stone structure replaced it.

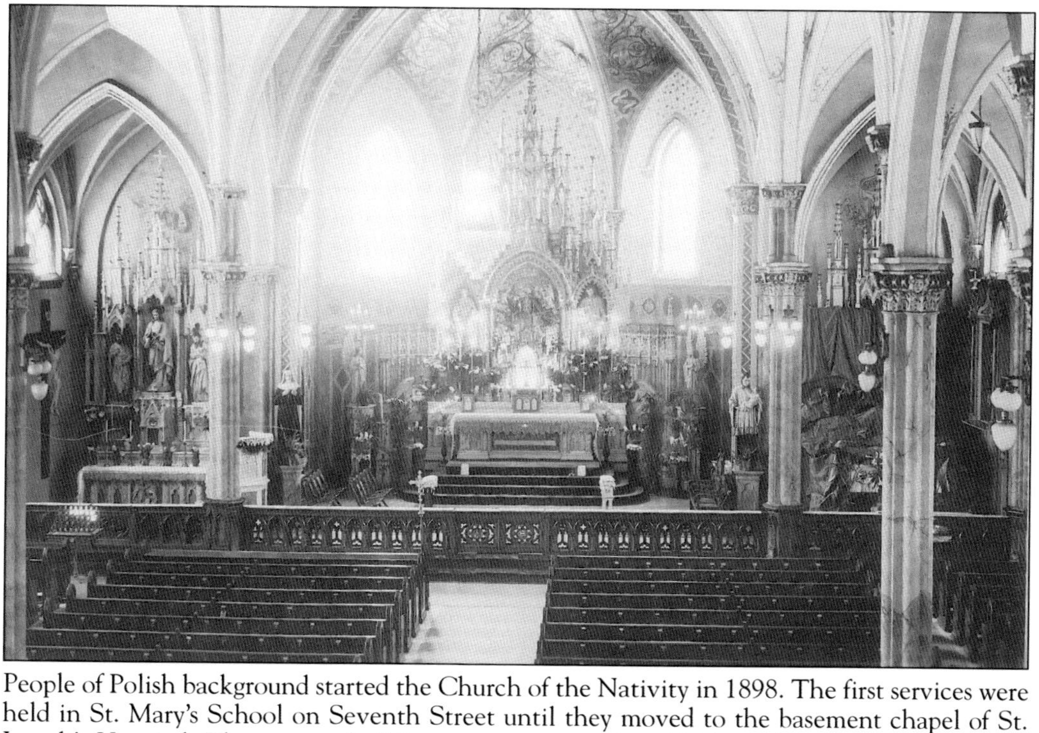

People of Polish background started the Church of the Nativity in 1898. The first services were held in St. Mary's School on Seventh Street until they moved to the basement chapel of St. Joseph's Hospital. The present building was constructed in 1915, in the Gothic style, and is named the Nativity of the Blessed Virgin Mary.

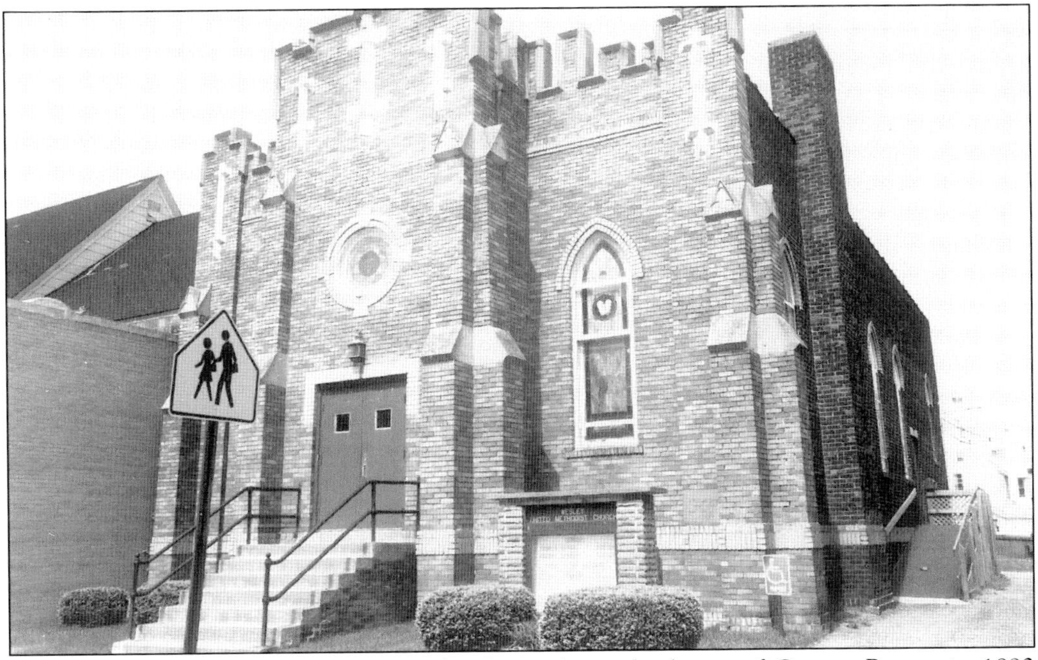

The Reverend R.L. Dickerson met with 15 people in the home of George Brown in 1893 and organized the Second Methodist Church in Lorain. A building was purchased on Seventh Street in 1894. That building was razed in 1910 and a new church was constructed. Again, the building was destroyed, this time in the 1924 tornado. The present structure was completed in 1927. The official name of the church was changed in 1978 to the Wesley United Methodist Church.

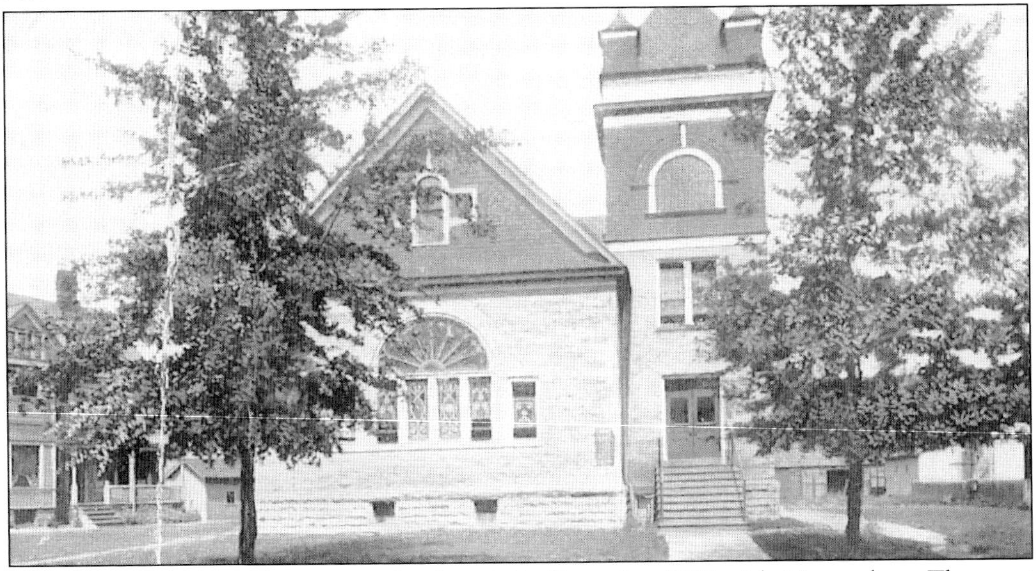

The Church of Christ was organized in Lorain in December 1876 with 18 members. They met in Edison Hall on Fifth Street and Broadway. Their first building was dedicated in 1878 and cost $1,753. It was located half a block from Broadway. This building was destroyed in the 1924 tornado. A new building was constructed in 1931, at the corner of Washington Avenue and Fifth Street, and is known as the Christian Temple Disciples of Christ.

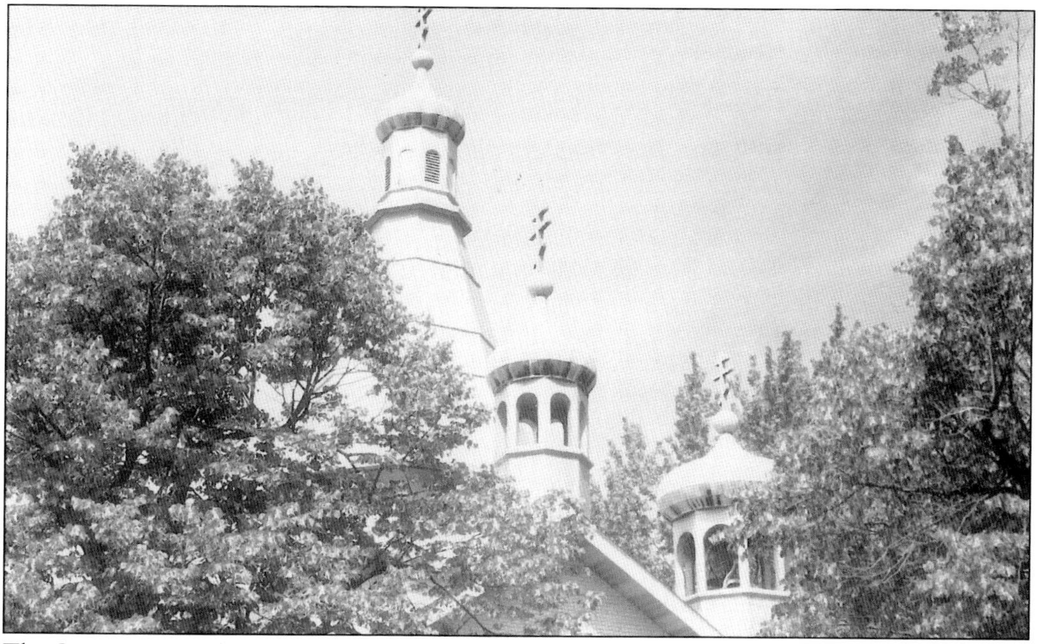

The Saint Peter and Paul Russian Orthodox Church was located in South Lorain at 2204 East Thirty-second Street. The early immigrants who came to Lorain to work at the steel plant were from Eastern Europe. Numerous ethnic groups helped make Lorain an international city.

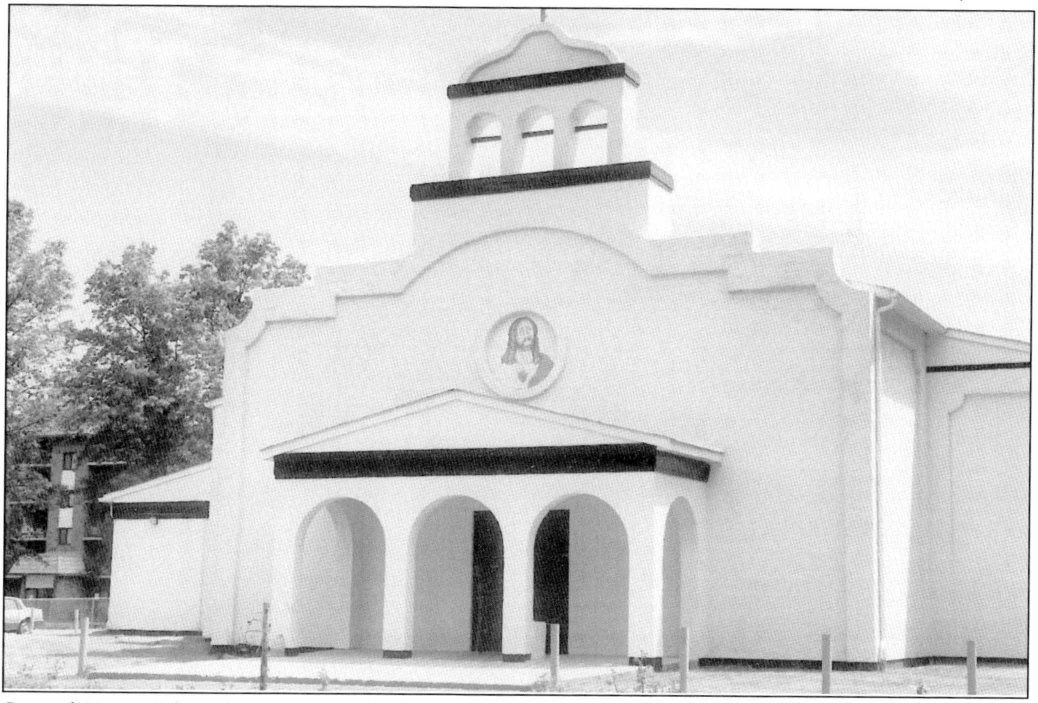

Sacred Heart Chapel was originally located on Vine Avenue. A meat market moved in when the church built a new building. On April 15, 1974, this church was dedicated. The priests were members of Missionary Servants of the Most Holy Trinity. The church was built for over half a million dollars and serves the Hispanic community in the area.

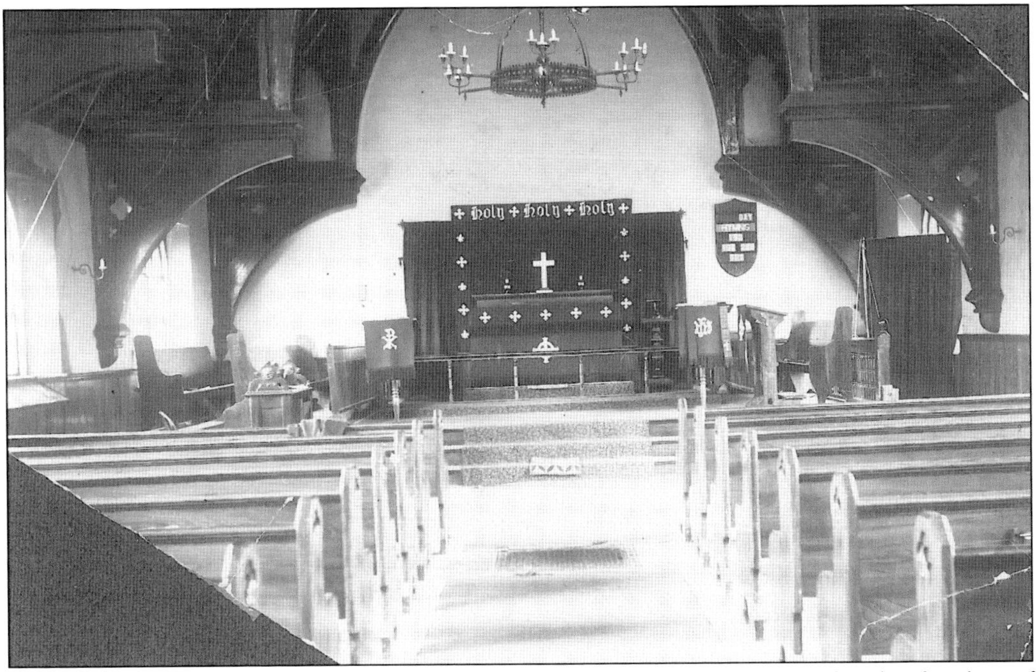

This is the interior of St. David's Episcopal Church, organized in 1895 by the families of prominent businessmen, Tom Johnson and Arthur J. Moxham, who were officials of the new Johnson Steel Rail Co. It was built on the northwest corner of what is now Pearl Avenue and Thirty-first Street. The church remained active until May 10, 1932, when it merged with the downtown Episcopal Church of the Redeemer, built in 1904 and located at Seventh Street and Reid Avenue.

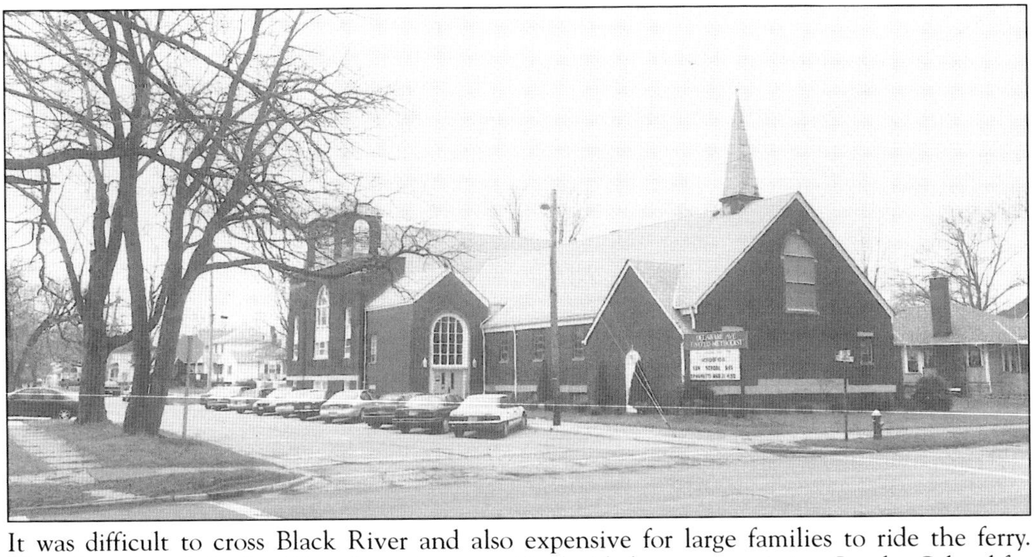

It was difficult to cross Black River and also expensive for large families to ride the ferry. Therefore, the Methodist Church on the west side decided to start a mission Sunday School for those who lived on the east side. The Sunday School started on August 6, 1899, and eventually grew into a full church. The building was constructed at the corner of Gawn Avenue and East Erie Avenue. When the street name was changed to Delaware Avenue, the church became known as the Delaware Avenue United Methodist Church.

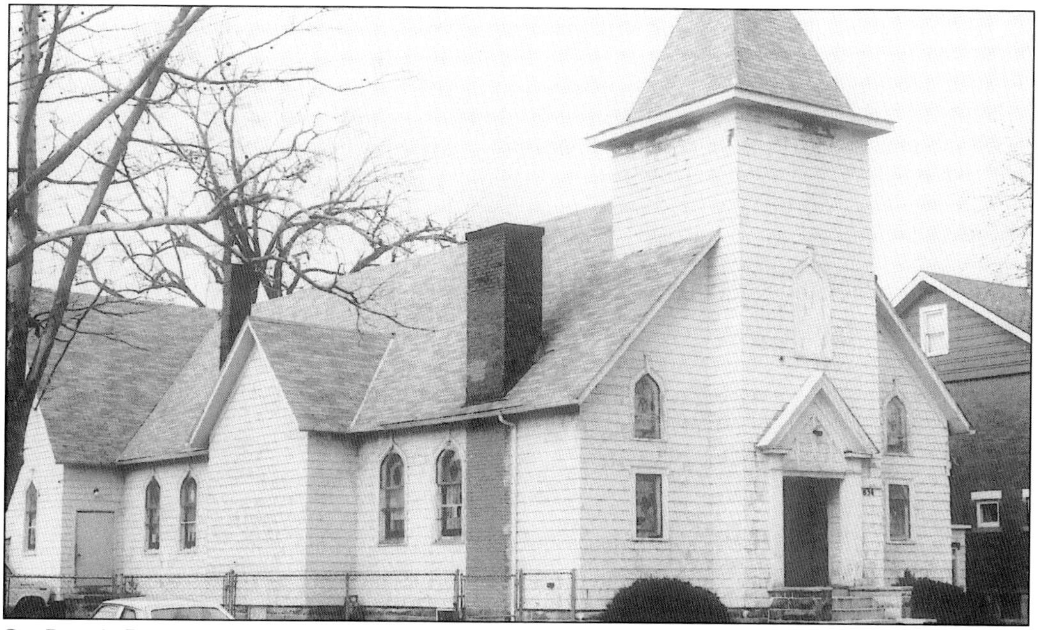

St. Peter's Roman Catholic Church started here in 1909 at 834 West Seventeenth Street. When the new church was built on Oberlin Avenue, the building was sold to the Compassion Baptist Church. A fire destroyed that building in February 1993 and a new church, located at 520 West Twenty-second Street, was built on the site of the Spang Baking Company.

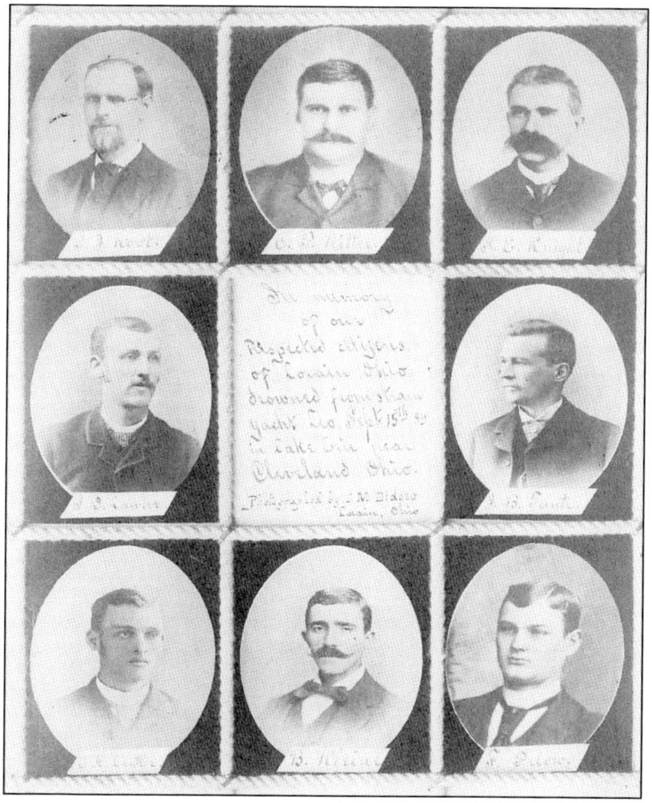

It was in 1889 that Lorain was plunged into great sadness with one of its earliest disasters. Some of the most prominent business leaders of Lorain had just bought a steam yacht, called the *Leo,* and were taking it to Cleveland for inspection. They also took other prominent Lorain businessmen with them for a nice outing. That was the last anyone heard from them. A storm did hit, but it is thought that the engine may have exploded, killing all eight businessmen plus the pilot of the boat. It was a great loss to the city.

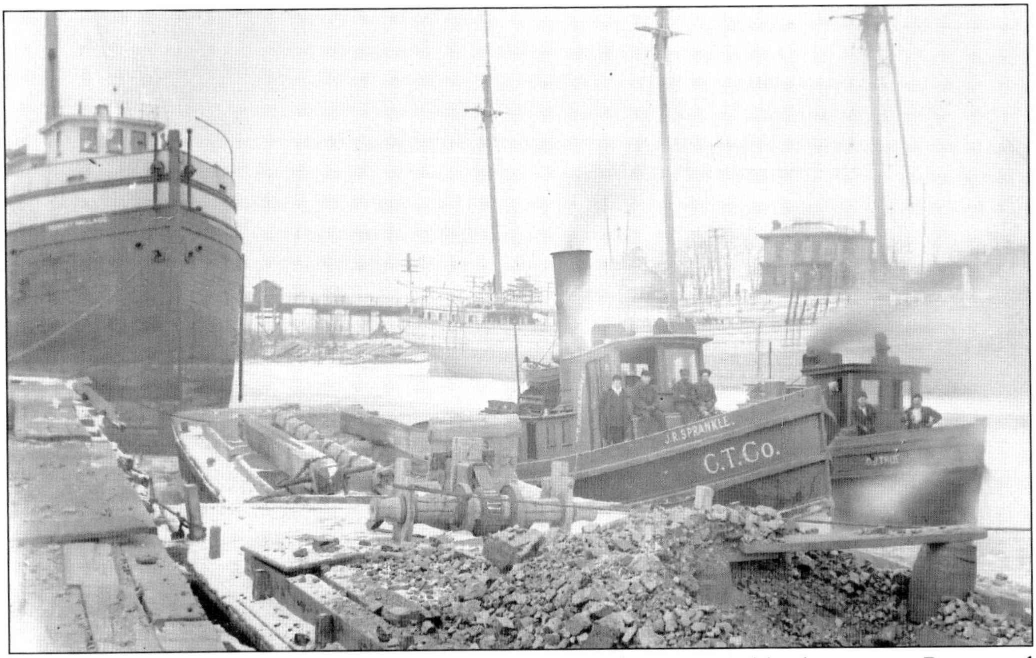

In January 1904, a 50-mph wind came out of the northwest with blinding snow. Boats and barges were torn from their moorings and drifted out into the lake. The tug *Cascade* (similar to the *Sprankle*, pictured here) started out to save what they could. They found a drifting barge loaded with fuel oil and while trying to save it, the storm worsened. The captain and his crew of 12 watched as wind-blown ice chunks slammed into the tug. With water pouring into the tug, they rammed it into the ice flow and abandoned ship. They wandered on the ice and finally came ashore west of the Lorain lighthouse.

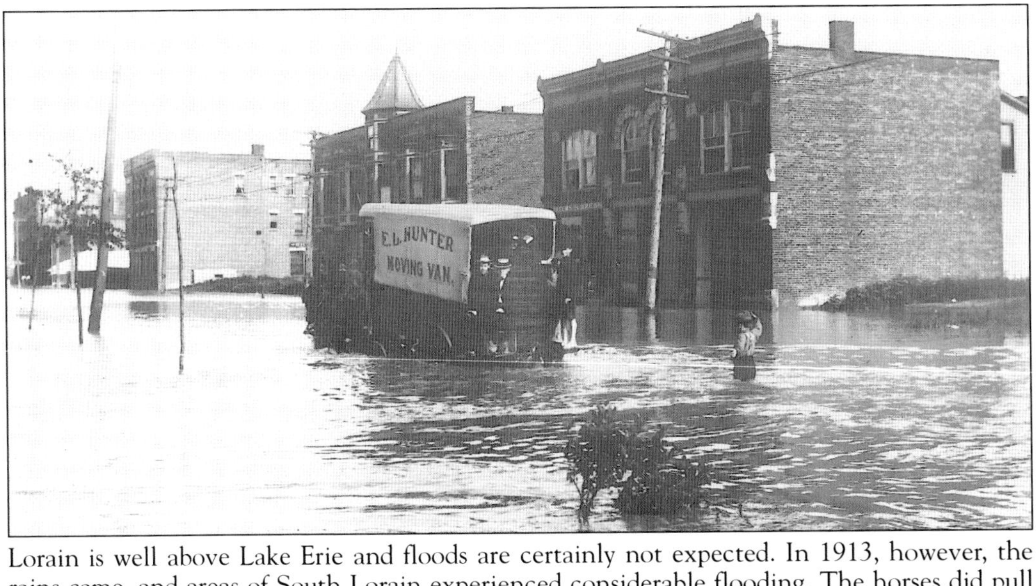

Lorain is well above Lake Erie and floods are certainly not expected. In 1913, however, the rains came, and areas of South Lorain experienced considerable flooding. The horses did pull the moving van through the flooded streets, and obviously, boys had fun wading through the high water.

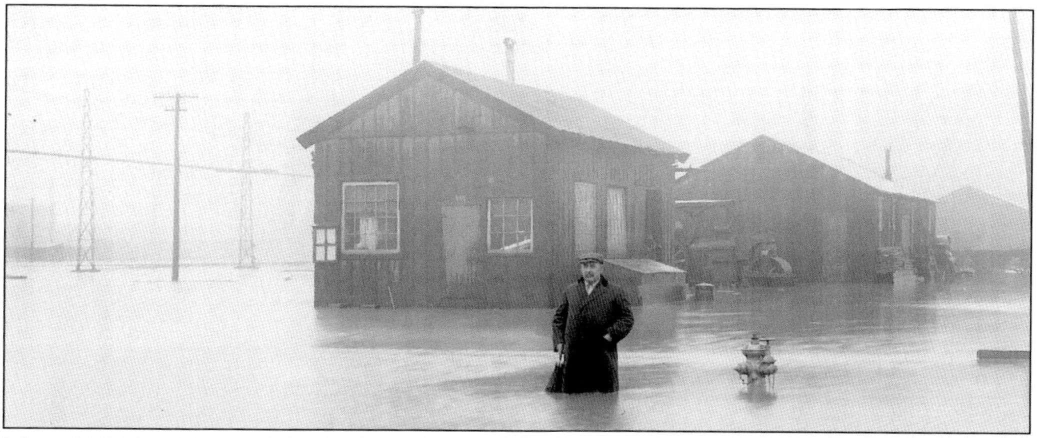

The 1913 Flood hit on March 25 and caused high water at Twenty-eighth Street and Pearl Avenue in South Lorain. In the background is the steel plant. The high water did much damage and prevented people from venturing out. The man in the picture, William Young, shows how deep the water was on this street. Notice the old, steam pavement roller between the buildings.

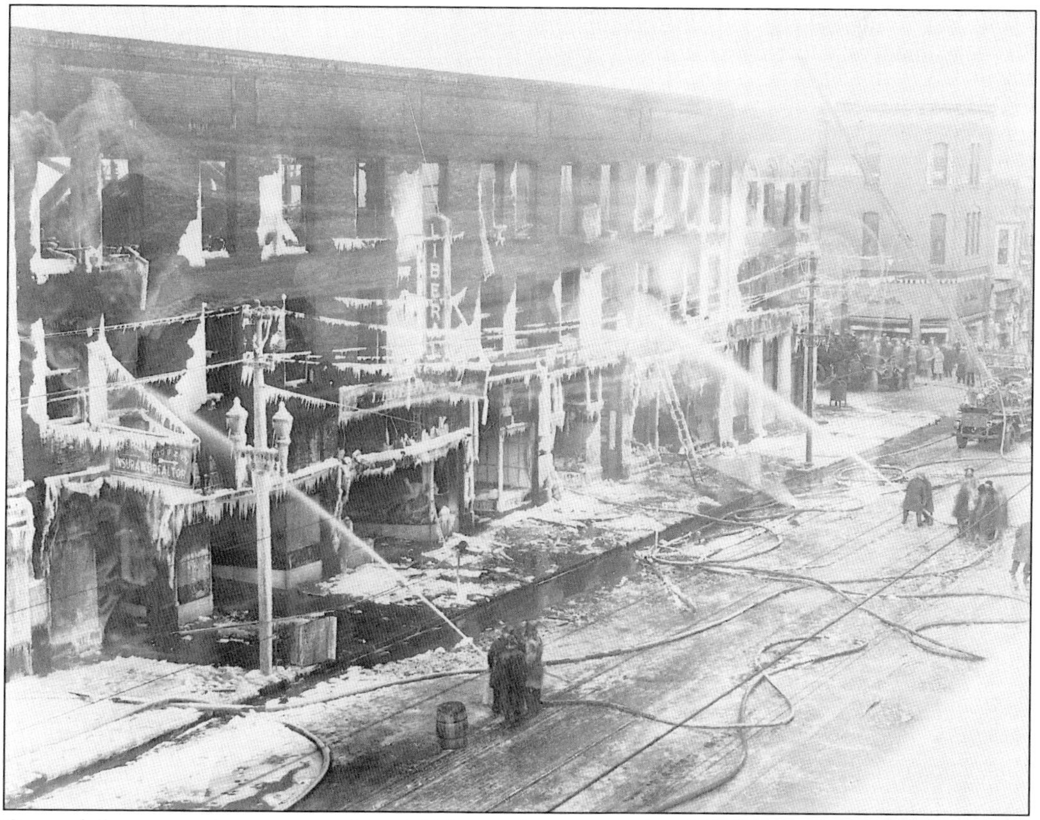

One of the worst fires occurred in 1926, on the west side of Broadway between Sixth and Seventh Streets. At the corner of Sixth Street was the Lorain Banking Co. Next to it was the Oehlke Clothing store, the Merit Clothing, Liberty Credit Clothing, J.C. Penney department store, Central Drugstore, George Meyer Men's Furnishings, Lorain Real Estate by Walker & Zier, and Ostrov's Shoes. Many of the small businesses never reopened.

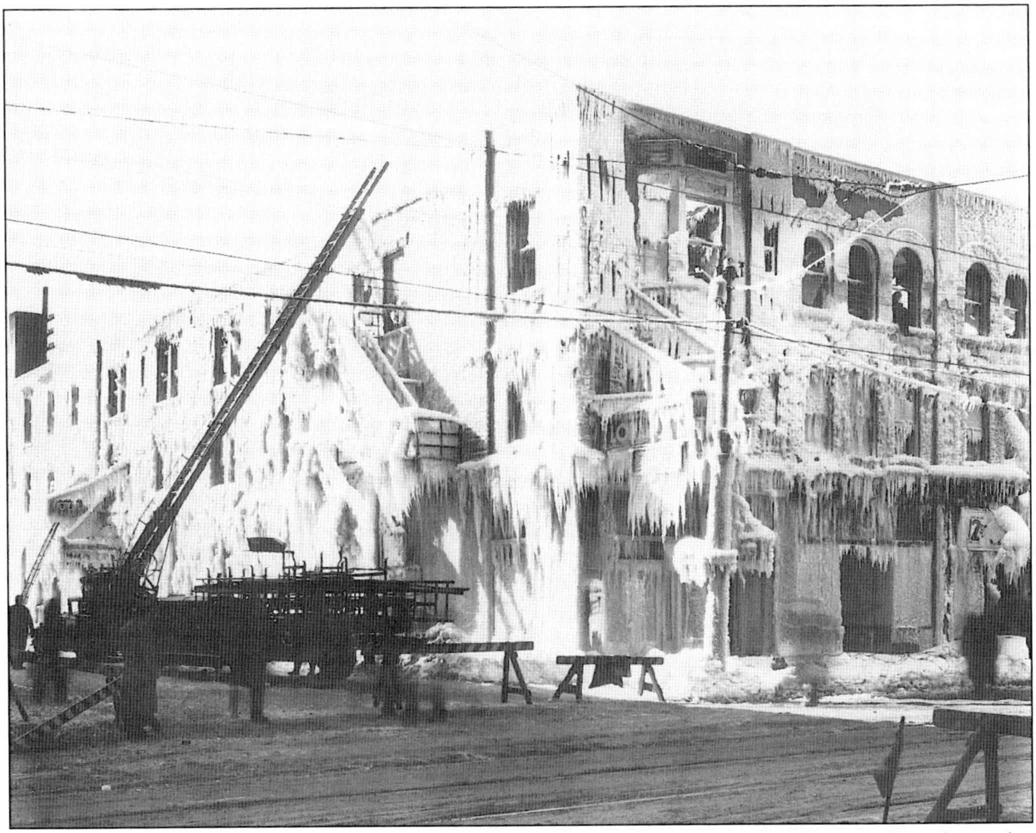

It was a cold November night in 1936 when a fire broke out at the Lorain Hotel, at the corner of Broadway and Seventh Street. The thermometer was reading 20 degrees below zero and the firemen were pouring water onto the roaring flames. The building was eventually restored and became the J.C. Penney Co. Later, Bobel's Office Products conducted business there for many years.

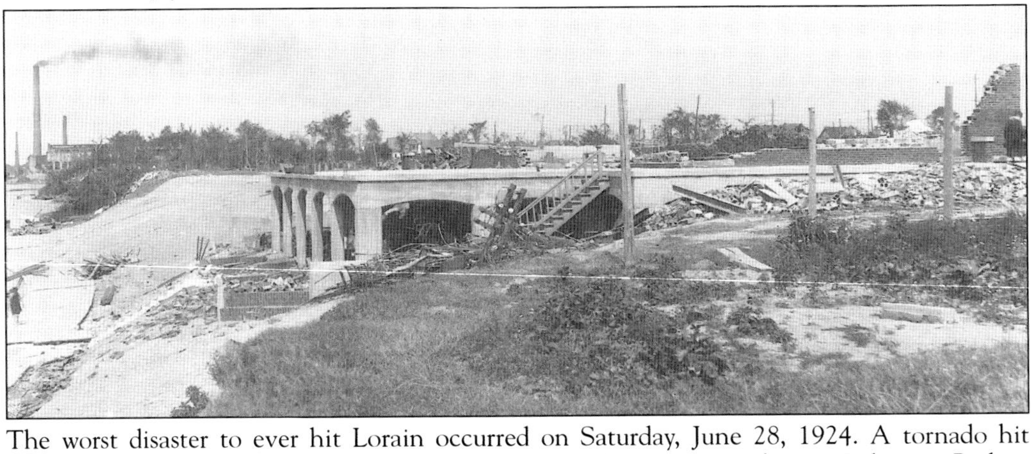

The worst disaster to ever hit Lorain occurred on Saturday, June 28, 1924. A tornado hit Sandusky, then proceeded along the shore of the lake, where it came ashore at Lakeview Park in Lorain. The swimmers saw it coming and rushed to the bathhouse. If they chose the basement, they lived. If they chose the upper floor, most of them were killed. This was the second-worst place to be in that tornado.

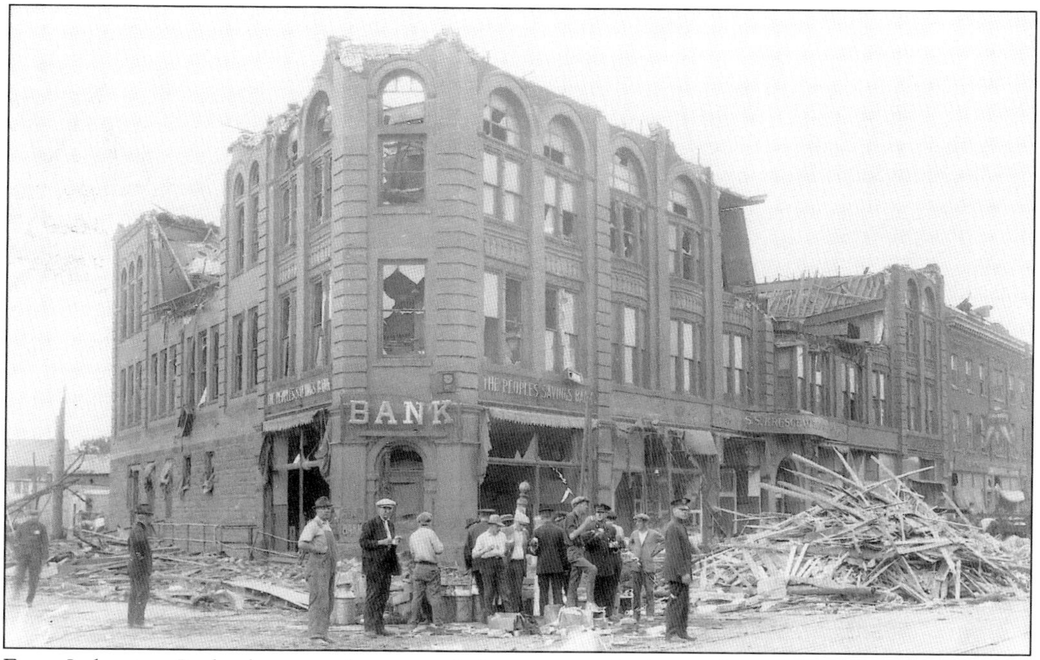

From Lakeview Park, the tornado proceeded east through the residential area, destroying many homes and killing people as it went. When it hit the business district, it seemed to gain in strength. Most of the business district was destroyed. The Peoples Savings Bank at the corner of Fourth and Broadway shows a sample of the extent of the destruction.

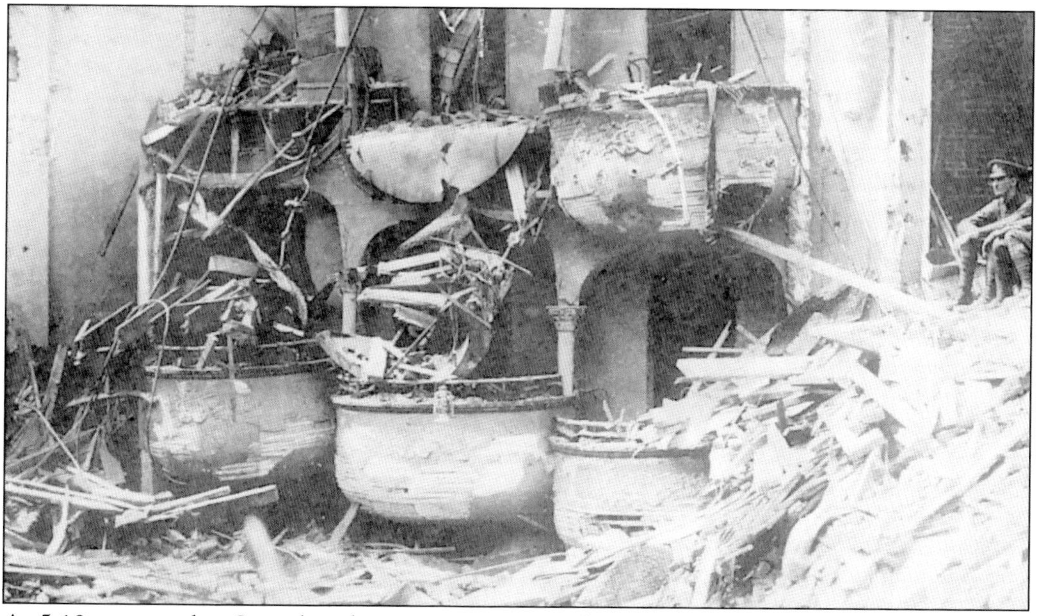

At 5:10 p.m. on that Saturday, there were many people attending a movie at the State Theater on Broadway. The tornado winds took off the top floor of the building next to it, and blew it onto the roof of the theater. The roof collapsed on all the people in attendance. There were more people killed at the State Theater than anywhere else.

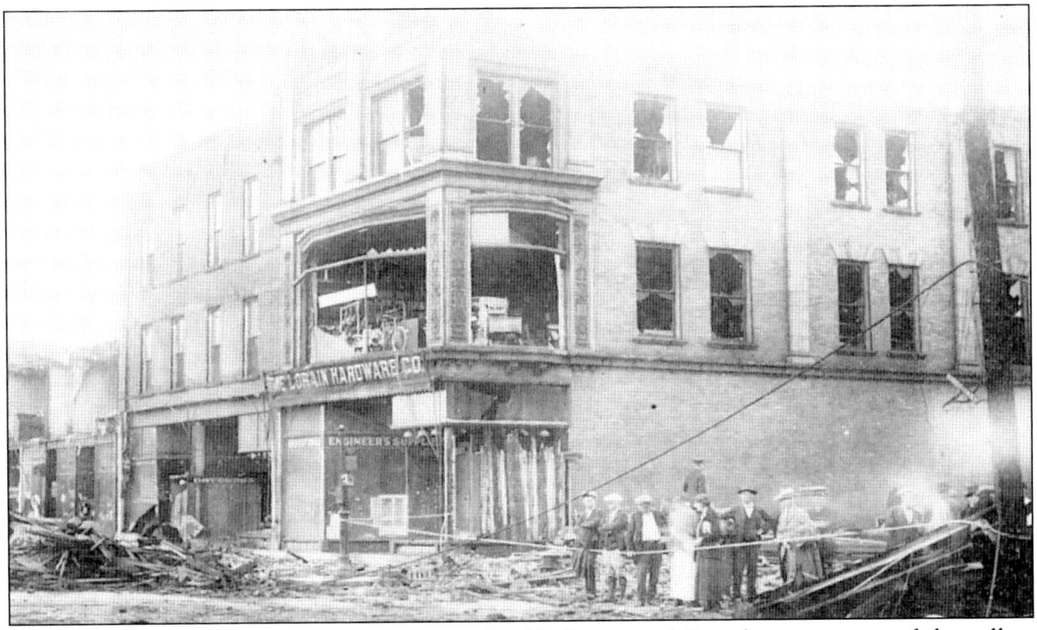

The Lorain Hardware Store at the corner of Fifth Street and Broadway was one of the tallest in town. It was four stories high! Count the floors! Of course, the tornado blew off the top floor and only three remained. The building was then roofed over and remained only three stories high.

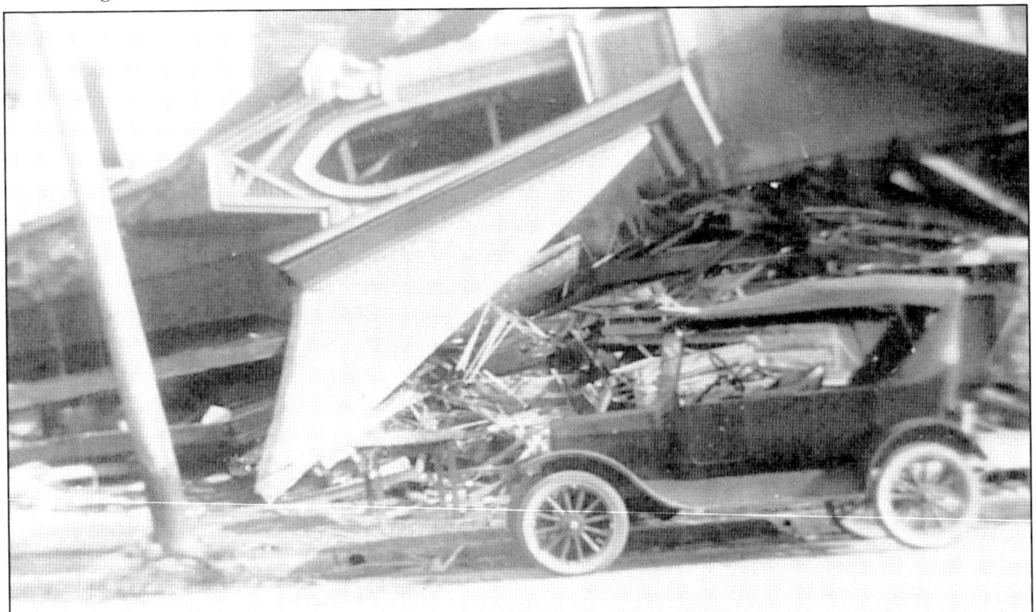

The First Congregational Church was a wooden structure at the corner of Fourth Street and Washington Avenue. The tornado blew the church and its steeple east onto the Number One Fire Station. The next day, services were held at Irving School to give thanks for those who survived, and to pray for those 78 people who were killed in the tornado. The members immediately started a campaign to raise money for the much larger brick church that was built on the same site.

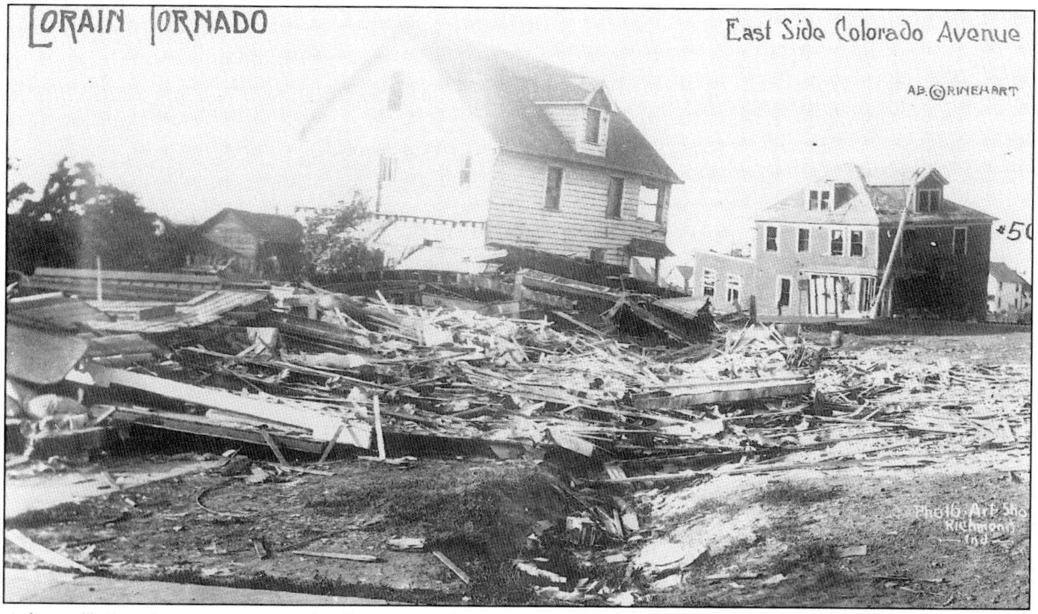

After all the destruction in the business district, the tornado continued east across Black River and hit the homes there. As in any tornado, some houses were blown off their foundations, some were turned to match wood, and some were bypassed by the winds.

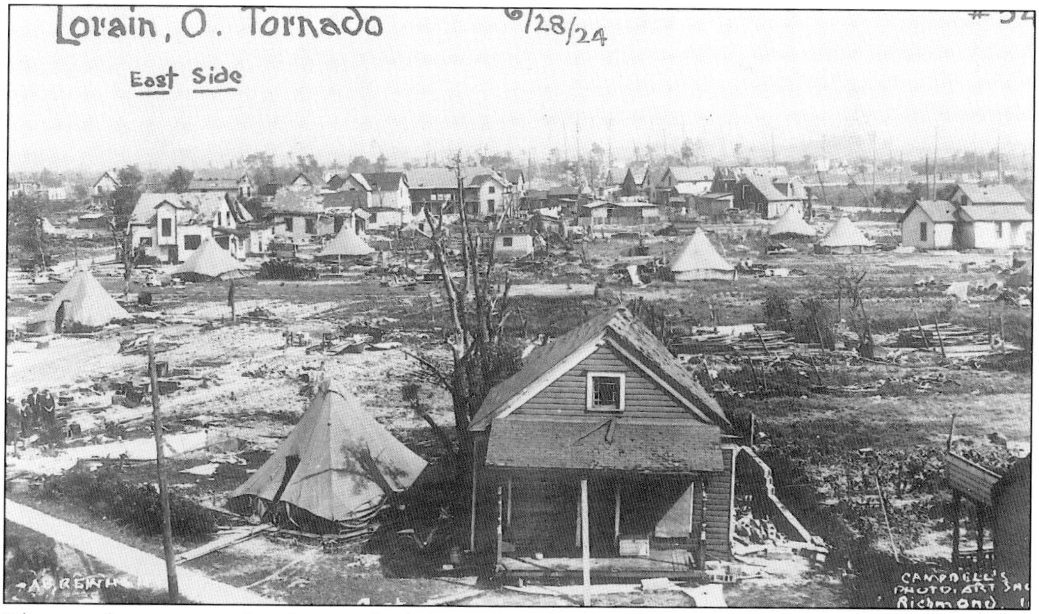

The word went out that Lorain had been wiped off the map. People in Cleveland formed emergency hospital crews and sailed into Black River to help the people. The governor of the state declared a national emergency, and the National Guard was called out to help the survivors. They brought tents for themselves and for the residents to use as temporary shelter.

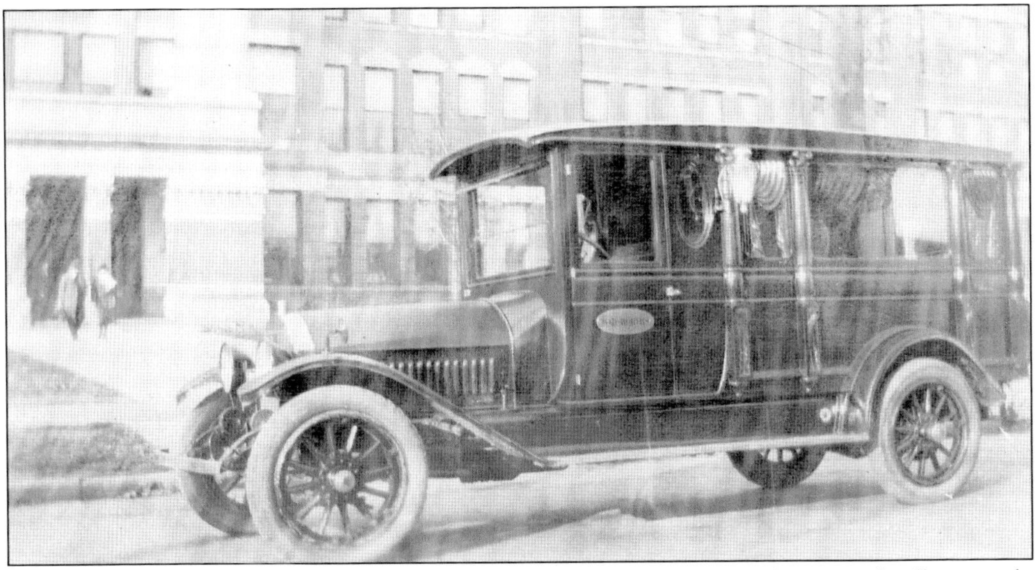

Seventy-eight people were killed in the tornado that day, making it the most deadly tornado to ever hit Ohio. Most deaths came from the State Theater, and the next highest was from the bathhouse. The Lorain High School, located at Sixth Street and Washington Avenue, was used as a hospital and morgue. Pictured above is a hearse in use that day.

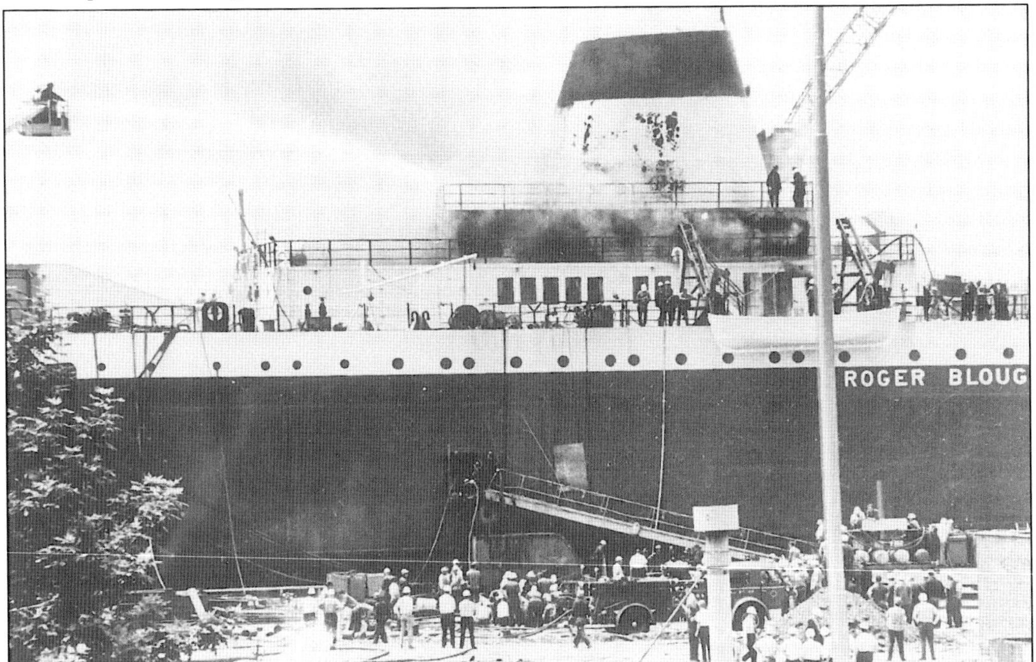

The American Shipbuilding Co. was constructing one of the largest ships to be built on the Great Lakes at that time. On June 24, 1971, the *Roger M. Blough*, an 858-foot ship, suddenly caught fire from a welder's torch and it spread to a 20,000-gallon fuel tank, which ruptured. Three explosions rocked the ship and temperatures reached 2,500 degrees. Four men were killed and 18 injured in the fire. The ship was restored and it was used on the Great Lakes for many years. (Photograph courtesy of *The Lorain Morning Journal*.)

Four

Our Government

Bridges, Lighthouses, Buildings, Parks, and Schools

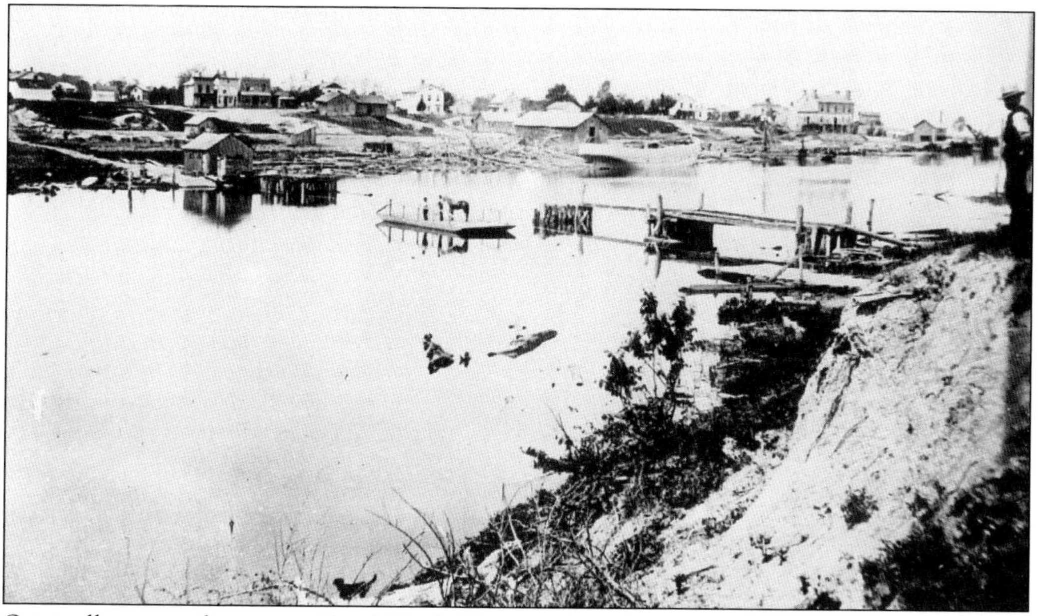

Originally, to get from one side of Black River to the other, it was necessary to walk across a sandbar near the mouth of the river. Later, a ferry was used to transport people, horses, and wagons. The first picture of a bridge is labeled 1873 and shows a barge taking people and a horse across. The spring rains caused the center section of the bridge to wash out into Lake Erie.

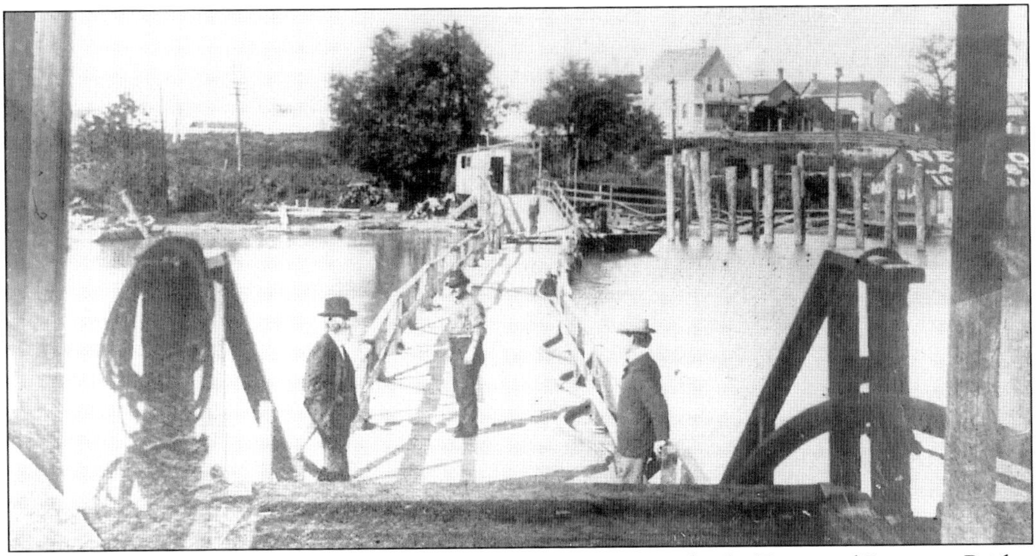

To replace the earlier bridge built by L.A. Fauver and G.A. Resek, the Ferry and Pontoon Bridge Company built a bridge using eight pontoons. The bridge carried passengers and water across Black River. Notice the fire hose slung across the floating structure. It had to be disconnected when there was a boat passing through. Those living on the east side learned to have extra water in tubs for just such times. It cost 2¢ to cross this structure, which operated for ten months in 1899. Pictured are Thomas Gawn (left) and G.A. Resek (right).

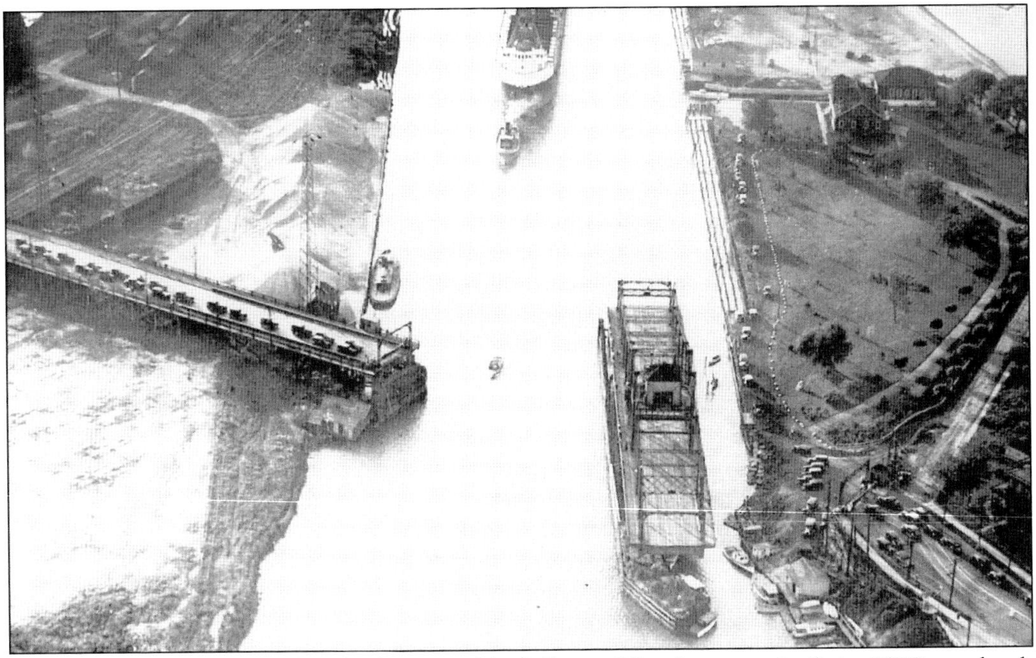

There were two swing bridges built across Black River. The first one, built in 1900, used oak planking for a floor and served for many years. When the streetcar era came, they found the cars were too heavy to run track and cars across the bridge. Passengers from the streetcars had to get off and walk across that bridge. A new swing bridge was built that could handle the weight. It was in service until 1940. Notice the ore carrier coming in from the lake.

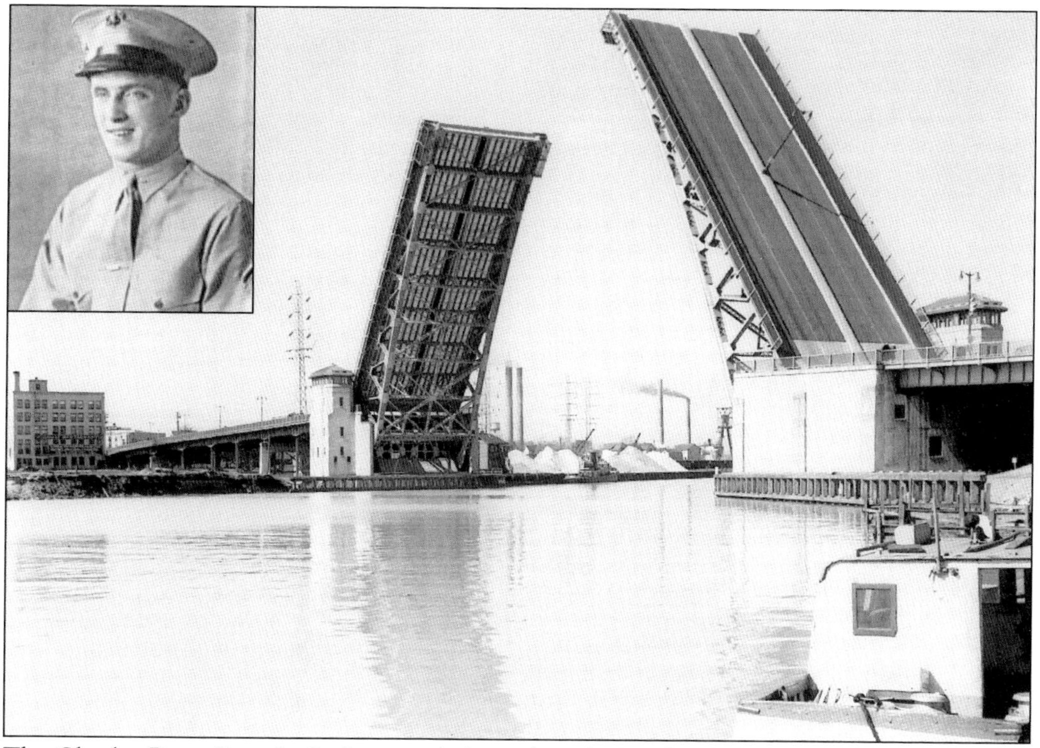

The Charles Berry Bascule Bridge was dedicated on September 25, 1940. The cost was about $1,400,000. The bridge was 1,426 feet long, including approaches, and at the time was the longest bascule-type bridge in the world. Lorainite Charles Berry heroically saved fellow soldiers by falling on a grenade that had been thrown into their foxhole during the WW II Pacific Campaign.

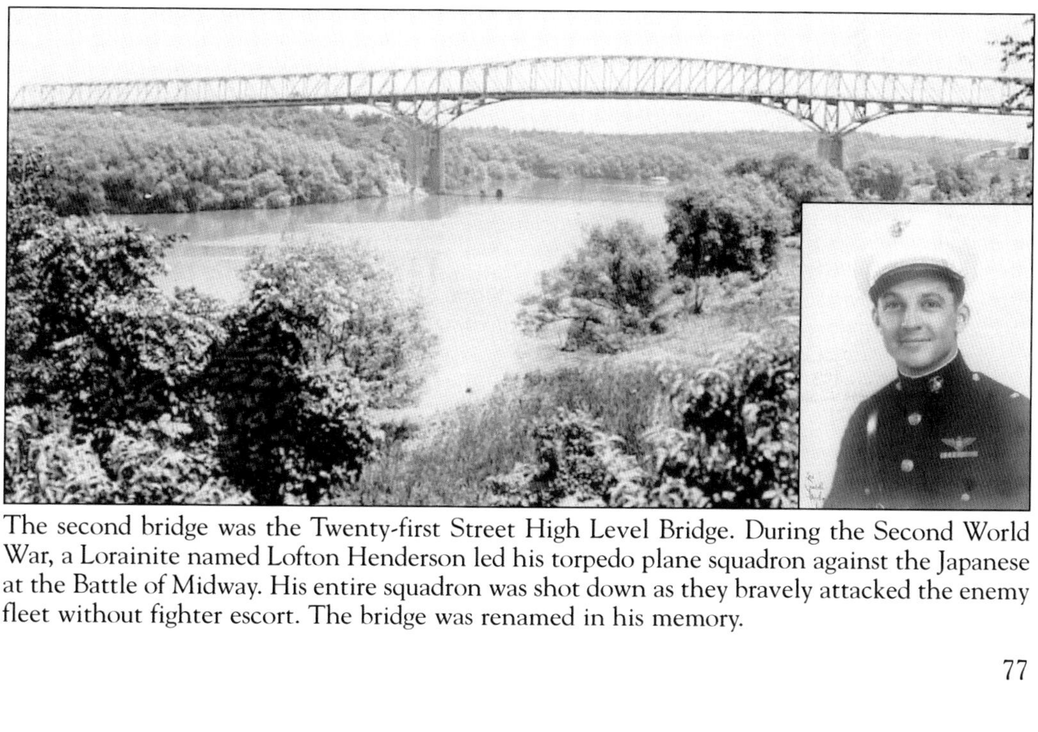

The second bridge was the Twenty-first Street High Level Bridge. During the Second World War, a Lorainite named Lofton Henderson led his torpedo plane squadron against the Japanese at the Battle of Midway. His entire squadron was shot down as they bravely attacked the enemy fleet without fighter escort. The bridge was renamed in his memory.

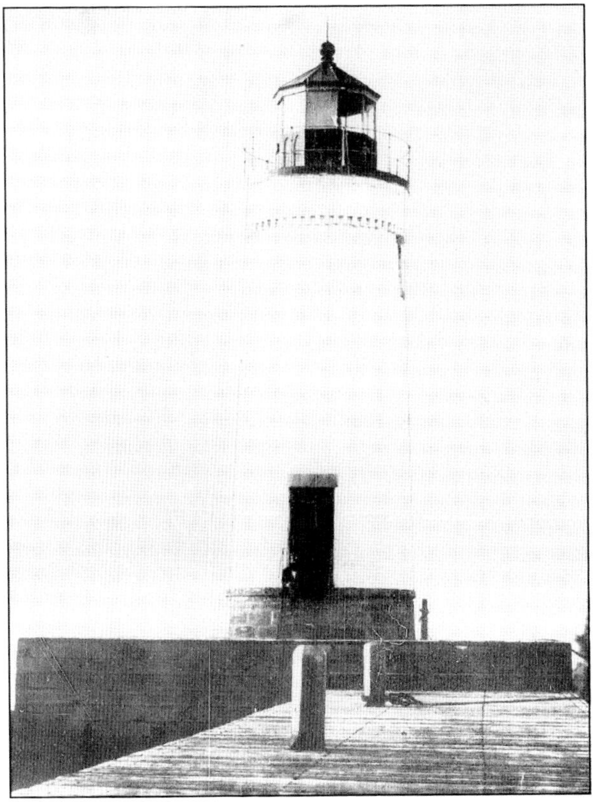

With Lorain being a lake port, there was a need for a lighthouse. In 1836 the first lighthouse was built on the shore of Lake Erie and next to the Black River. Oil had to be carried to the light every day during shipping season.

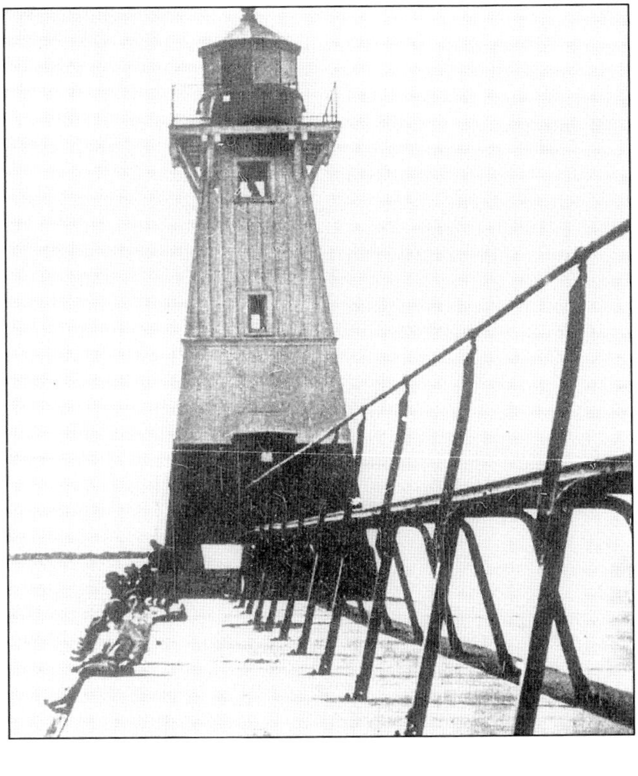

The second lighthouse in Lorain was built on a 350-foot pier. Again, the keeper had to take oil to the lamp every day. Storms from the northeast often pounded the pier, and at two different times, the keepers were washed overboard from the pier and drowned. After the second incident, a steel catwalk was constructed so "green water" would pass under the keepers; thus they could remain safe by holding onto the railing. A few years later, a "range light" was built at the base of the pier so captains could line up the two lights and sail directly into the harbor.

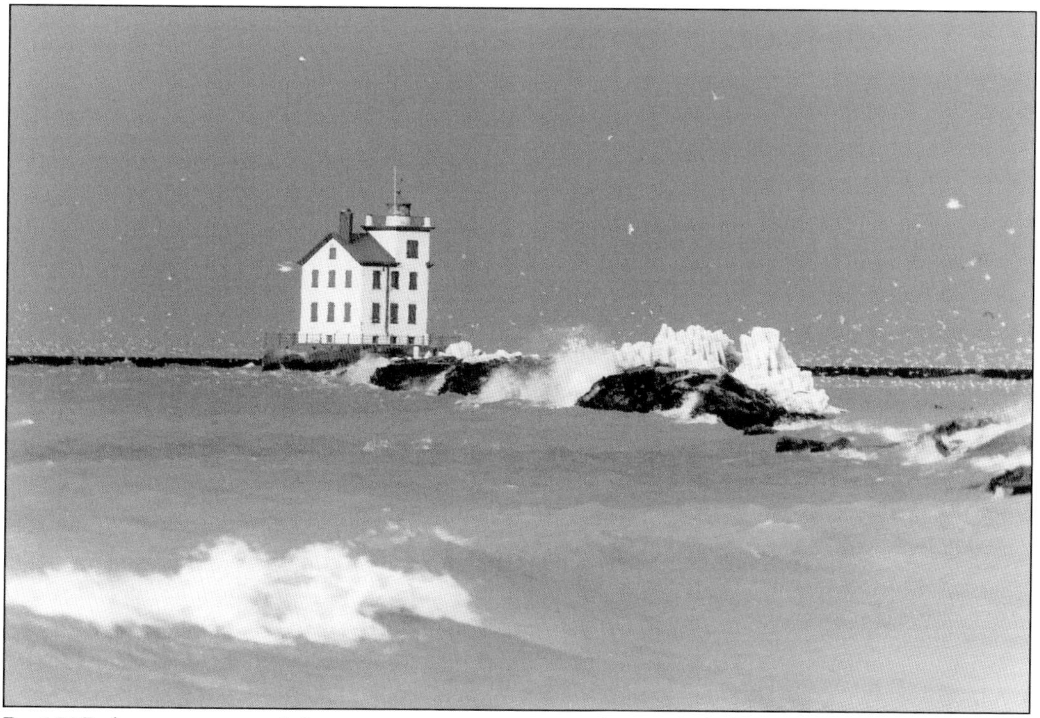

By 1917 there was a need for a major improvement. A new lighthouse was built farther out, with a channel breaking the pier. The lighthouse keeper had to live there and care for the light, which was now electrical, and help rescue those in trouble on the lake. That lighthouse was deactivated and is now in the process of being restored so tourists may visit it.

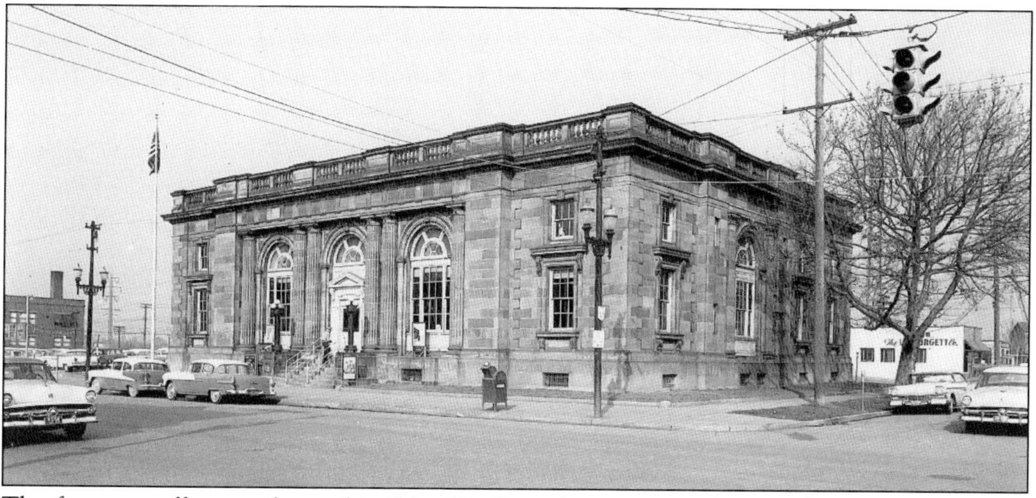

The first post office was located in John Reid's trading post, on the west bank of Black River, in 1811. The post office was named "Mouth of Black River," and that name also served as the village's name. By 1898 the office had moved to Fourth Street. A few years later, it moved to a wooden building on Fifth Street, and later still, it was located in a brick building on Sixth Street in the back of the Lorain Banking Co. By 1914 a new and larger facility was built on Broadway at Ninth Street, as seen in the above photograph. In 1999 a new distribution center was constructed on the east side, near Colorado Avenue and Root Road.

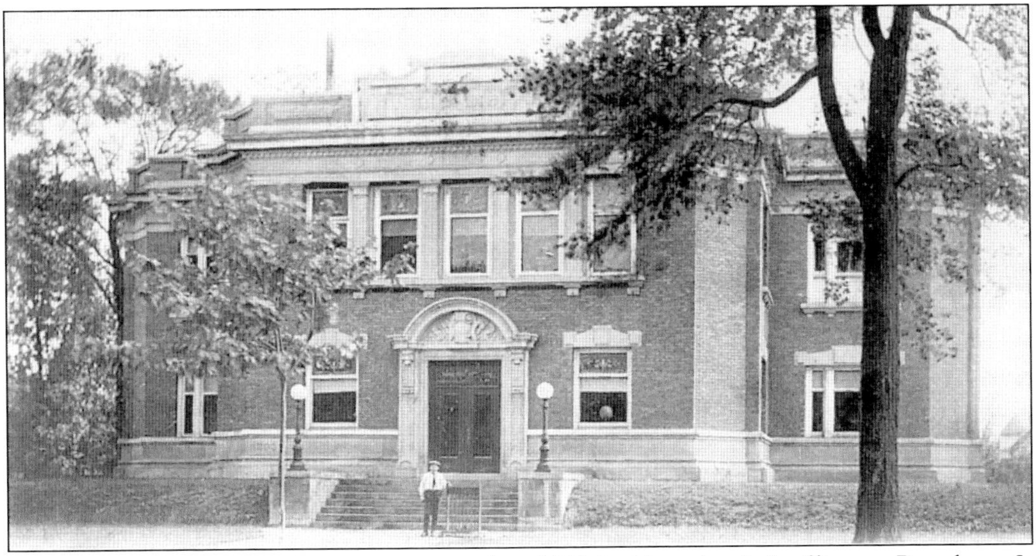

The first public library in Lorain was started in 1883 inside a dentist's office on Broadway. It lasted three years and the books were donated to the school system's library. In 1900 another major effort was started. In 1904 the library, shown above, was built on Tenth Street and Long Avenue. Andrew Carnegie (of Carnegie Steel Co. fame) donated $30,000 to help with the construction. The building served Lorain for over 50 years as a center of learning.

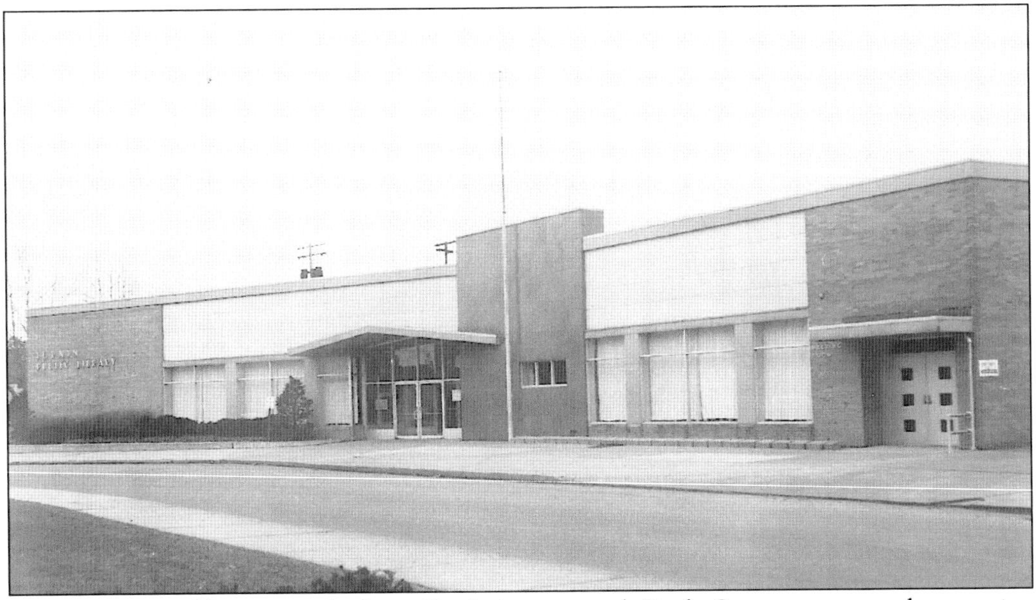

In 1957 a new library was built at Reid Avenue and Sixth Street to serve the growing population. New services were added and many branches were built throughout the city to provide local availability to the public. After Toni Morrison received the Nobel Prize for Literature, a room at the library was dedicated to her. She had used the old library as a center for her learning, and it was felt most appropriate to name a study room after her. Toni Morrison attended the dedication.

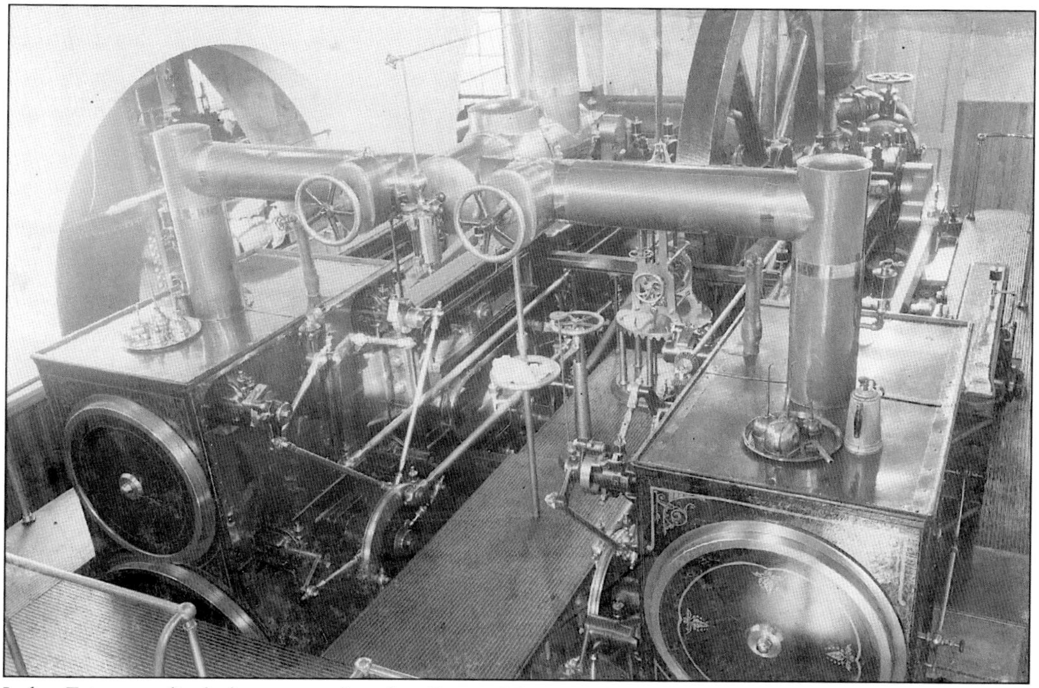

Lake Erie supplied the water for the City of Lorain. Water was pumped raw to the houses through wooden pipes that were held together by iron bands. Steam-powered pumps, shown above, served Lorain for years. In 1892 the first sewer system was installed. It dumped into Black River and mixed with the intake pipe in Lake Erie, resulting in many cases of typhoid fever. Dr. Hug, the health commissioner, insisted the water be cleaned up. By 1901 Lorain had installed the first water-filtration plant in the United States.

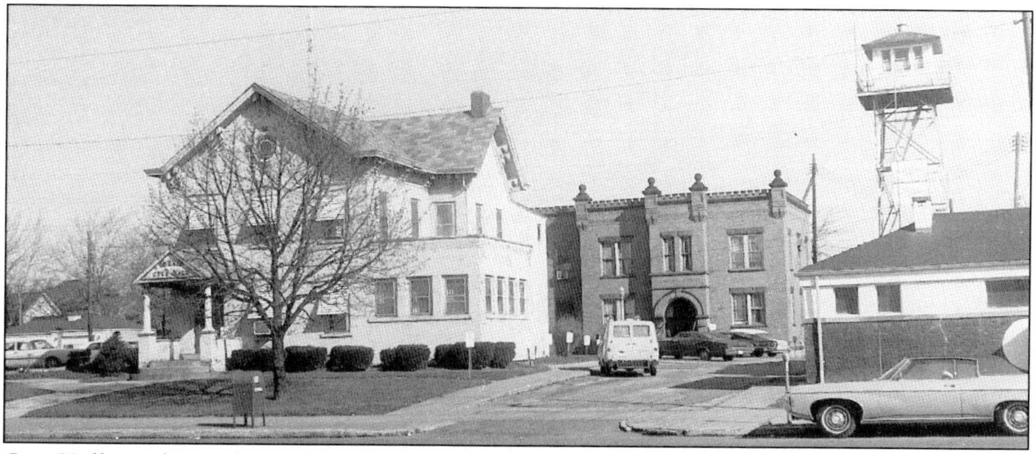

City Hall was located in a few offices in the Wagner Building, at the corner of Broadway and Erie Avenue until the tornado destroyed the building in 1924. The city administration moved to the Stang house, formerly the Jones Homestead, as shown on Erie Avenue. A police station and jail were built behind City Hall. In the war years of the 1940s, a Civil Defense tower was built behind it, with an airplane spotter's lookout and air raid siren. This picture was taken during the 1960s.

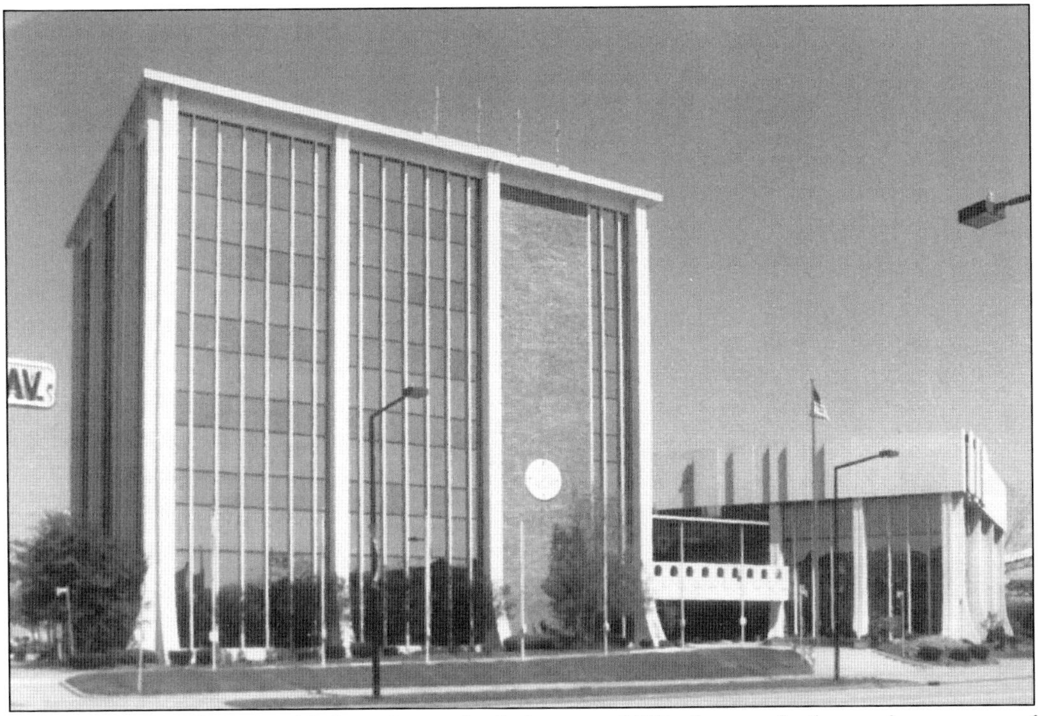

A new City Hall was added to Lorain's skyline in 1973. It was built at the corner of North Broadway and West Erie Avenue. Many buildings were torn down to make room for it. The building provided expanded facilities for the administration, the police department, and a jail facility.

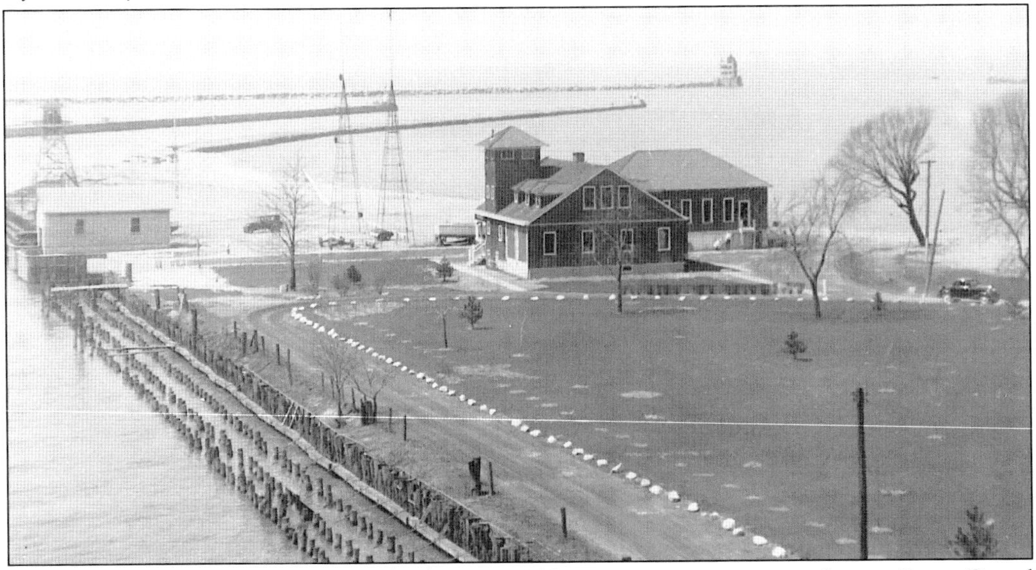

Lorain has long been known for its harbor. In 1908 construction was started on a Coast Guard Station on the east side of Black River. The land around it was a swamp. Fill-dirt brought the level up so the land could be drained, and the station was in full operation around 1910. Crews working from this building made many rescues. In 1989 a new and enlarged Coast Guard Station was built on the same site.

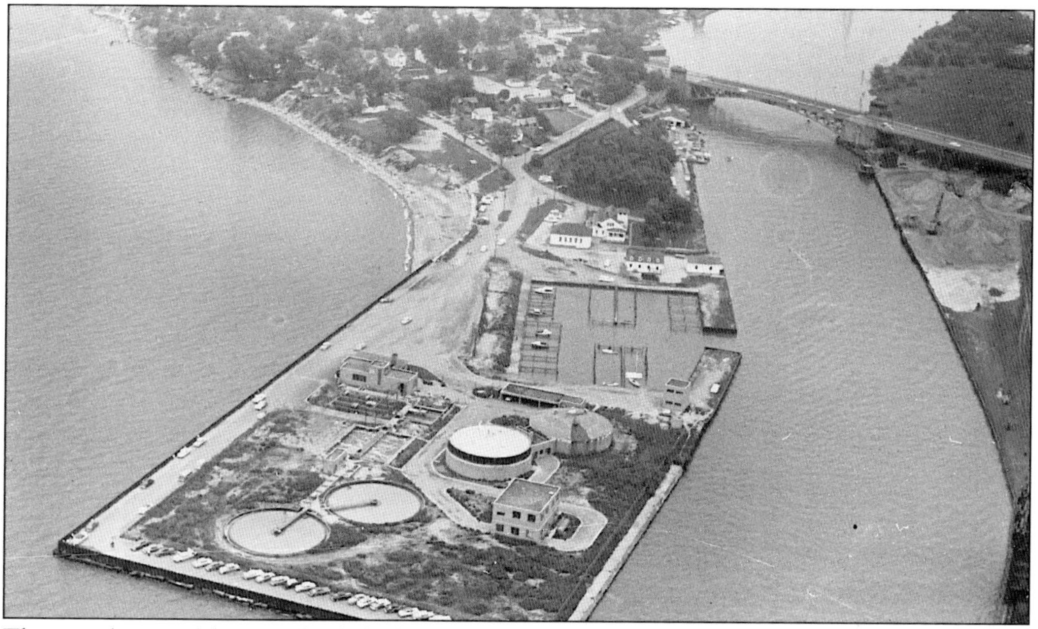

This aerial view of the mouth of Black River shows the Bascule Bridge in the background and the new Black River Wastewater Plant (built on the east side of the river) in the foreground. This facility went into operation in 1955 and has helped to clean the waters of Lake Erie and Black River. Just above the plant is a marina for small boats and beside it is the Coast Guard Station. Many of the houses on the left have been torn down and a park area has replaced them.

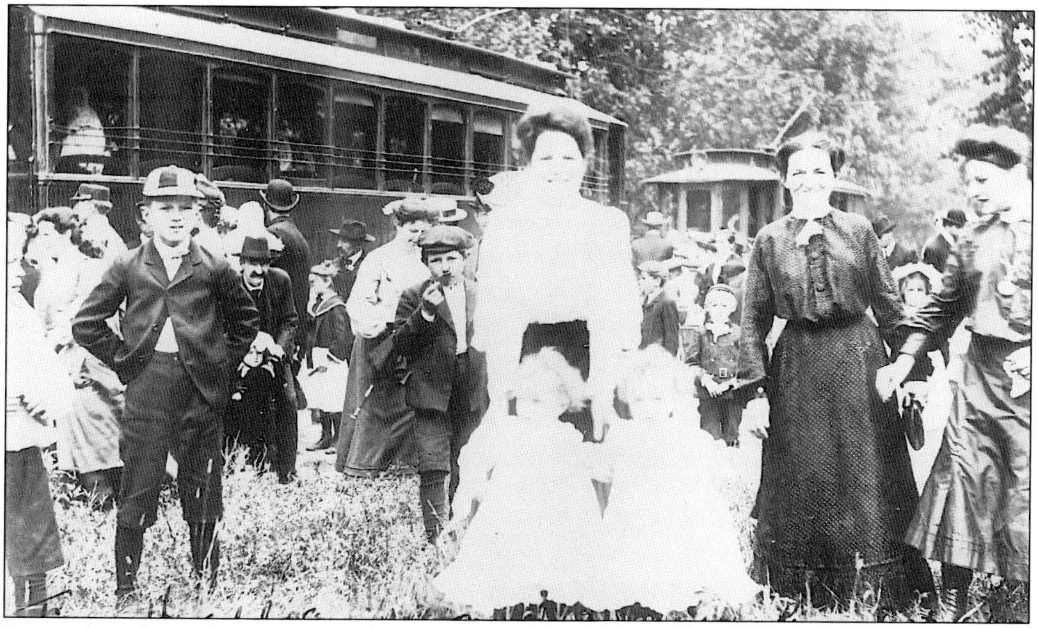

Lorain has always been interested in its parks. One of the earliest ones was Randall's Grove, located at East Erie and Euclid Avenues. After the Civil War, Henry Randall let the 103rd Ohio Volunteer Infantry have their first reunion on his farm. It soon turned into a resort for picnics, fishing, games, and outings. People even came by train, horse-drawn car, and the inter-urban streetcar to the large dance hall. This picture shows an excursion in 1891.

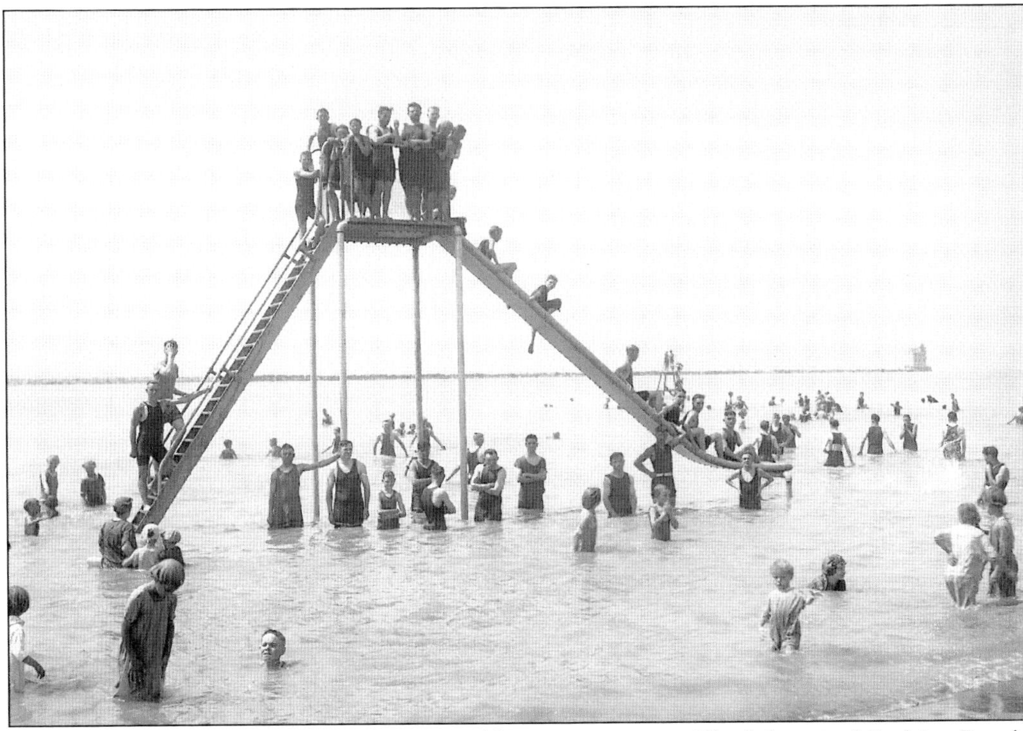

Lake Erie provided wonderful swimming and boating activities. The Municipal Bathing Beach, at the foot of Oberlin Avenue and First Street, provided many hours of entertainment for Lorainites. In those days without air conditioning, it also provided a chance to cool off. This picture from 1917 shows the latest in swimwear. The Lorain lighthouse is in the background, just after its completion.

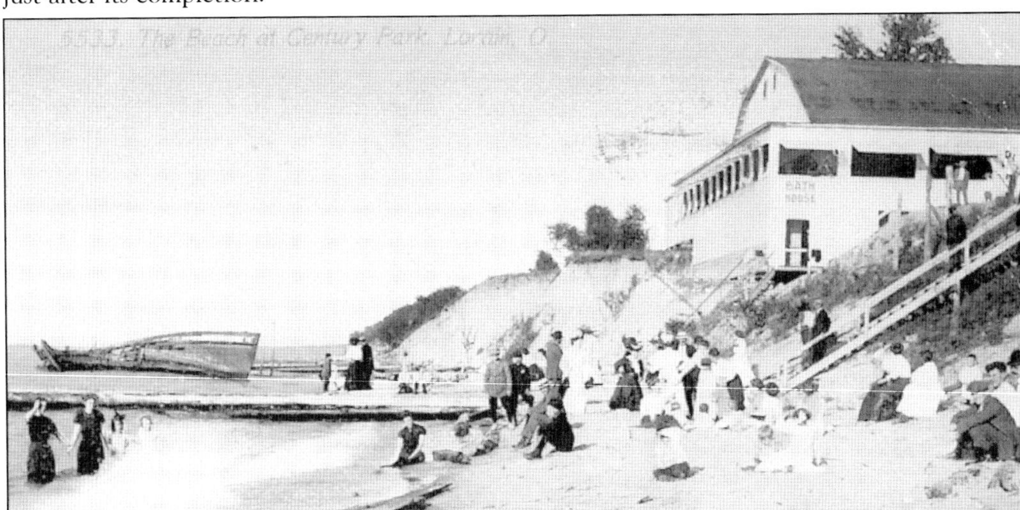

Century Park was located at East Erie and Michigan Avenues. Originally, the beach had a dance pavilion that was privately owned. Later it became a city park. This 1912 picture shows many people enjoying the park and its view of Lake Erie. Is that a ship that was driven ashore long ago?

One of the earliest parks in town was Washington Avenue Park. It was included in the original plot for Charleston in 1834. Couples had a chance to sit and enjoy the summer day in front of the bandstand, as seen in this picture from 1913. In 1983 the name was changed to Veteran's Park, in honor of the Lorain Veterans' Council for Civic Improvement. A new fountain and pavilion were built here.

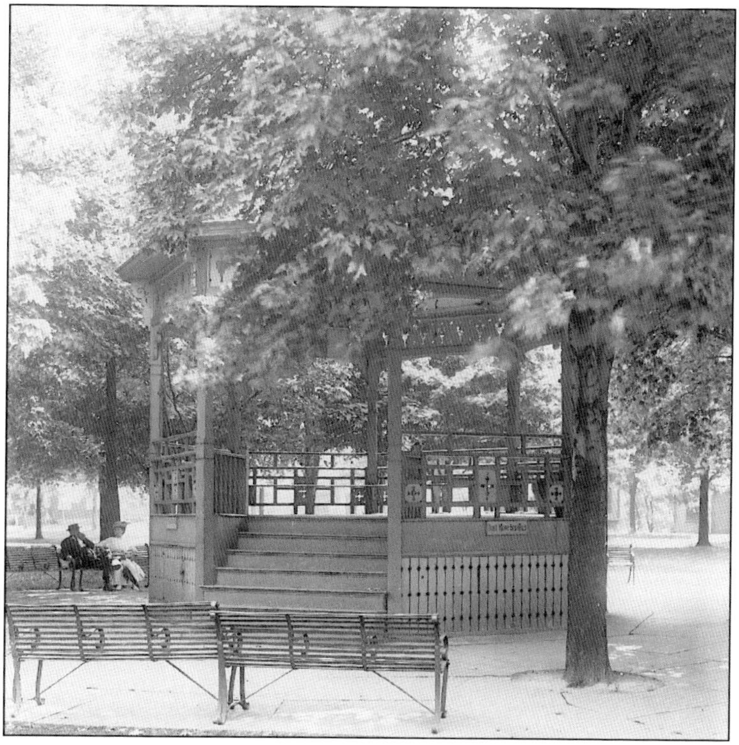

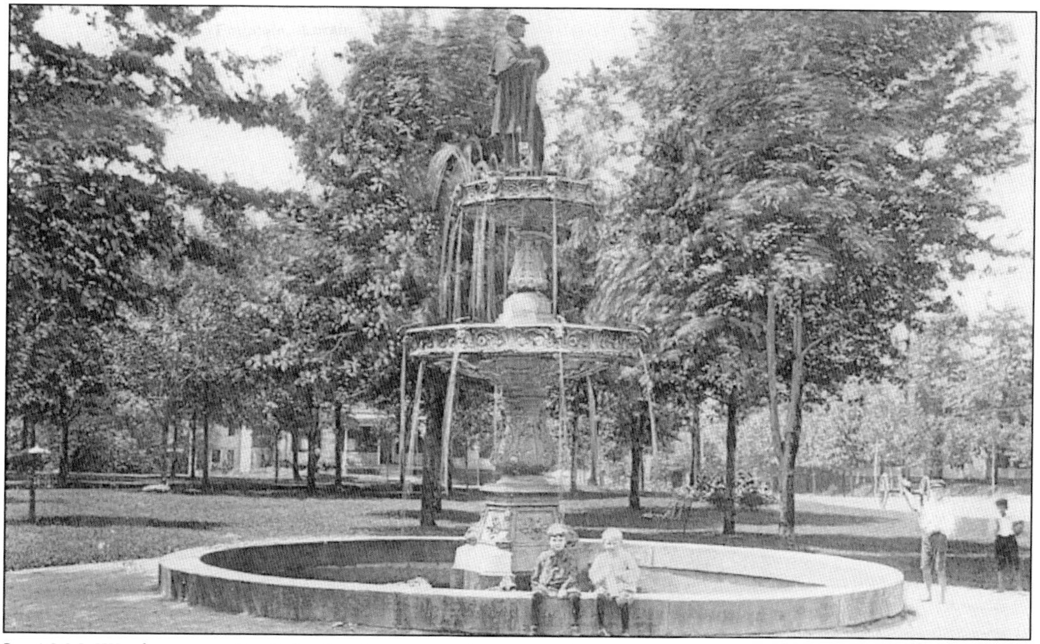

In 1908 Washington Park had a fountain that was also very attractive. A statue of a Civil War soldier was placed on top of it. The boys on the right were dressed in knickers, which was the usual dress for boys under 12. Once they were "of age" they were allowed to get long trousers (a mark of being grown-up). The statue was later taken down and sent to the 103rd Ohio Volunteer Infantry complex in Sheffield Lake.

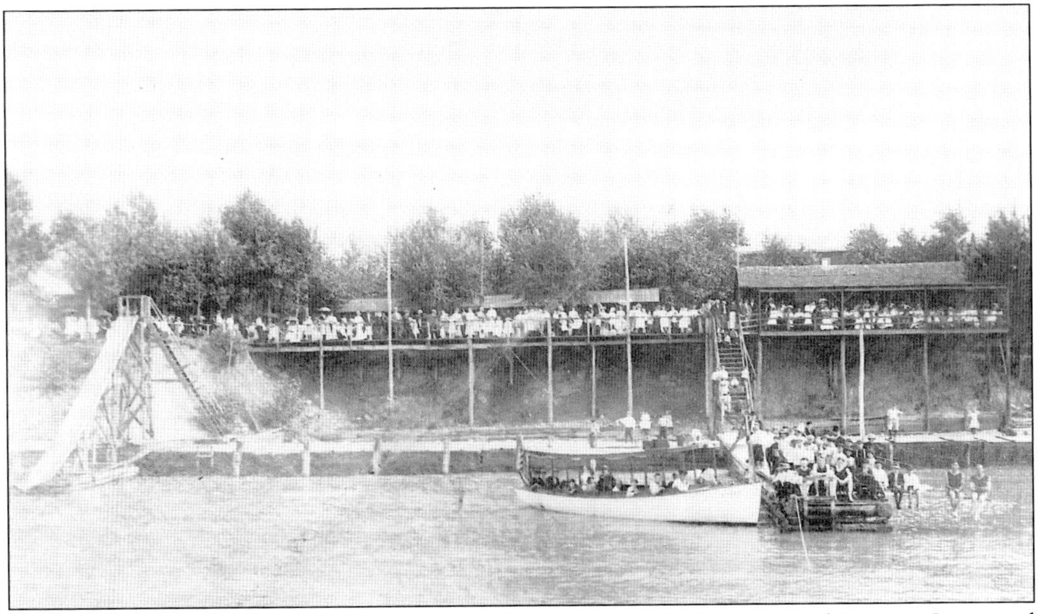

Glen's Beach was a park situated on Lakeside Avenue, near the Coast Guard Station. It opened June 4, 1907, and attracted many swimmers to the nice beach. Roller-skating and dancing were held in the building; it had the largest dance floor in Lorain County. Many tables outside provided places for picnics and lunches during band concerts.

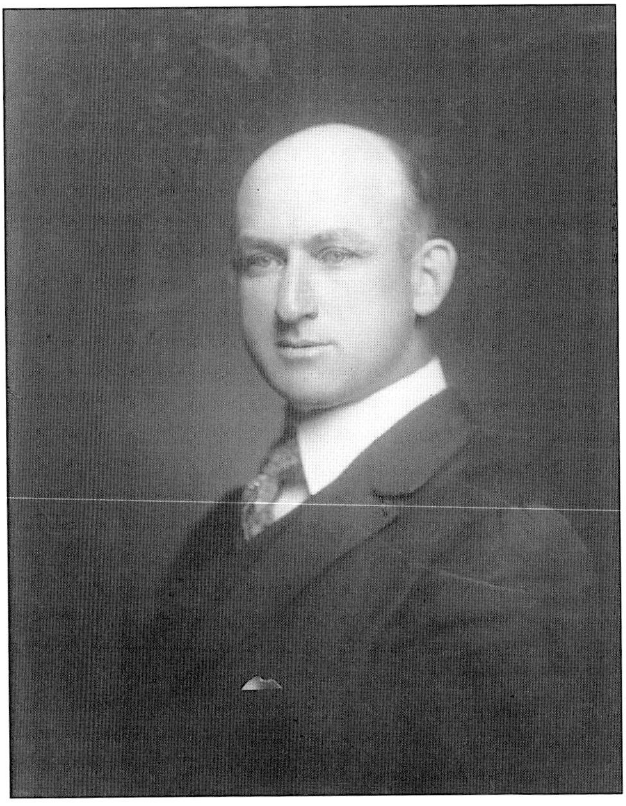

Leonard Moore became mayor of the City of Lorain in 1916. He persuaded the City Council to purchase property west of town, and there he founded Lakeview Park. It has become one of the largest and most developed parks in the city. Mayor Moore was Secretary-Treasurer of the Lorain Lumber & Manufacturing Co. before becoming mayor.

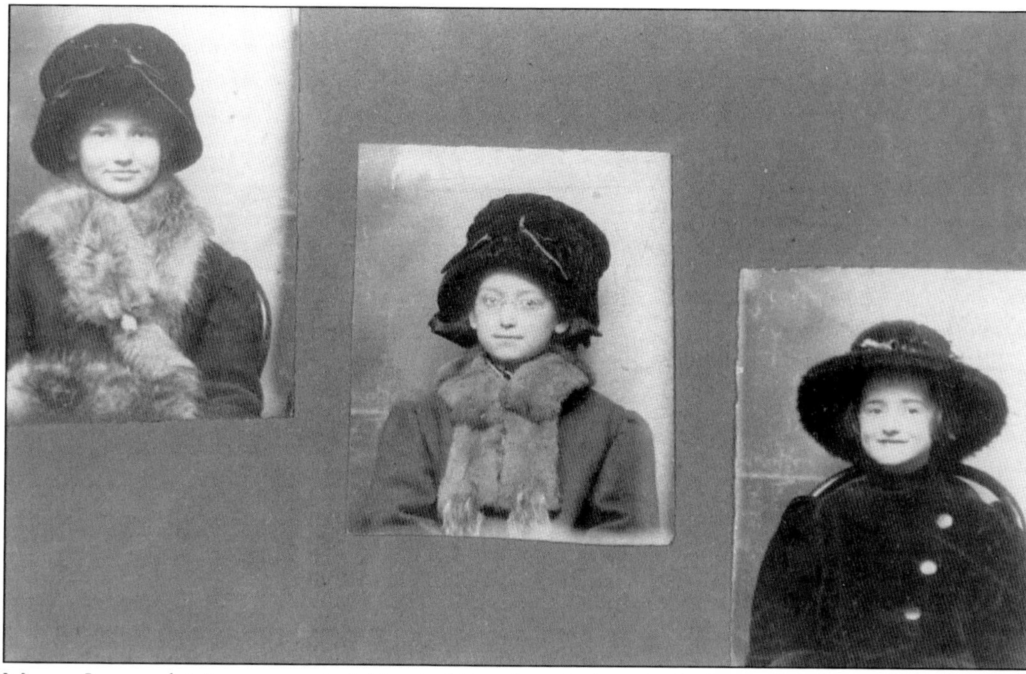

Mayor Leonard Moore married Carrie Friend and they had three daughters. In this 1913 photograph are, from left to right, Ruth, Eleanore, and Helen. They lived in a large home at 309 Fifth Street. Eleanore was the youngest. She married and moved to California and had two sons. Helen Moore was the oldest. She stayed in the home until her death in 1981. Ruth, who was the middle child, was the first to die. A few years after the death of Helen, the City of Lorain purchased the house. It became the home of the Black River Historical Society in 1993 and was placed on the National Registry.

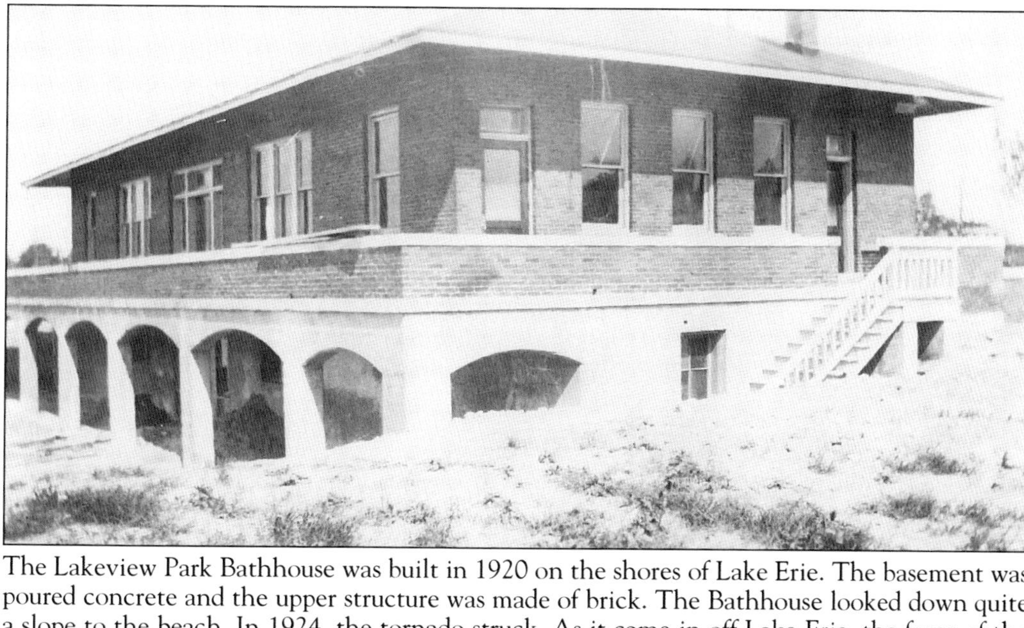

The Lakeview Park Bathhouse was built in 1920 on the shores of Lake Erie. The basement was poured concrete and the upper structure was made of brick. The Bathhouse looked down quite a slope to the beach. In 1924, the tornado struck. As it came in off Lake Erie, the force of the winds blew the top floor completely away. Later, a new top floor was built.

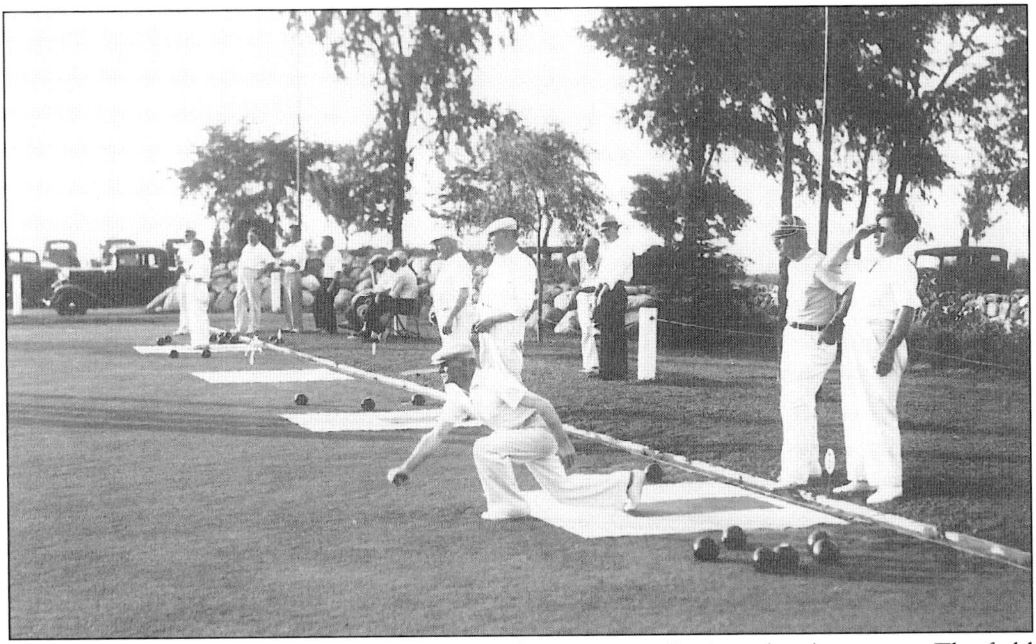

One of the first improvements to Lakeview Park was to install a lawn bowling green. The field had lighting installed and was used by the Lorain Lawn Bowling Association for their sport, which is of Scottish origin. The green is 300 feet square, and play runs on weeknights and Sundays from May into the fall, weather permitting.

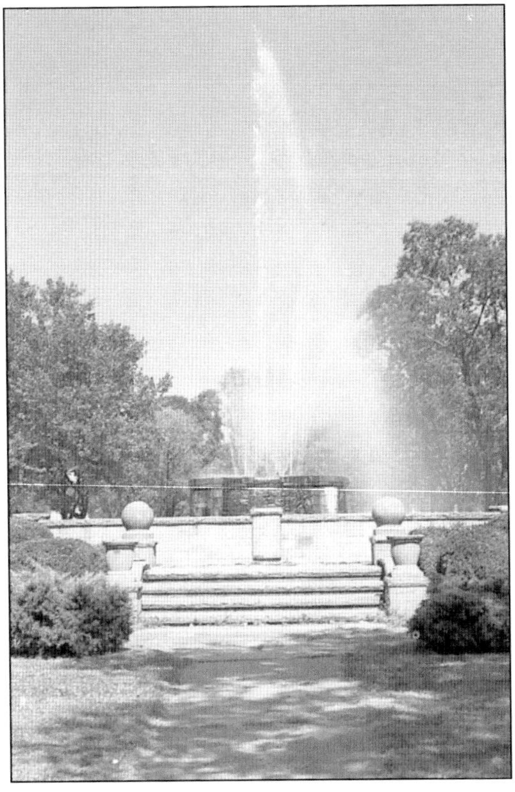

One of the most beautiful fountains in the area is the one at Lakeview Park. This fountain was completed and dedicated in 1935 and was a project of the National Youth Association. The fountain is especially beautiful in the evenings, when a computerized system runs the lights of various colors, and the spray formation varies on a six-minute repetitive cycle.

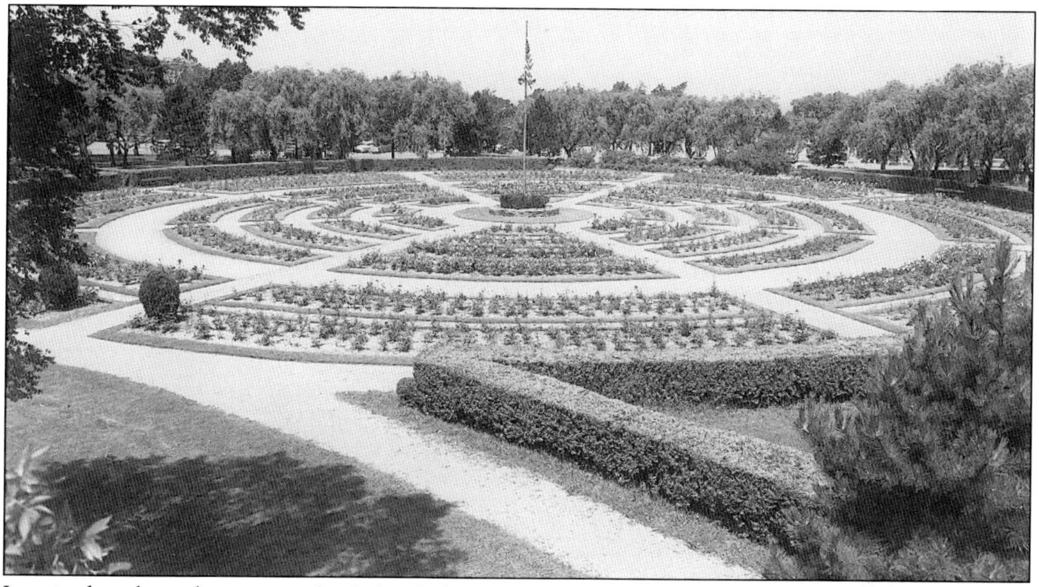

Lorain has long been proud of the Lakeview Park Rose Garden. Records indicate that it dates back to 1933, when the Rotary Club of Lorain laid out the wheel-pattern, and 35 civic organizations, along with the City Park Department, planted over 3,000 rose bushes in 48 beds. With the extreme heat of the summer of 1959, many bushes suffered severe damage and had to be replaced. The Kiwanis Club of Lorain led that restoration project with the City Park Department.

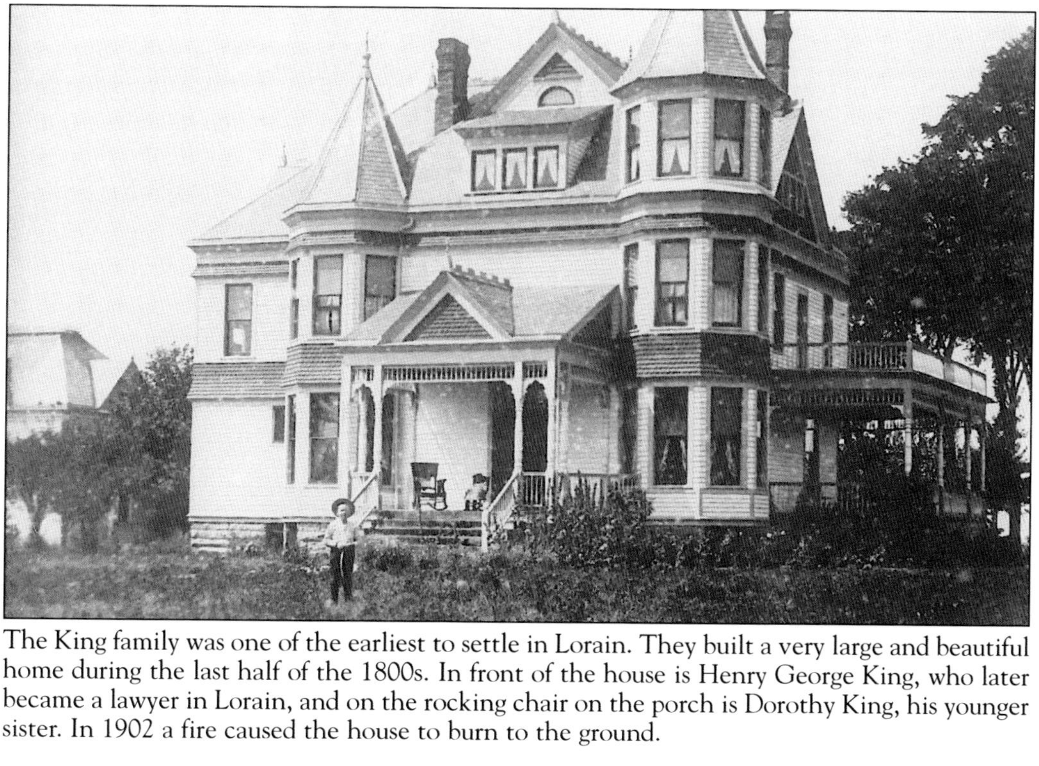

The King family was one of the earliest to settle in Lorain. They built a very large and beautiful home during the last half of the 1800s. In front of the house is Henry George King, who later became a lawyer in Lorain, and on the rocking chair on the porch is Dorothy King, his younger sister. In 1902 a fire caused the house to burn to the ground.

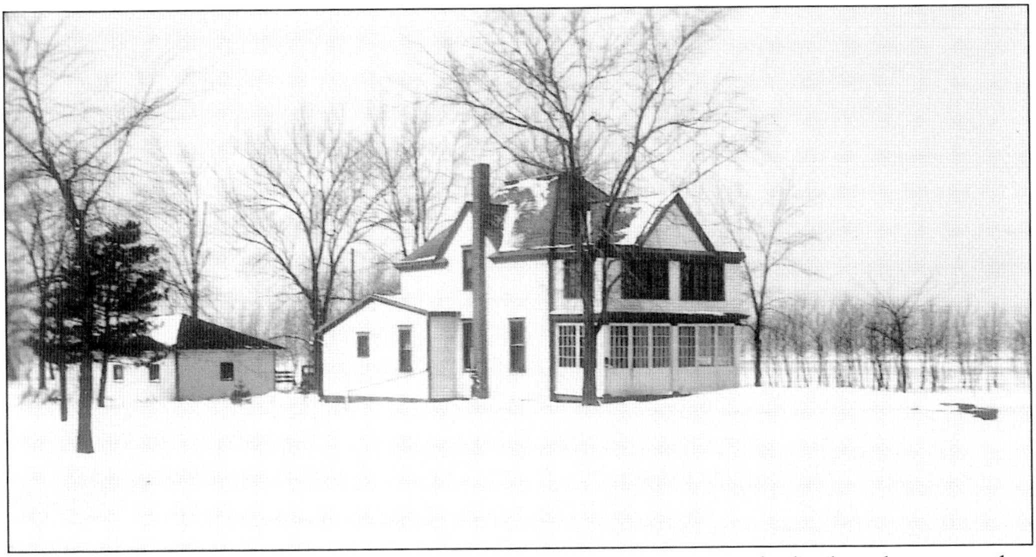

After the fire, the family moved into the remodeled carriage house in the back and continued to live there until the last family member, Elizabeth King, died in the late 1990s. Upon her passing away, the city bought the property, which added many acres to Lakeview Park.

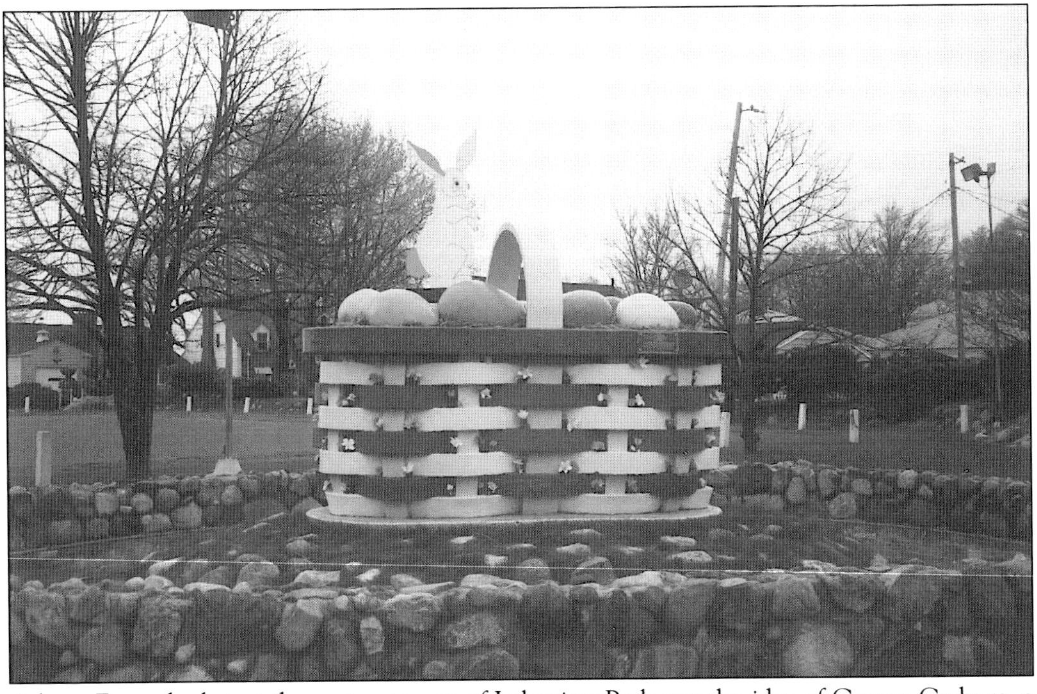

A large Easter basket at the east entrance of Lakeview Park was the idea of George Crehore, a former park superintendent. David Shukait, a Park Department employee, proceeded to design the basket. In 1937 he received a patent on the design. The basket is made of concrete and is painted with colors depending on the holiday. Each of those Easter eggs weighs about 200 pounds. Parents bring their little children to have their picture taken in front of the basket. There is another basket at Oakwood Park.

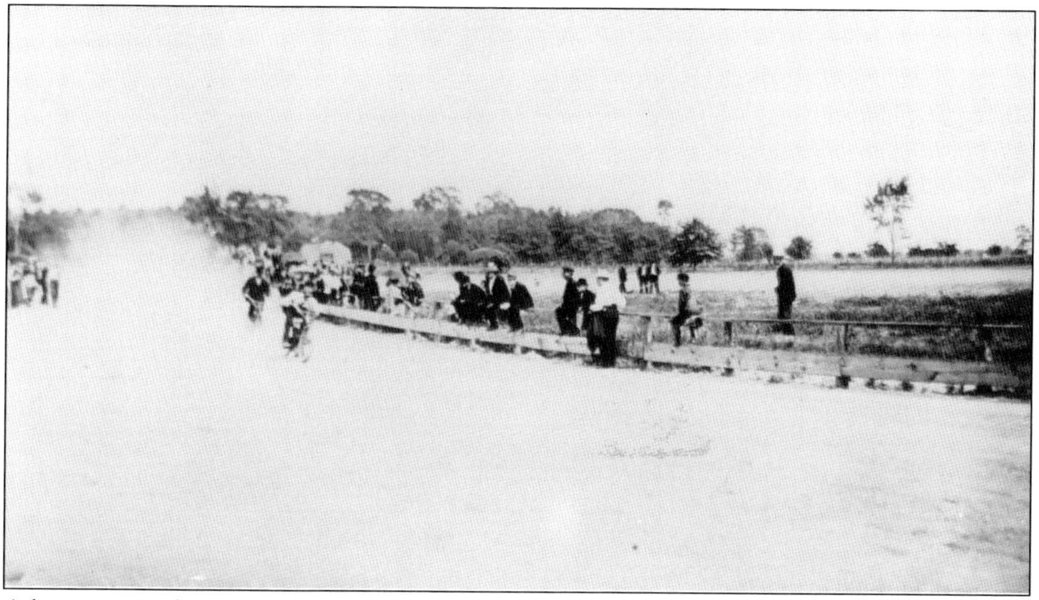

A large racetrack was built in western Lorain, just east of Leavitt Road and north of the railroad tracks on land that was owned by the King family. Races of all kinds were held there, including horse, auto, and bike races. On weekend afternoons crowds would gather to see the race and congratulate the winner. One of the frequent auto race drivers was Otto Carlson, who had a job as chief mechanic at the Buick garage on Broadway.

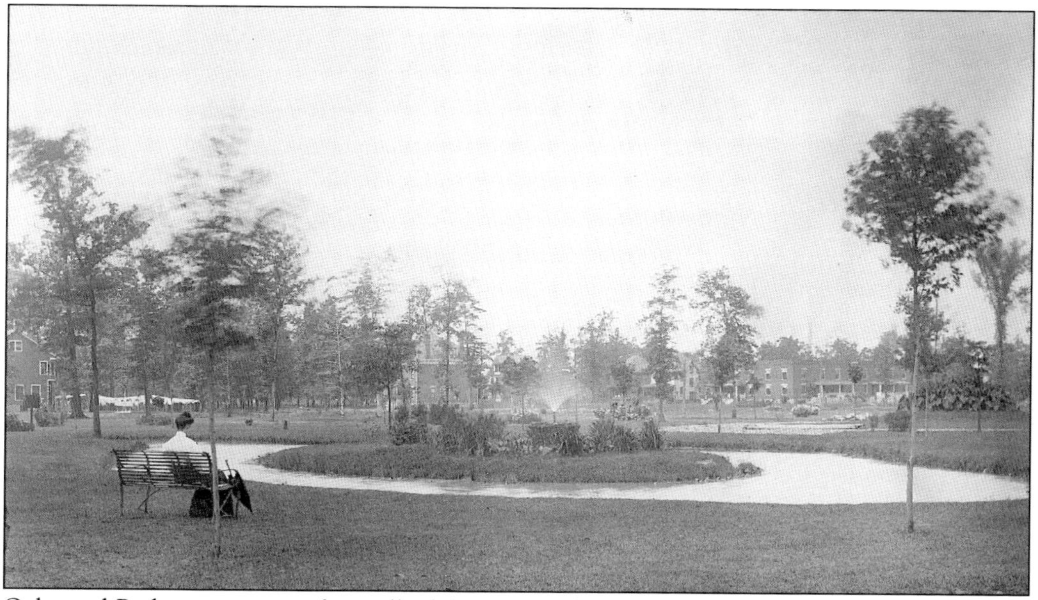

Oakwood Park got its name from all of the giant oak trees that strove to reach the heights of the smokestacks of the National Tube Co. that was just down the street. This piece of land was dedicated to the City of Lorain for a park in 1894, the year the Johnson Steel Rail plant came to town. Some 42 National Youth Administration boys helped drain the swamp land and built the lagoon and island. They had the help of C.E. VanDeusen, then the City Prosecutor, and George Crehore, then the Park Superintendent.

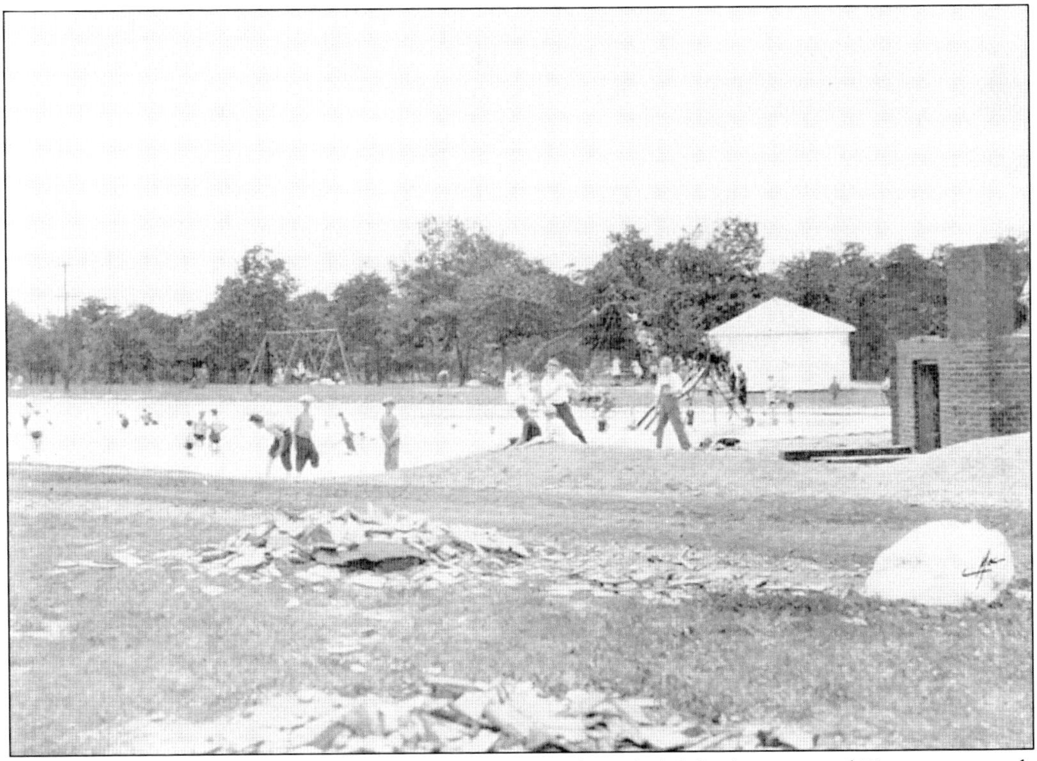

Central Park, also known as Highland Park, is located on Oakdale Avenue and Twenty-seventh to Thirtieth Streets. Land was purchased by the City in 1910 at a cost not to exceed $9,000. The site was formerly a stone quarry operated by the Lorain Stone Company at the turn of the century. The park provided the people of the area with a pool, picnic area, and ball diamonds. This 1930s picture also shows swing sets in the background.

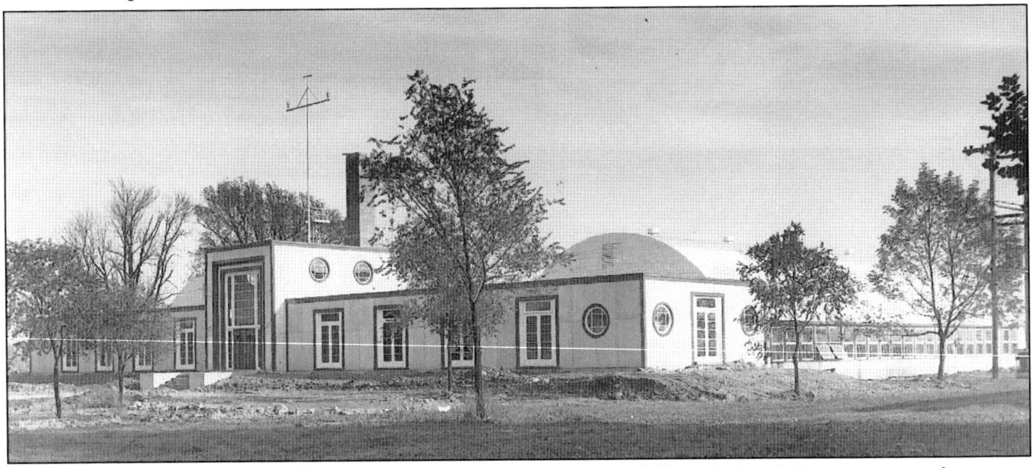

The Naval Reserve Station was on the east side, near Longfellow School. It was in use for many years. The picture also shows the mast of the USS *Arizona*, a battleship sunk at Pearl Harbor. No records exist as to how it got to Lorain. The best guess is that Admiral King had it sent to Lorain. It was here for many years, taken down, and laid in a neighbor's yard during the 1950s or 1960s. After ten years, the city of Lorain said they did not want it. It was sold to the State of Arizona, where it is on display at the state capitol building.

Victory Park is located at the corner of West Erie Avenue and Fifth Street. The World War I memorial was dedicated on April 6, 1922, when schoolchildren and adults came to participate. There are four bronze plaques on the statue. One side says, "They are not dead who died for liberty, but live forever in the hearts of their countrymen." The tornado of 1924 caused the loss of the blade on the sword and the olive branch. Showing civic pride, Mr. Schonebarger, owner of Best Tool and Equipment Repairs, had the statue re-bronzed, and the law firm of Wickens, Herzer & Panza planted the flowers.

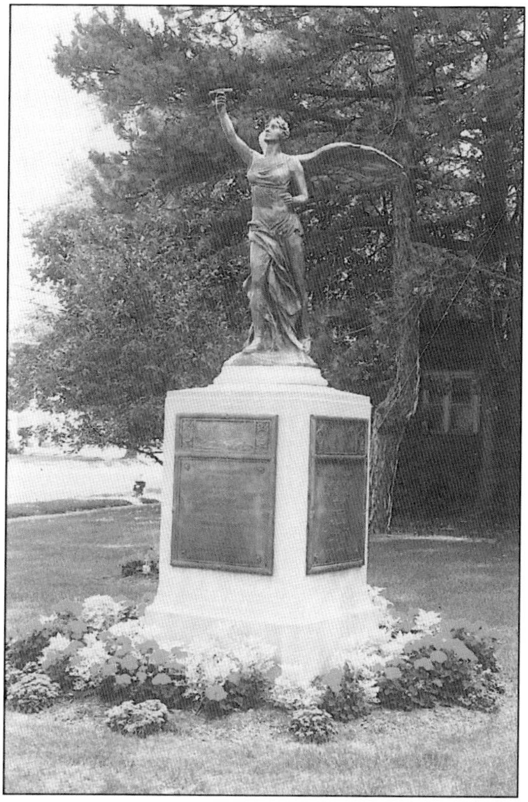

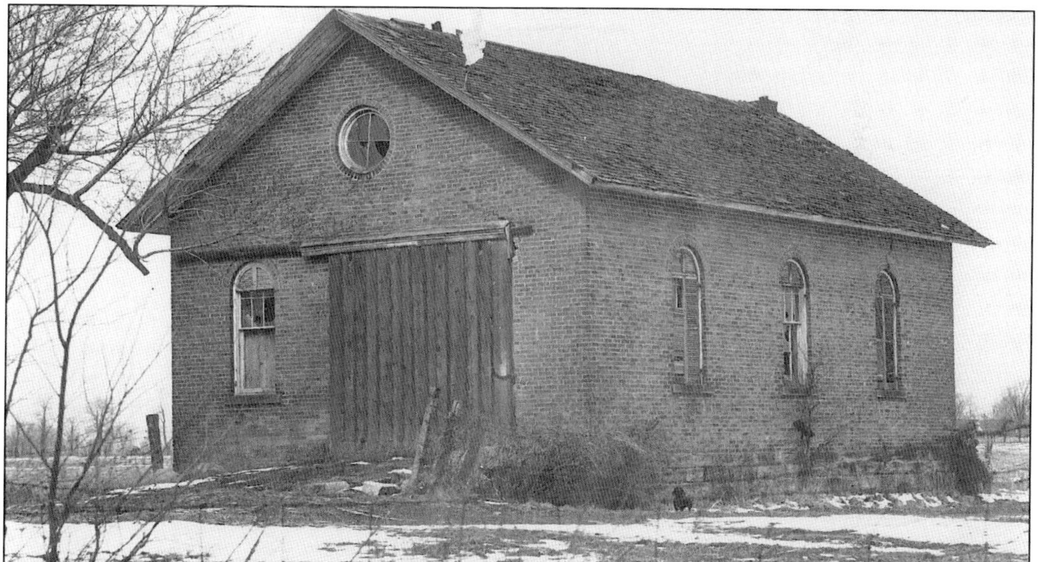

On November 9, 1827, the first school board for Black River Township was elected and $200 was appropriated for the construction of the schoolhouse. It was located on the northeast corner of Meister and Leavitt Road in the township. At that time it was not a part of what was to become Lorain, but the site was later added to the city. The brick building served students for 20 years and was replaced with a fire station.

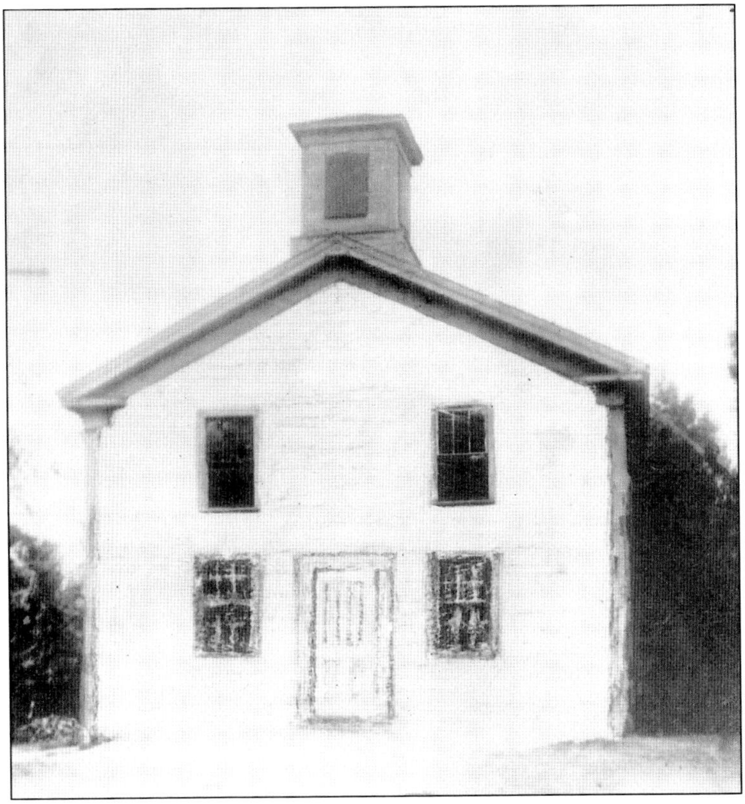

Later, a private subscription school served the town of Black River. Responding to a need for an increasing school population in 1853, a two-story schoolhouse was built on Duane Street (Fourth Street) near Washington Avenue, where the Number One Fire Station stood. In 1911 it was moved from that location to Washington Avenue and Eighth Street, where it was remodeled and used as a private home. It was recently demolished.

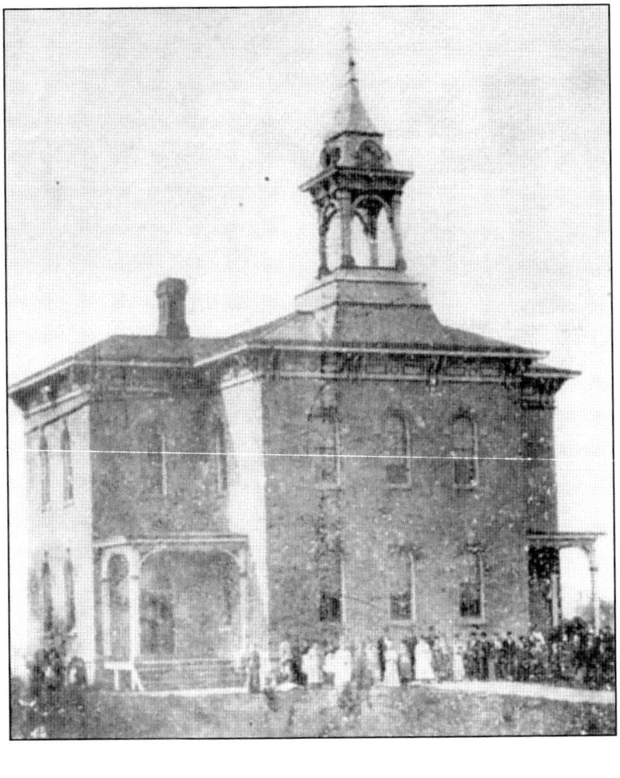

Union School was located at the southwest corner of Sixth Street and Washington Avenue. This school cost $15,000 to build and the land was valued at $2,000. As the town prospered, a much larger building was needed, so Lorain High School was built on the same site.

The first part of Lorain High was built south of the Union School. When that half of the building was completed, the students moved in and the Union School was torn down. Then the northern part of the school was built. Lorain High School served the community for 118 years, until the building was converted to Lorain Middle School in 1995 .

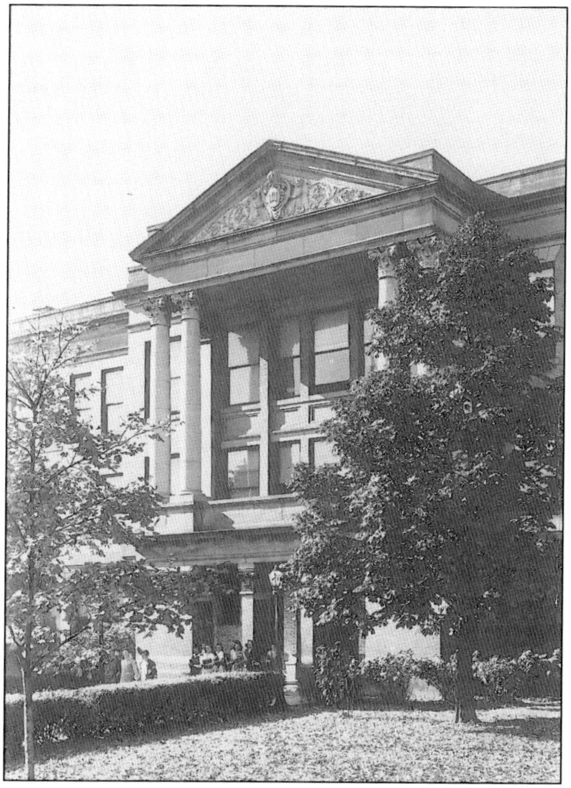

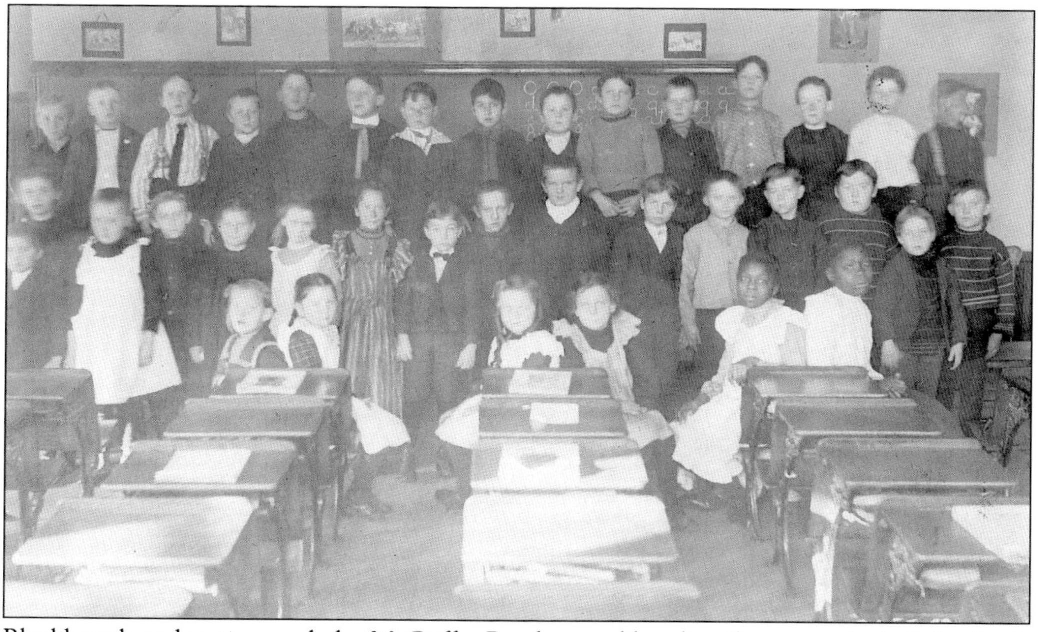

Blackboards and stationary desks, McGuffey Readers, and lunch pails were typical of all schools of the 19th century in Lorain. The Zion Lutheran German School at Seventeenth Street and Reid Avenue illustrates the ethnic variety of the Lorain school population and one of the parochial schools active in town at that time.

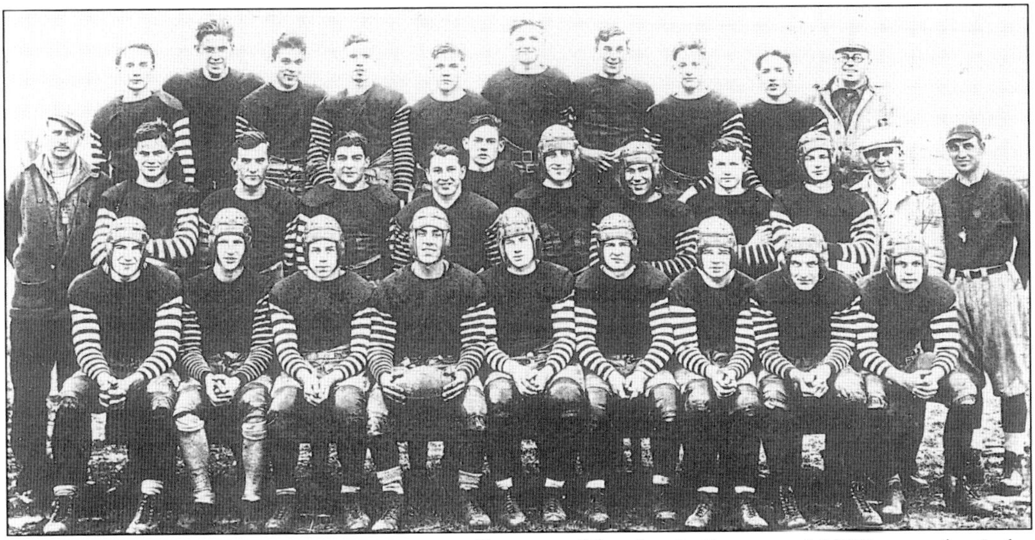

Lorain High had many winning teams in all sports. The football team of 1927 won the Lake Erie League championship. The team included the following: (first row) Joe Fitzgerald, Bill Andorka, Harry Traub, Vincent Glorioso, Al Fauver, Foster Armstrong, Frank Towner, Forest Newman, and George Crehore; (middle row) assistant coach Spencer Myers, Charles Delceg, Ed Skolnicki, Joe Temerario, Amby Kissel, Les Burge, Paul Shade, Nunzio Ceresa, Dan Smith, George Stephenson, Clarence Wolfe, and Coach E.M. McCaskey; (back row) Tom Giasomo, James Bauer, Jim Chazer, Leo Flynn, Carl Hageman, Pat Wright, George Vinovich, Bob Willowby, Jim McGue, and trainer Doc Waterhouse.

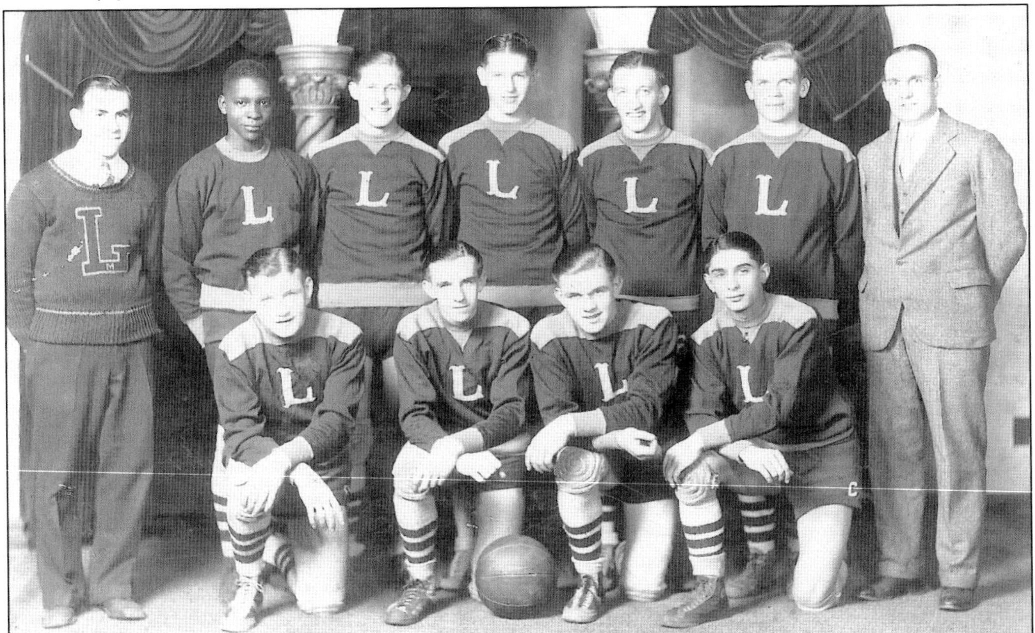

The Lorain High Varsity Basketball team of 1929 had a successful season in the Lake Erie High School League. The team tied for second place. The lettermen are as follows: (bottom row) Hageman (captain), Horkay, Ursic (captain-elect), and Andorka; (top row) unidentified, Andrews, Smith, Giasomo (captain), Woods, Davevich, and Coach E.M. McCaskey.

Concurrently with the public schools, Lorain had a network of parochial schools. St. Mary's Academy began meeting in a room in St. Joseph's Hospital in 1873. They later moved into their own building and are still functioning as a school. In 1903 the academy had 230 pupils. Academy High School opened in 1906, and the current building was opened in 1924 at the corner of Seventh Street and Reid Avenue.

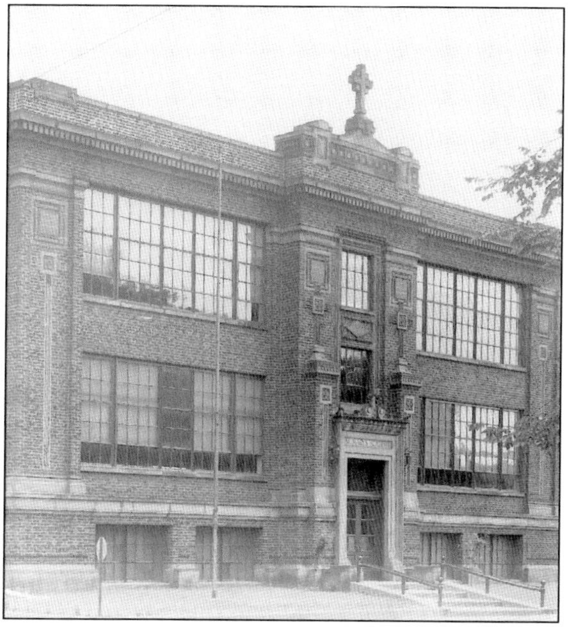

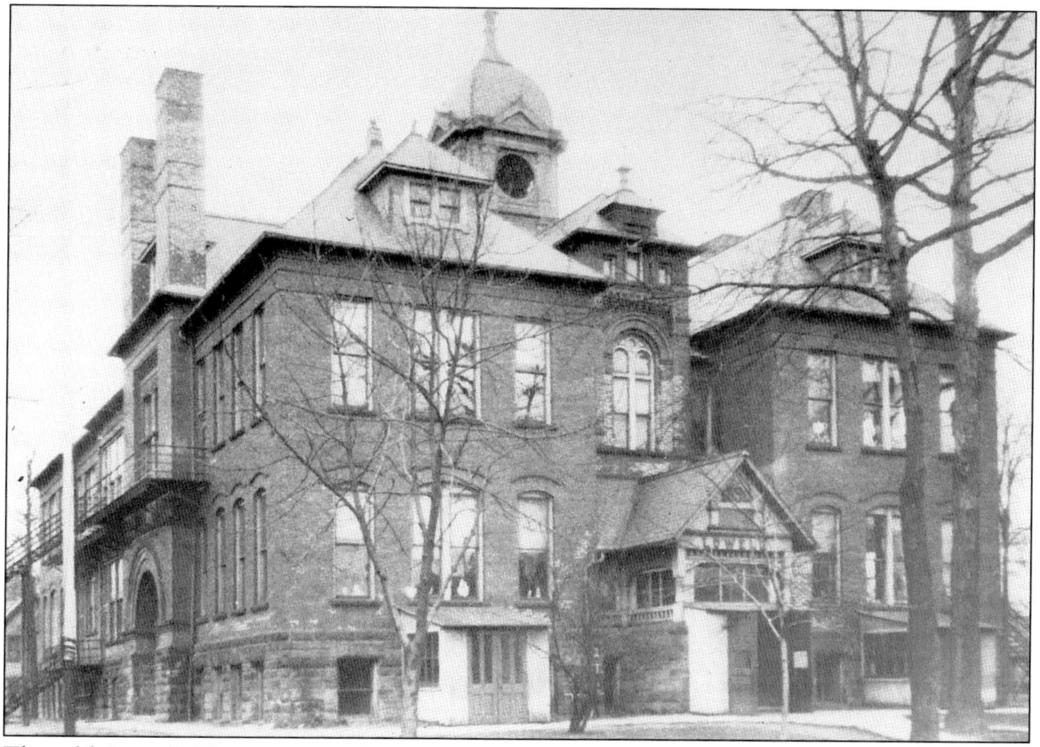

The old Lowell Elementary School represented the older architecture of schools built to accommodate the children of the growing population. The schools included Garfield, Oakwood, Harrison, old Lowell (pictured), old Lincoln, old Fairhome, Garden Avenue, Boone, Brownell, and old Charleston (known as Bank Street or Sixth Street School) which was destroyed by the tornado of 1924. The use of the word "old" indicates new buildings with the same names that have been built recently.

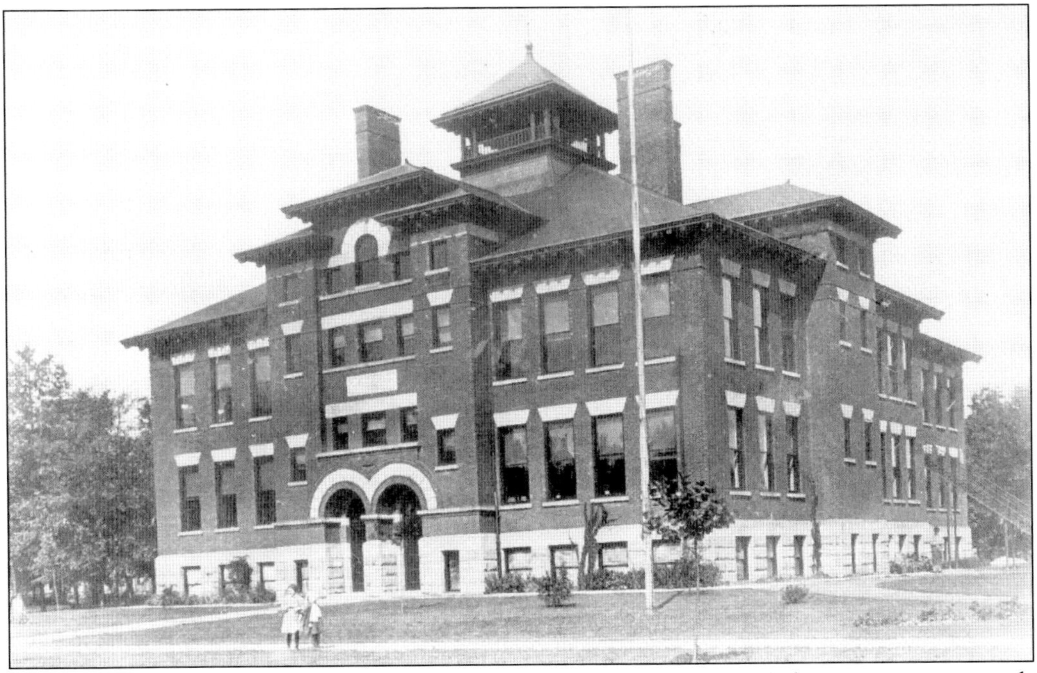

Oakwood School at Grove Avenue was torn down in the late 1960s. A fire station now stands on its location. Many of the older schools were replaced with more modern buildings and the same names were used. New elementary schools include Lakeview, Palm Avenue, Homewood, Jane Lindsay, Emerson, Masson, Larkmoor, and Meister Road School.

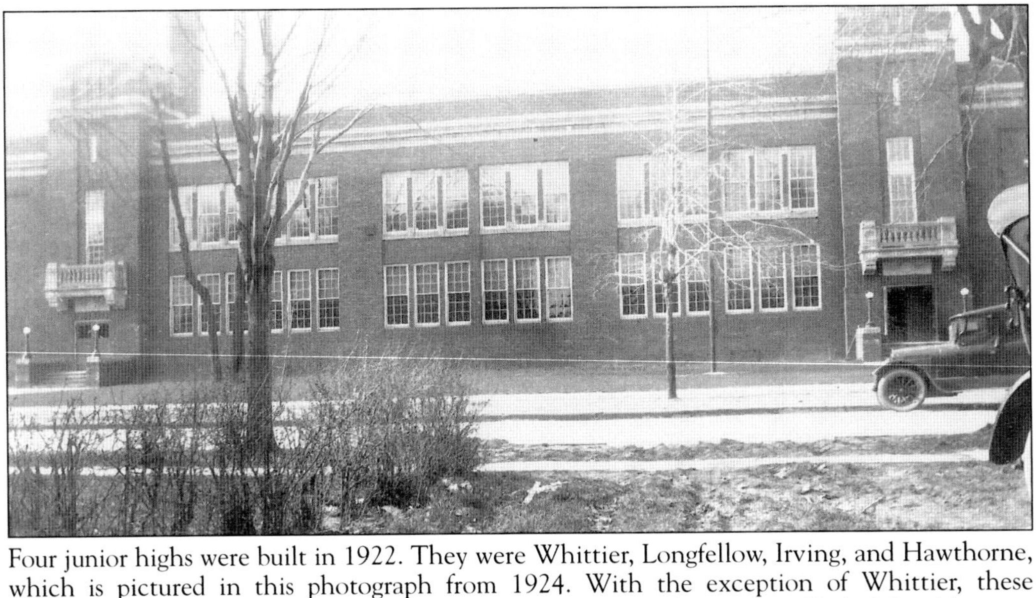

Four junior highs were built in 1922. They were Whittier, Longfellow, Irving, and Hawthorne, which is pictured in this photograph from 1924. With the exception of Whittier, these buildings were converted to elementary buildings in 1995, when Lorain High School became Lorain Middle School as part of a new reorganization.

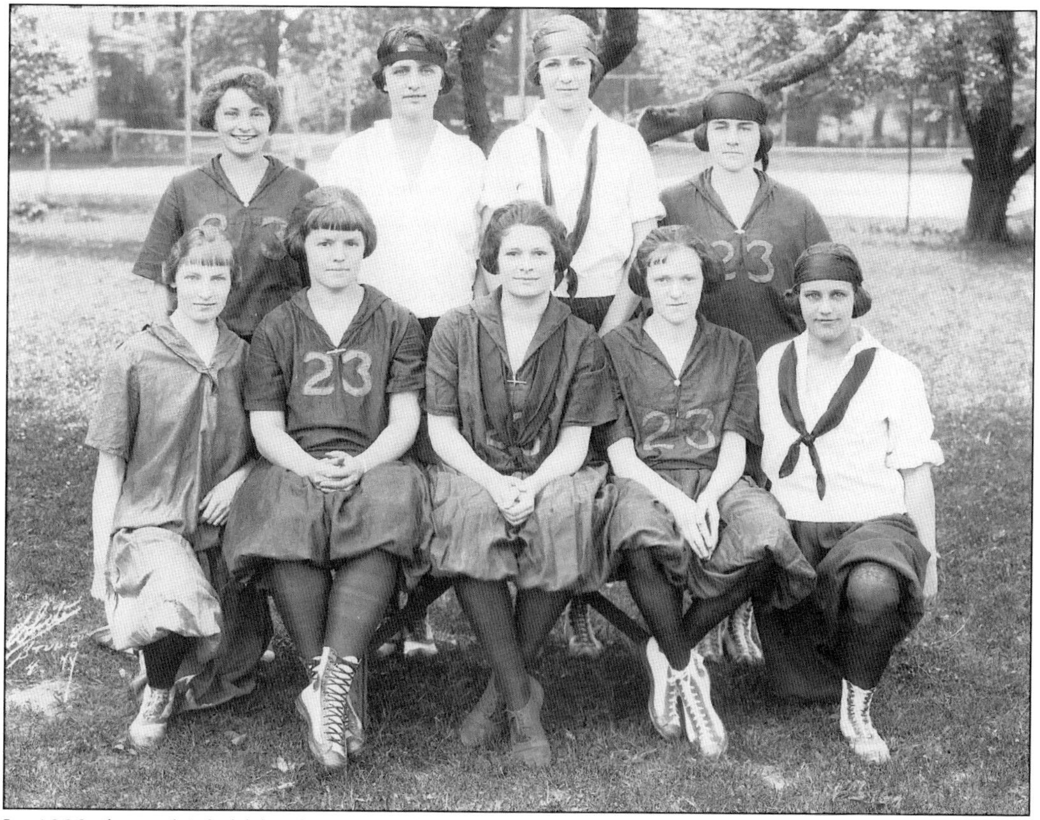

In 1923 the girls' field hockey team for Lorain High won many games. Pictured here are the All-Stars coached by Miss Will. The seniors on the team were Helen Beck, Ruth Marsac, Elizabeth Sakett, and Donna Virtue. The other girls were underclass members. The names of just two are known. In the first row, the second person from the left is Marian Fisher, and the last person is Rachael Rowley. That same year the Boys Basketball team won the championship of Class A.

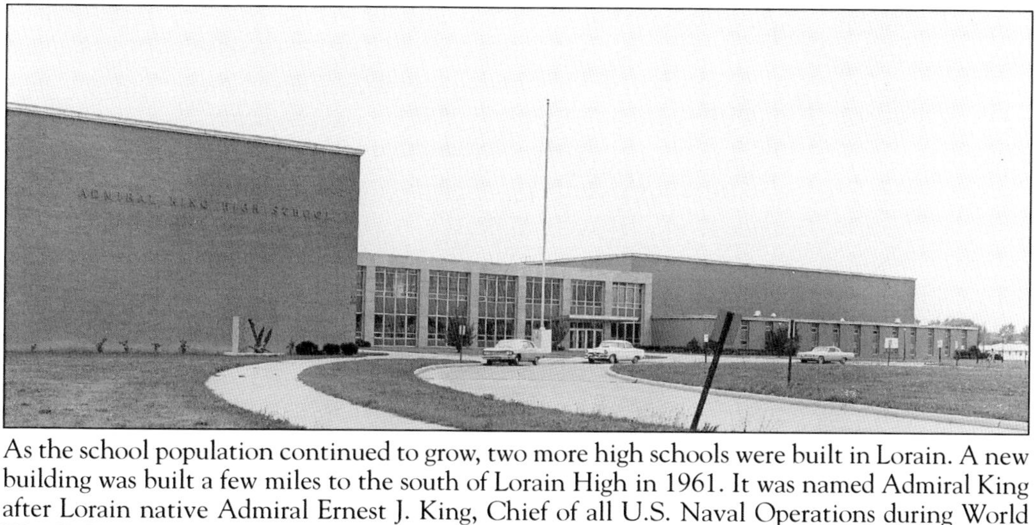

As the school population continued to grow, two more high schools were built in Lorain. A new building was built a few miles to the south of Lorain High in 1961. It was named Admiral King after Lorain native Admiral Ernest J. King, Chief of all U.S. Naval Operations during World War II. Dr. Joseph Calta was the first principal of the school.

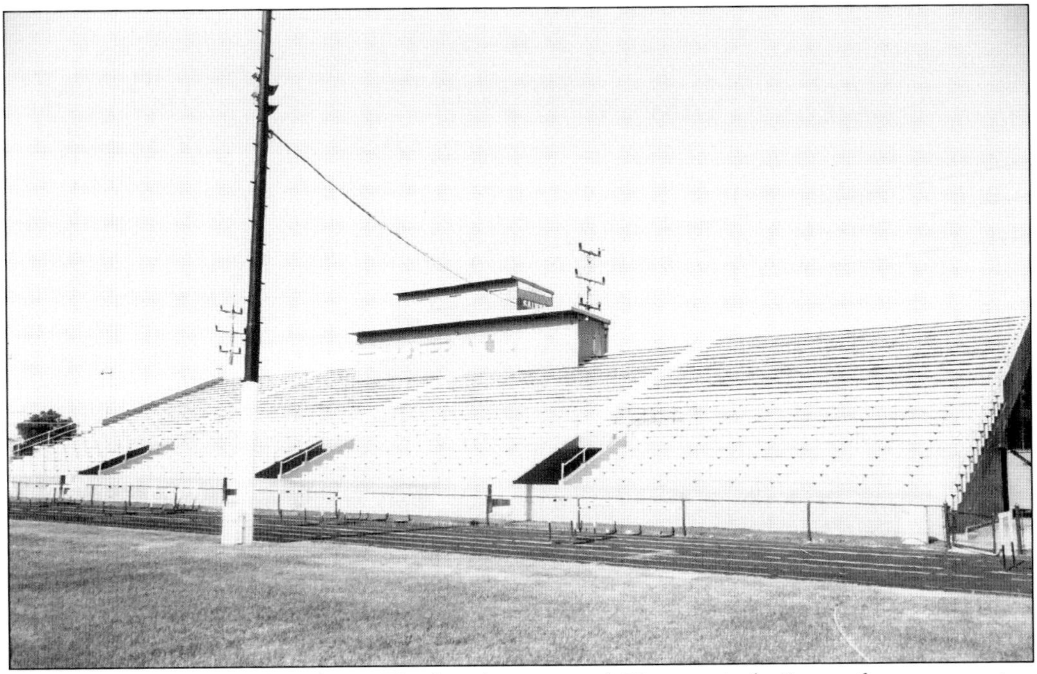

In 1927 land was purchased on Oberlin Avenue and Twenty-sixth Street for a recreation stadium. At first it was just a field for sporting events. During the Depression, concrete stands were built for the fans to watch football games. Many other events were held outdoors for the city, and most graduations from the high schools in Lorain took place there. This later became George Daniel Stadium, named for George Daniel, who was the first supervisor of physical education until 1985, when he retired.

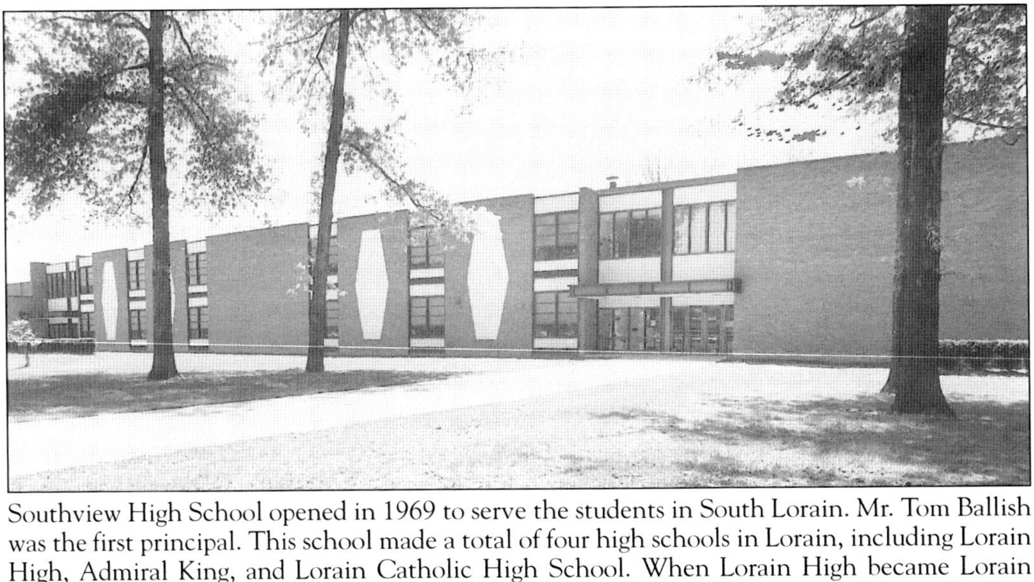

Southview High School opened in 1969 to serve the students in South Lorain. Mr. Tom Ballish was the first principal. This school made a total of four high schools in Lorain, including Lorain High, Admiral King, and Lorain Catholic High School. When Lorain High became Lorain Middle School in the late 1990s, the names of the three high schools in Lorain were changed to Lorain Admiral King, Lorain Southview, and Lorain Catholic High School.

Five

Our Industry

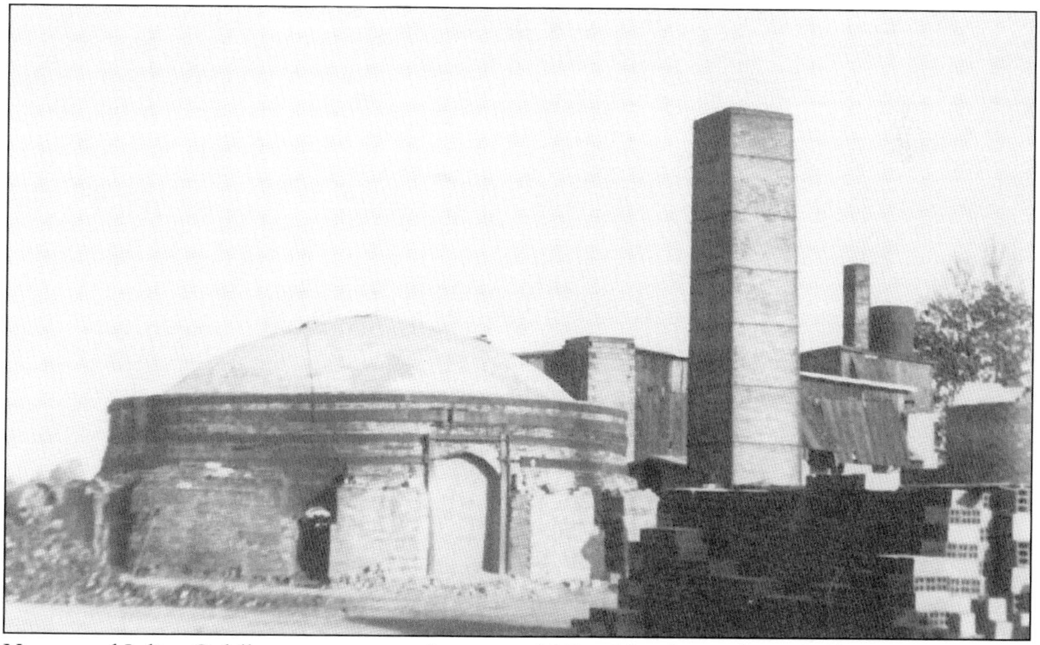

Henry and Julius Oehlke ran a pottery factory at 66 Franklin Street (now Fifth Street) just west of Hamilton Avenue. The factory made pottery and bricks from 1891 to 1899. The Oehlke home was on Hamilton Avenue. The family later operated a business on Broadway.

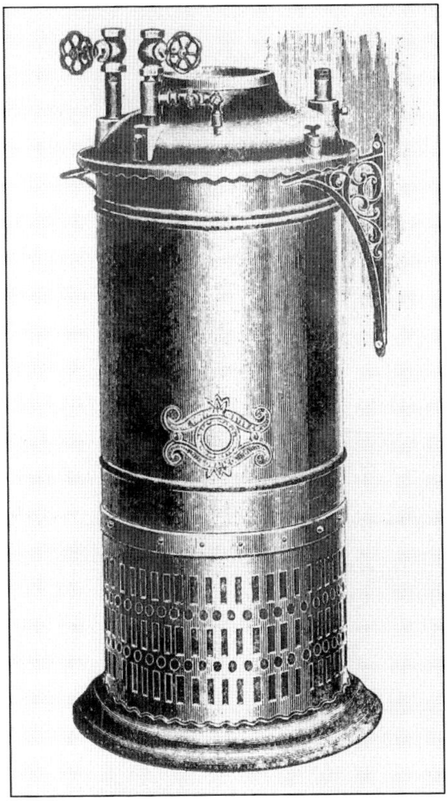

The Hoffman Heater Co. offices and factory were at the Nickel Plate Railroad and Washington Avenue. The first hot-water heater was made on January 19, 1905. When the hot-water faucet was turned on, a large gas flame in the center of a copper coil would heat the water for as long as the faucet was on. Mr. Thomas McGeachie had the franchise to sell the Hoffman Heaters at 324 Fourth Street. The water heaters were priced from $15 up to $100.

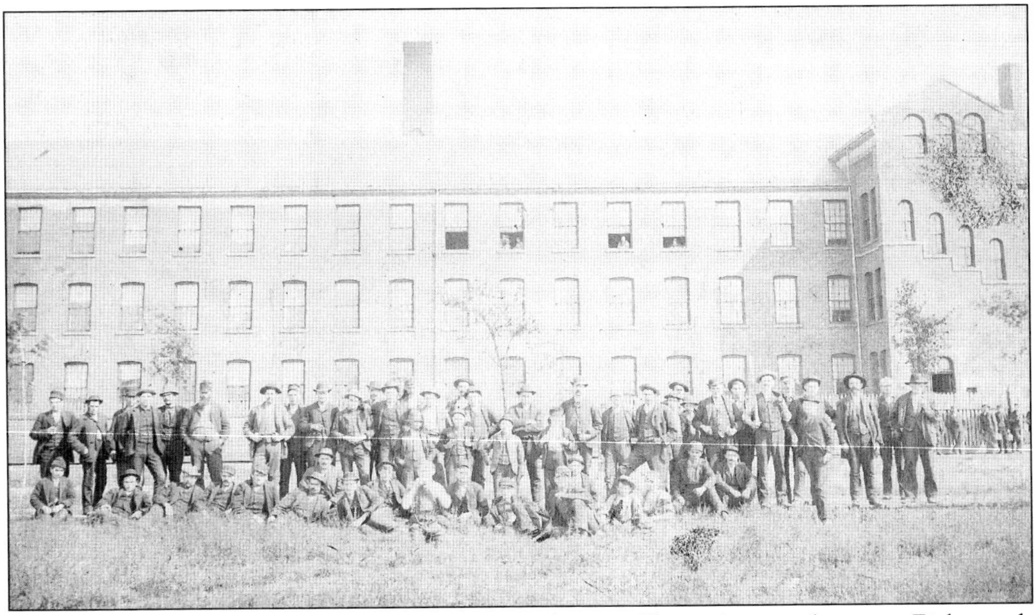

The Hayden Brass Works was located from Broadway to Elyria Avenue, between Eighteenth and Twentieth Streets. Started in Haydenville, Massachusetts, by Joel Hayden, it was moved to Lorain in 1881. The L-shaped building made brass fixtures, such as hose nozzles, tools, and gaslights. The factory had about 400 employees and was the major industry in town for years.

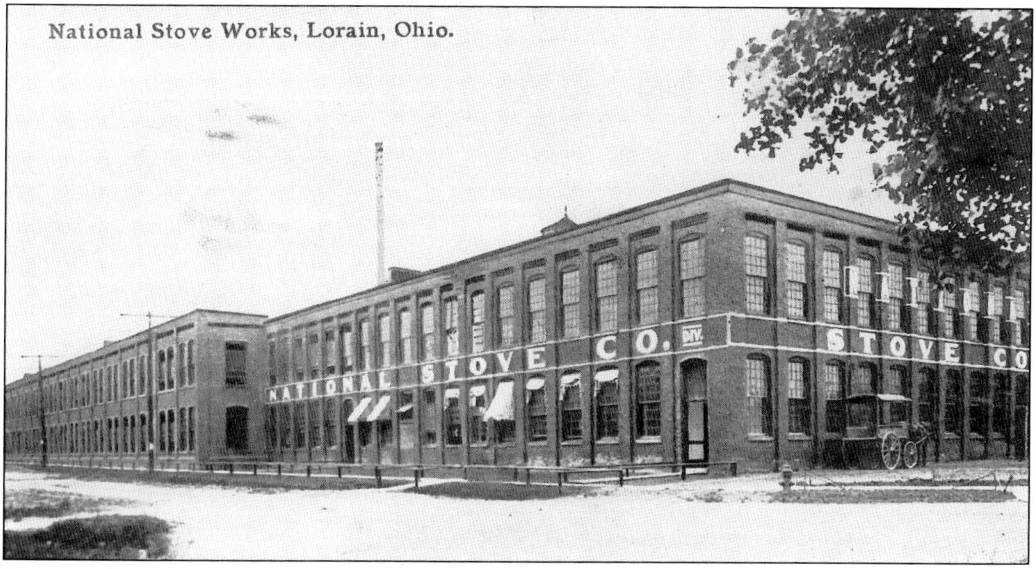

In 1895 the National Vapor Stove and Manufacturing Co. was built on Long Avenue and Twelfth Street. They made kerosene heaters and furnaces. Later, the name was changed to the National Stove Works, and in 1902 it was sold to the American Stove Co. The company made Magic Chef stoves at the St. Louis plant. The Lorain plant closed in the mid-1950s and some of the workers went to the Cleveland plant. The plant operation is now in Tennessee.

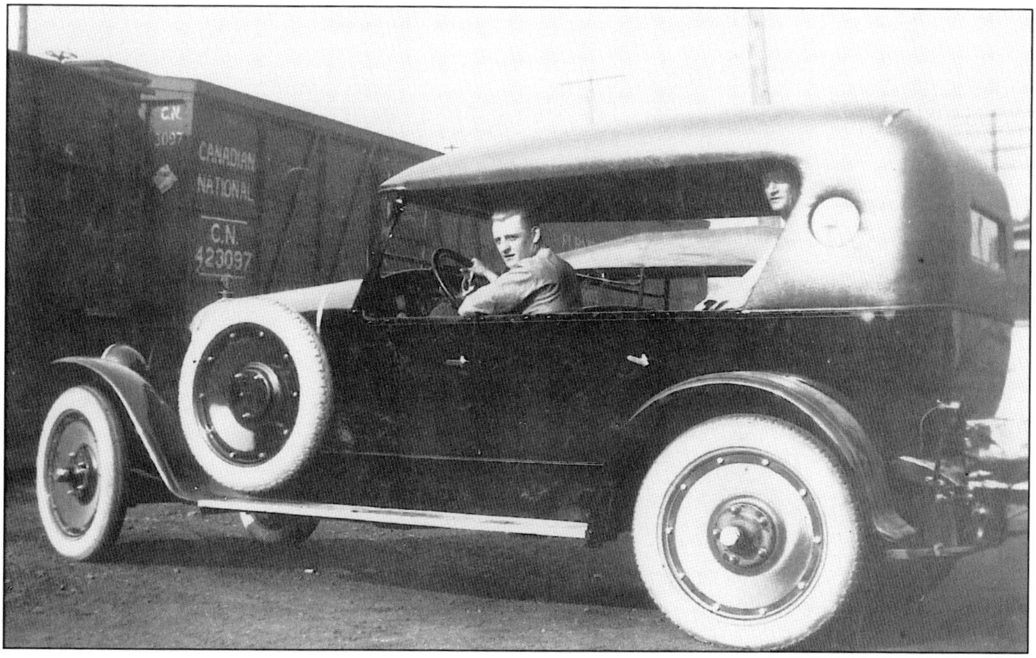

The Carroll Car Co. at Washington Avenue and the Nickel Plate tracks were in operation from 1920 to 1923. They assembled about 600 cars in three years. Shortly after the plant went into operation, a recession hit the country and they had a difficult time making money. In 1923 they got a large order from California. They made the cars and shipped them by train. The train went through a bad snowstorm around Chicago. When the train got to California, all of the engine blocks had frozen and the cars were useless. The company went out of business.

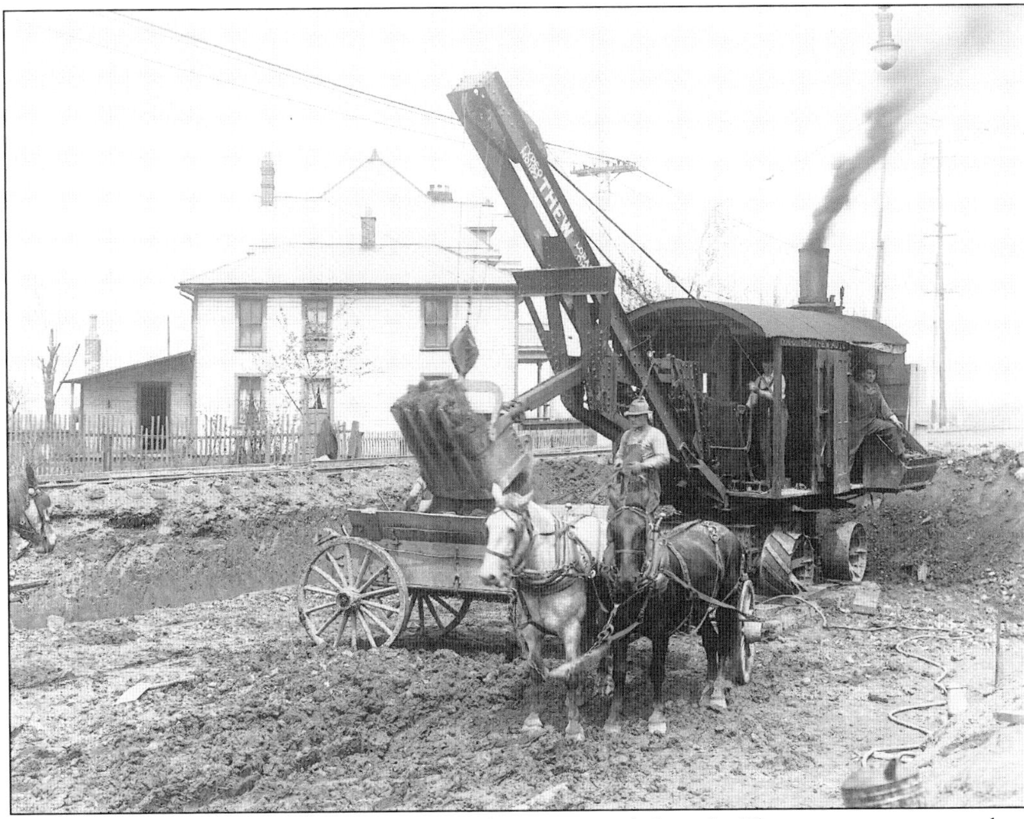

Captain Thew invented a new gear system for cranes and shovels. The purpose was to unload his ship faster. He soon changed from being a captain on the lakes to a captain of industry by building the Thew Shovel Co. in Lorain. The company prospered for many years and supplied many of the cranes and shovels for the Panama Canal and World War II. The picture shows a Thew Shovel at the start of excavation for the Twenty-eighth Street undercut.

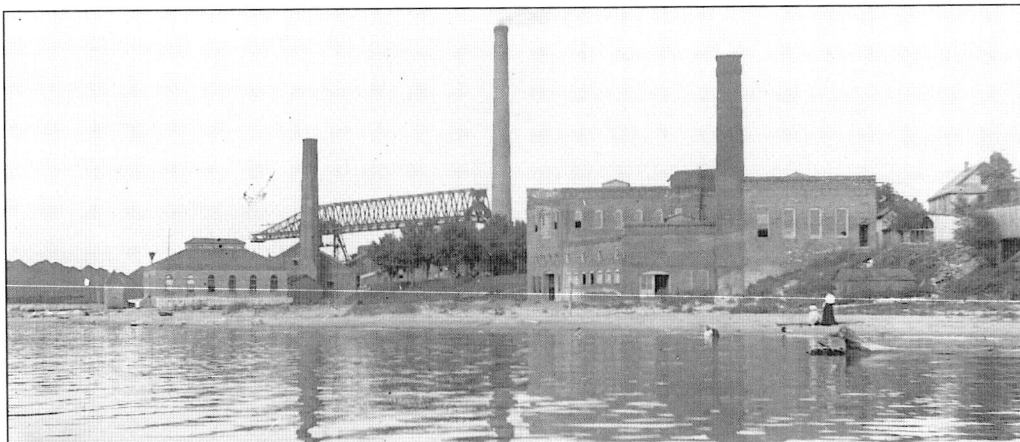

This photograph shows one of the views of the lakefront of Lorain in the 1920s. On the left is the Lorain Water Works, and in the center of the picture is the brick building of the Crystal Ice Co. On the right is the bathing beach, which later became the site of the Ohio Public Service, the new electric company.

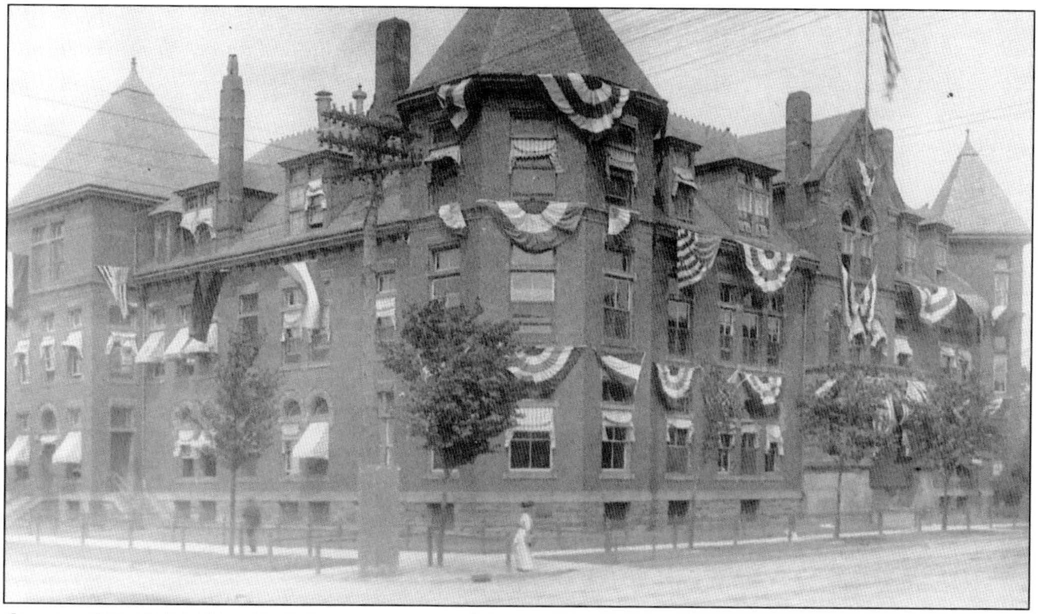

On April 2, 1894, Tom L. Johnson went to Mayor George Wickens Sr. and the Village Council to procure a site to erect a steel plant. The main office building was completed by the next year and the plant was in production. This picture shows the office as decorated for the 100th anniversary of the Perry victory against the British on Lake Erie in 1813. The steel mill was the most important industry in Lorain for many years.

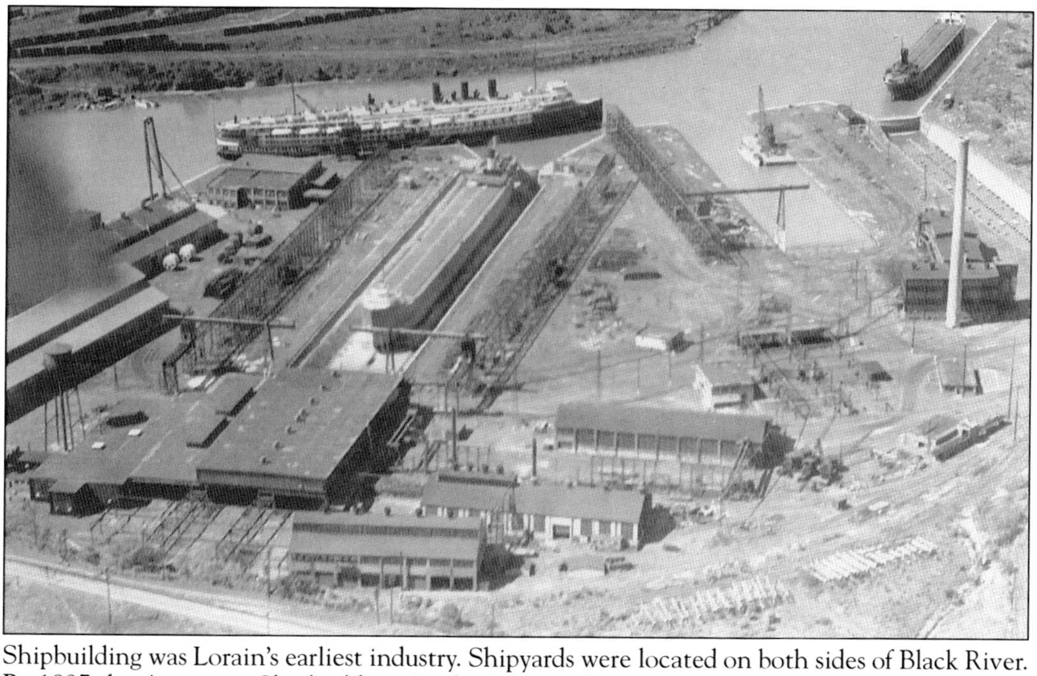

Shipbuilding was Lorain's earliest industry. Shipyards were located on both sides of Black River. By 1897 the American Shipbuilding Co. had shipyards on the east side; in 1898 they built the first steel-hulled ship on the Great Lakes. In Lorain, the American Shipbuilding Co. built some of the largest ships on the Great Lakes—some over 1,000 feet in length—before going out of business in the 1980s.

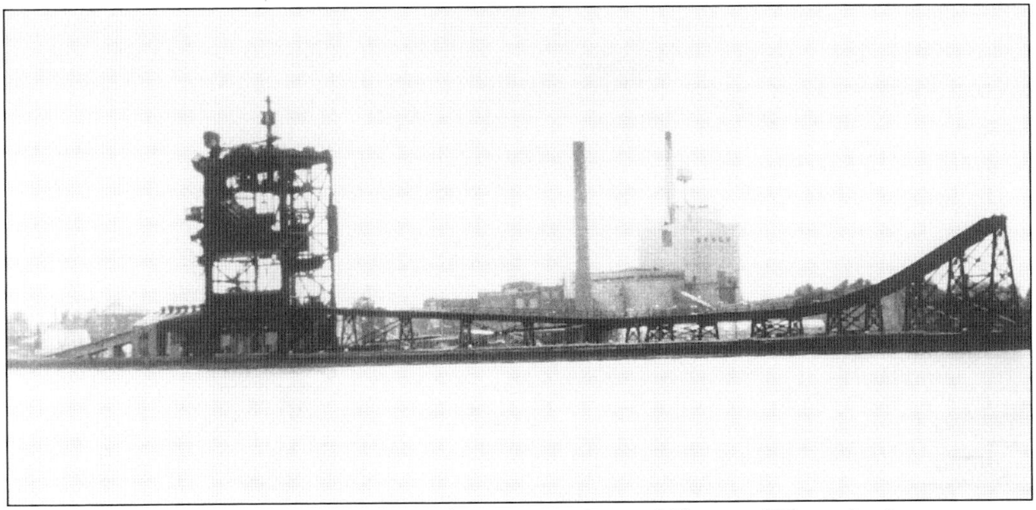

The first electric company in Lorain was the Citizens Gas and Electric. When the first generator was put into operation, electricity was on from dusk until 10:00 p.m. The Ohio Edison Co. was formed after 1930. The plant is seen near the center of the picture. To the left are the B&O coal-loading docks. Railroad coal cars were lifted by the tower, turned upside down, and the coal was emptied into a ship. The car was then lowered to the tracks and run by gravity to the right tower, where it was switched to the rail yards.

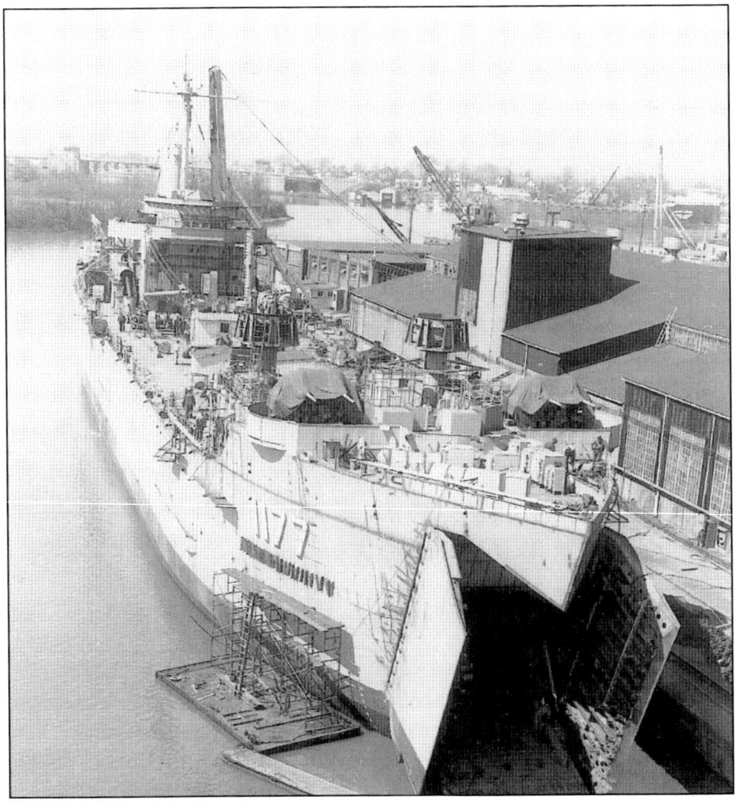

The USS *Lorain County*, an LST, was built at the Lorain yards in 1958. This ship was designed to carry troops, tanks, and other equipment, and land them on the beach of the enemy-held territory. This ship has recently been decommissioned. The navy will decide soon what to do with it. A group is trying to organize a drive to return it to Lorain.

In 1944 the Lorain yards of the American Shipbuilding Co. launched the USS *Lorain*, a frigate named for the city. Admiral Ernest J. King was present with Mrs. Fred Henderson, the mother of Lofton Henderson of Midway fame. She smashed the bottle of champagne to christen the ship.

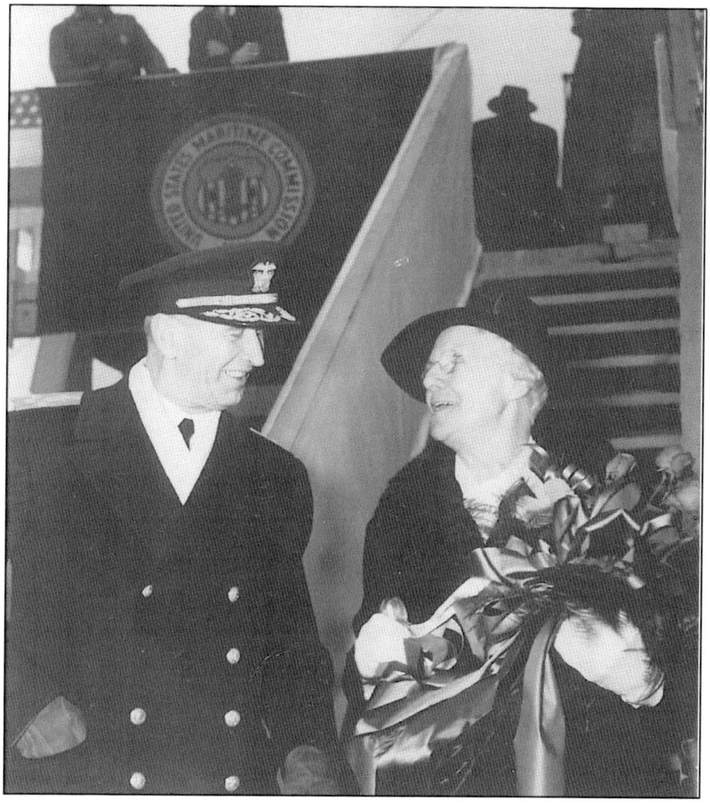

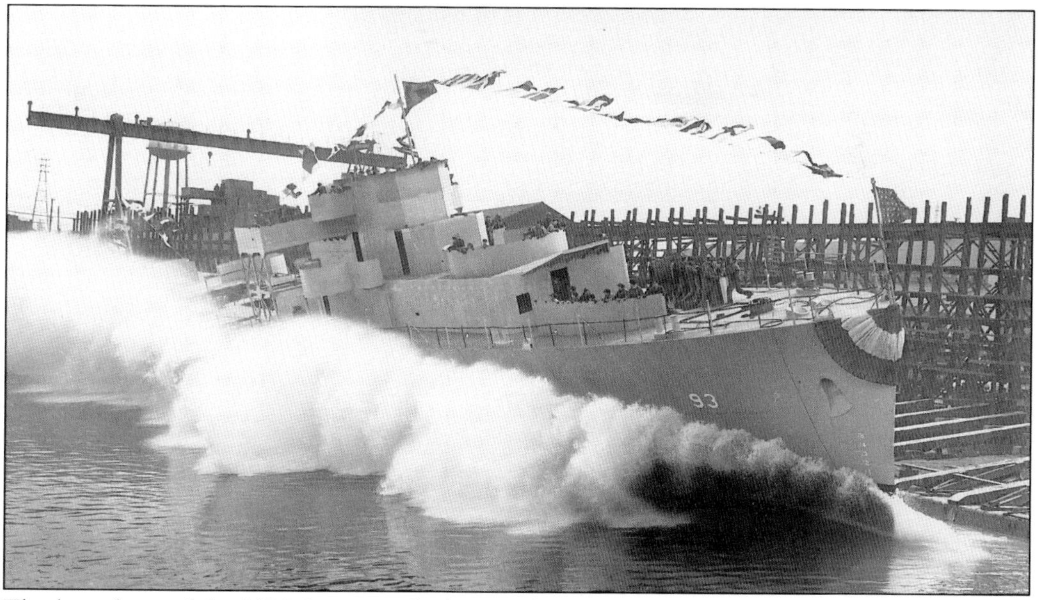

The launching of the USS *Lorain* took place at the Lorain yards in 1944. The ship was used as an anti-submarine and escort vessel for troop ships in the Atlantic Ocean. Mrs. Fred Henderson was the mother of Lofton Henderson who, as a Marine pilot, sighted the Japanese Fleet at the Battle of Midway and in an heroic effort, led his torpedo planes, unescorted by fighters, against the enemy. All of the U.S. planes in his squadron were shot down.

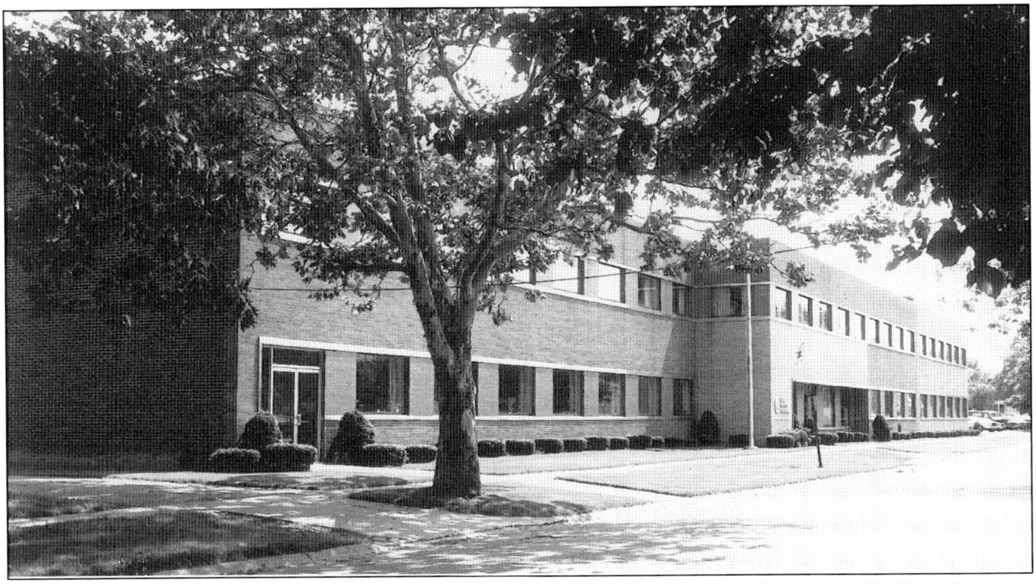

Lorain Products began in a one-room office located on the second floor at 669 Broadway in 1936. By 1937 C. Paul Stocker and F.J. Heavens purchased a building at 200 Seventh Street to design and manufacture power equipment for the communications industry. As the company became more successful, it moved to larger facilities at 1122 F Street. More factories were later built in Canada, California, and Mexico.

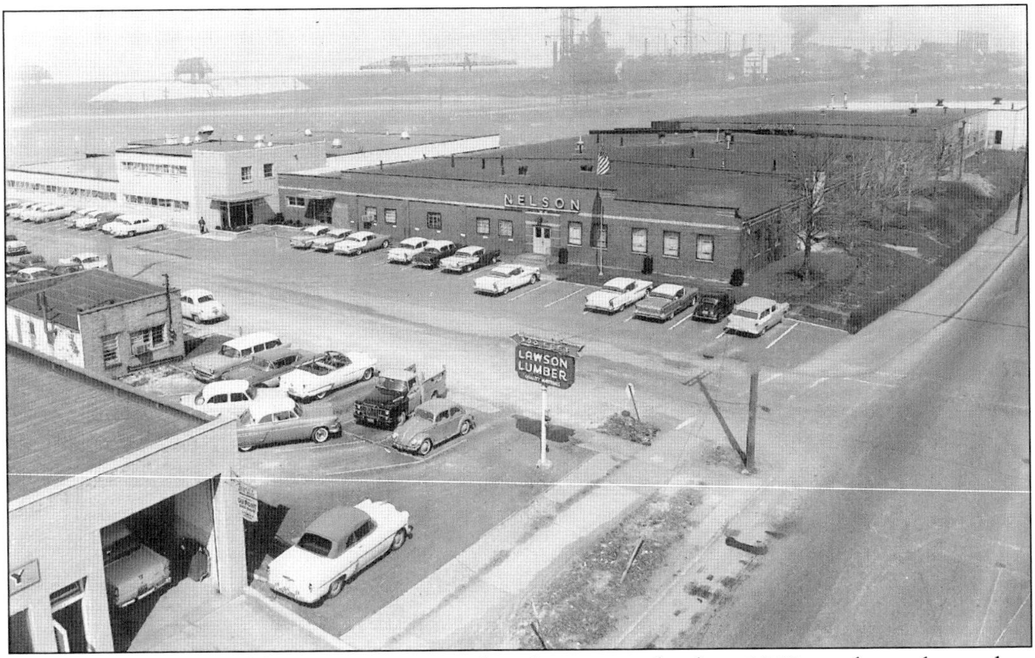

The Nelson Stud Welding Co. was started in Lorain in the late 1940s and was located at East Twenty-eighth Street and Toledo Avenue. In 1948 the Morton Gregory Co. purchased the company. Then, in 1969, a Cleveland company called TRW Inc. bought it. The business expanded and a new facility was built in Elyria, Ohio.

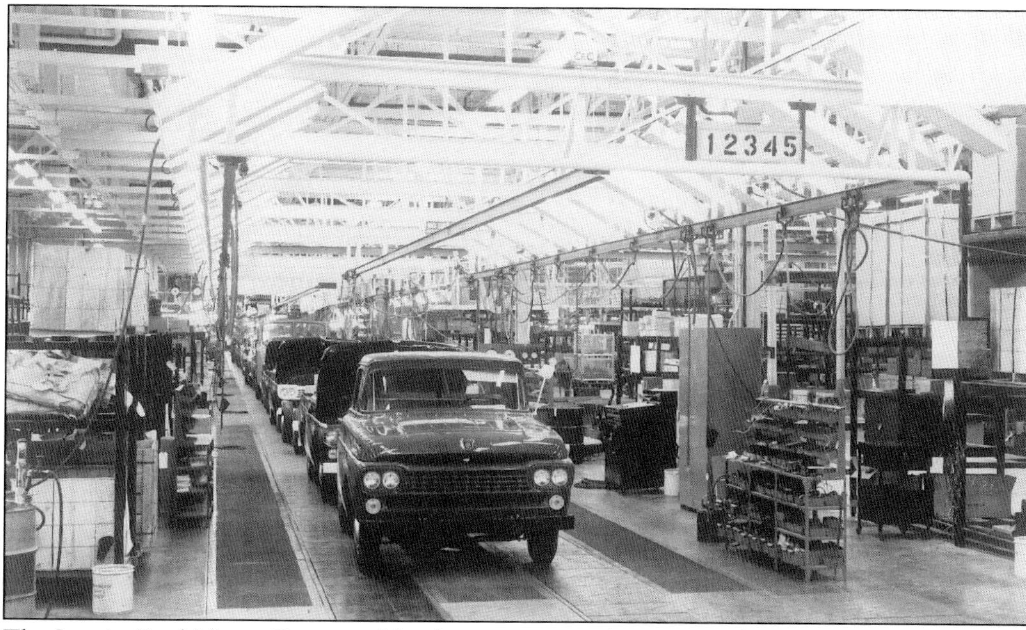

The Lorain Ford Motor Co. assembly plant was opened in 1958. The first vehicle off the line was an F-100 pick-up truck purchased by the Doane Electric Co. in Lorain. The plant has undergone major expansion. Ford was the first U.S. manufacturer to enter the van market. Recently, the company has downsized the production at the plant, but there are hopes for a new line to be added.

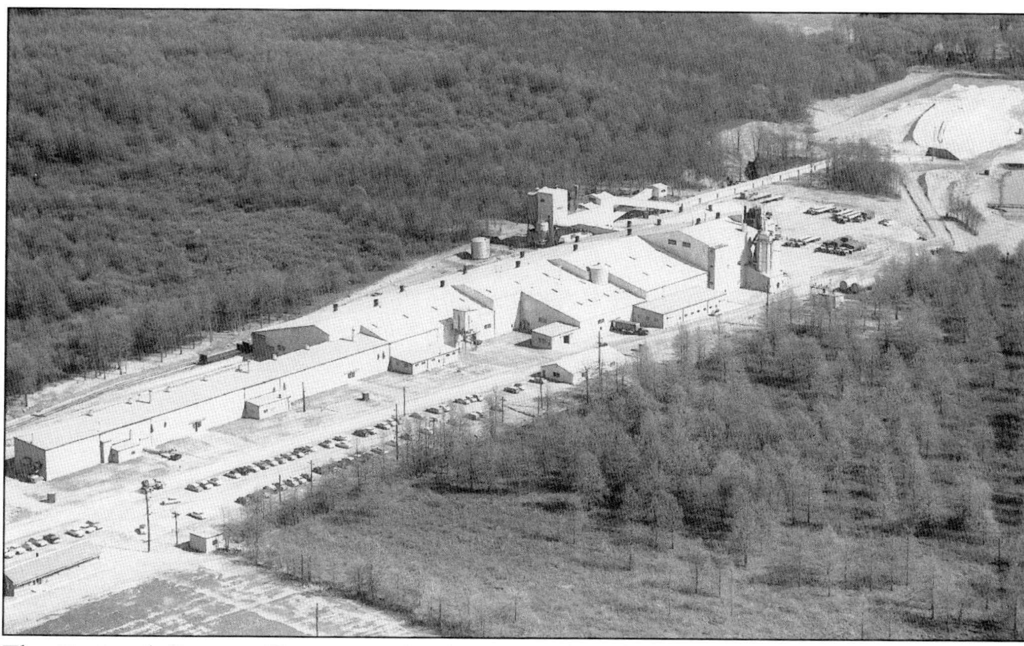

The National Gypsum Plant opened in Lorain in March 1960. The plant is located on the Black River, where ore carriers unload the crushed minerals that were pit-mined in Michigan. The company makes wallboard, lath, and specialty plaster products.

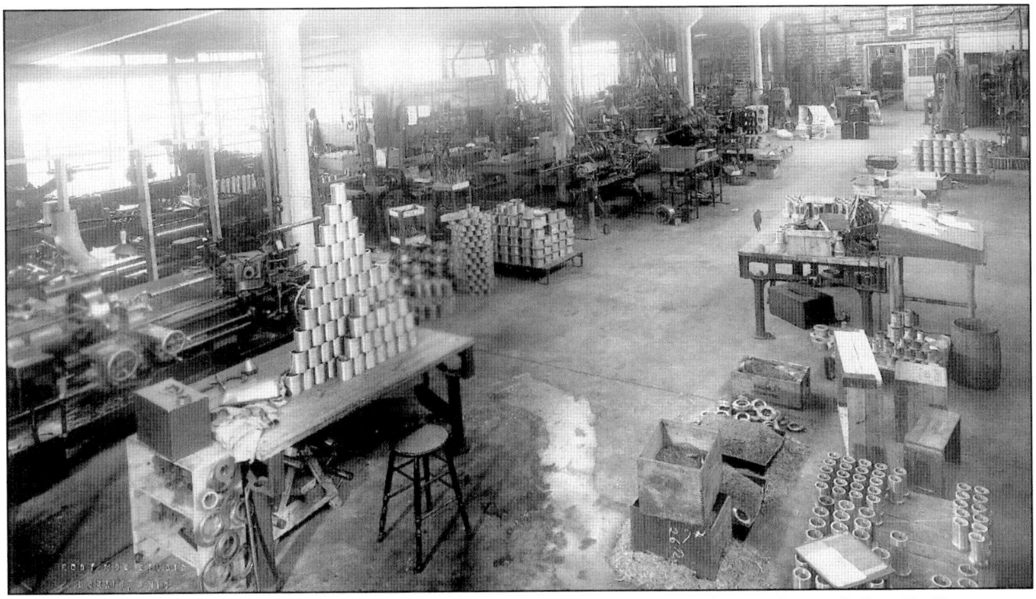

The interior of the American Crucible Products Co. of Lorain is shown here. John G. Dorn was a principal owner in the 1920s. His sons, J. Richard Dorn (president) and Randolph J. Dorn (vice president) operated the company in 1934. The plant made bronze, aluminum, and brass castings, as well as traffic signals. Charles H. Herzer was the manager.

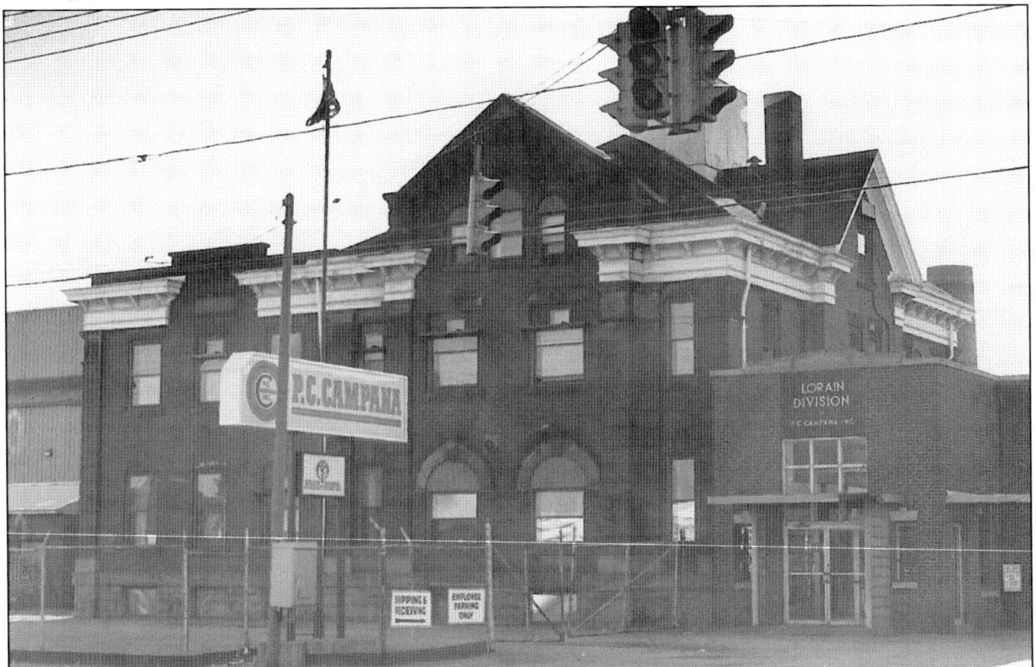

Patsie C. Campana founded P.C. Campana Inc. of Lorain in 1969. The company is a service and product conglomerate servicing the steel foundry and tubing industries. The company is continuing its expansion with the purchase of additional mills. Pictured is the company office on Twenty-eighth Street, which was originally the Lorain Thew Shovel Co., producers of power cranes and shovels.

Six

OUR TRANSPORTATION

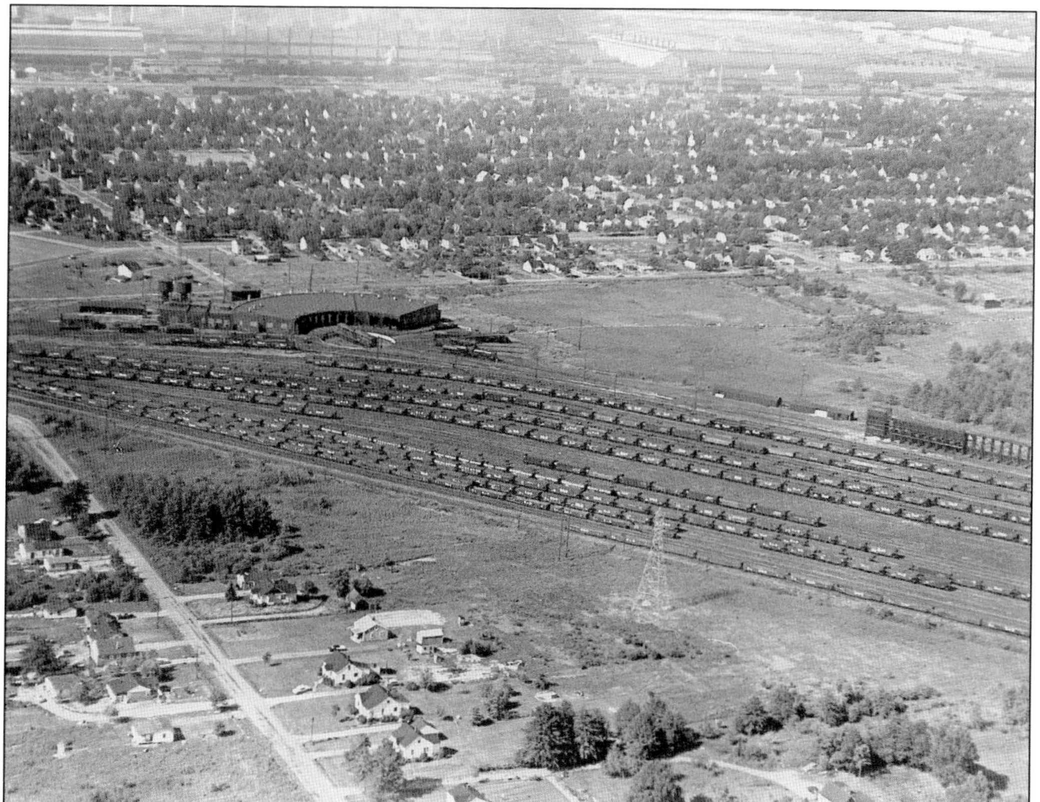

The new Round House was built after a 1904 fire destroyed the old one on East Twenty-first Street. Modern facilities were included at its new location on Thirty-sixth Street and Vine Avenue. In this 1936 photograph can be seen the marshaling yards for the trains, the Round House, and the U.S. Steel Plant at the top of the picture. The facility has long since been torn down as the railroads consolidated.

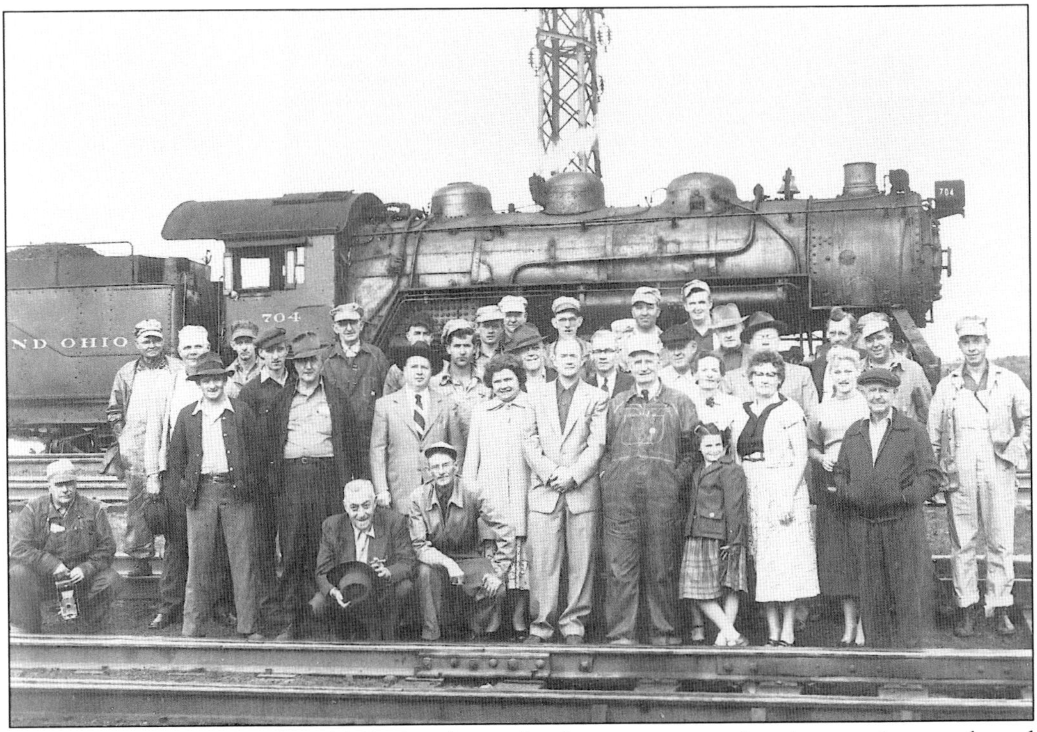

The Baltimore & Ohio (B&O) Railroad was the first to come to Lorain, running north and south. That August 1872 event marked a great advancement for the town. The community was little more than a small fishing village; the railroad brought with it the promise of industry, and therefore jobs and growth. The railroad car shop on Twenty-first Street (now Henderson Drive) did all the repairs on the coal cars for the trains.

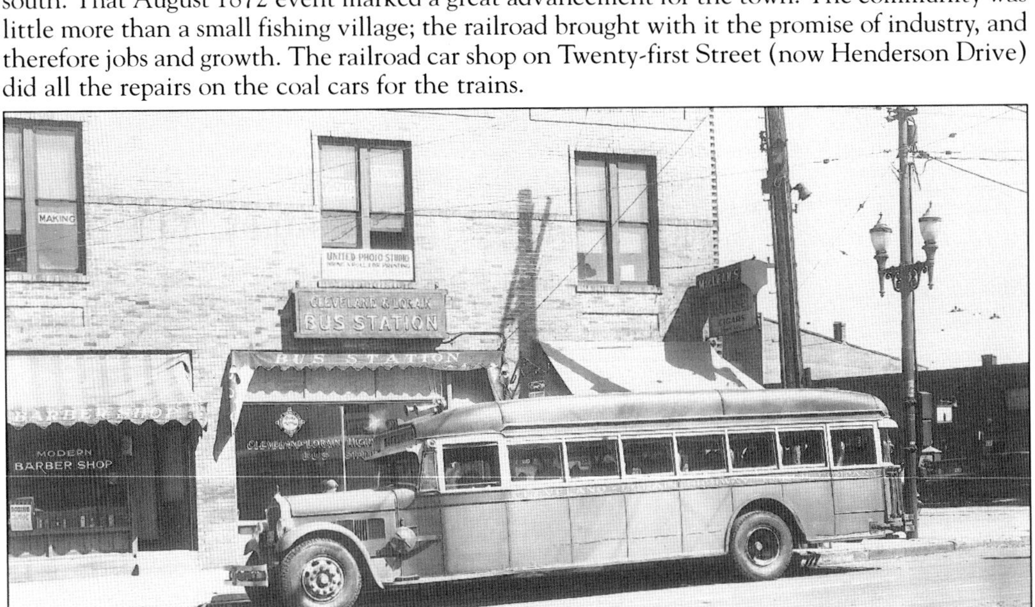

William Dunn and Ralph Sanborn incorporated the Cleveland-Lorain Highway Coach on March 21, 1923. The buses ran between Cleveland and Lorain by way of French Creek, which is east of South Lorain. The initial value of the company was set at $100,000. The picture shows the bus station that was located near the northwest corner of Broadway and Erie Avenue. The company served Lorain until the 1960s or 1970s.

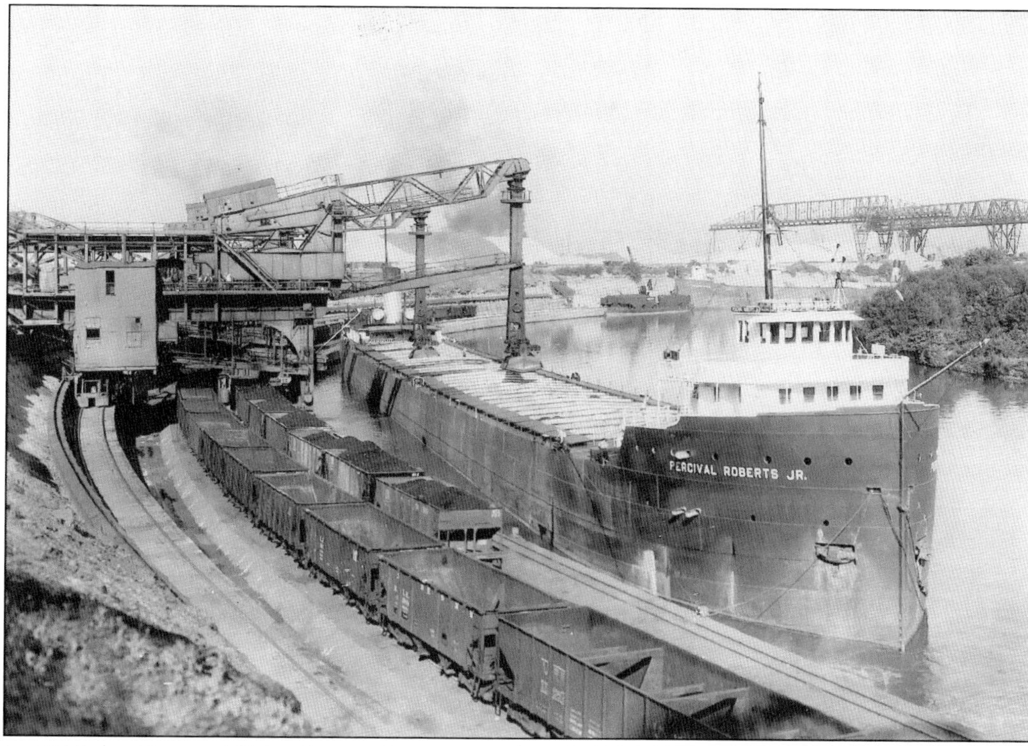

In 1934 the National Tube Co. produced more than 1,500,000 tons of steel ingots and employed nearly 10,000 workers. Shown in this 1930s view is the ship *Percival Roberts Jr.* unloading iron ore at the National Tube Co.'s ore docks. Note the Hulett ore unloaders. The operator would ride the clamshell down into the hold of the ship, grab the ore, and empty it into rail cars. The iron ore was shipped in from the Minnesota area on the upper Great Lakes and used at the steel plant in Lorain.

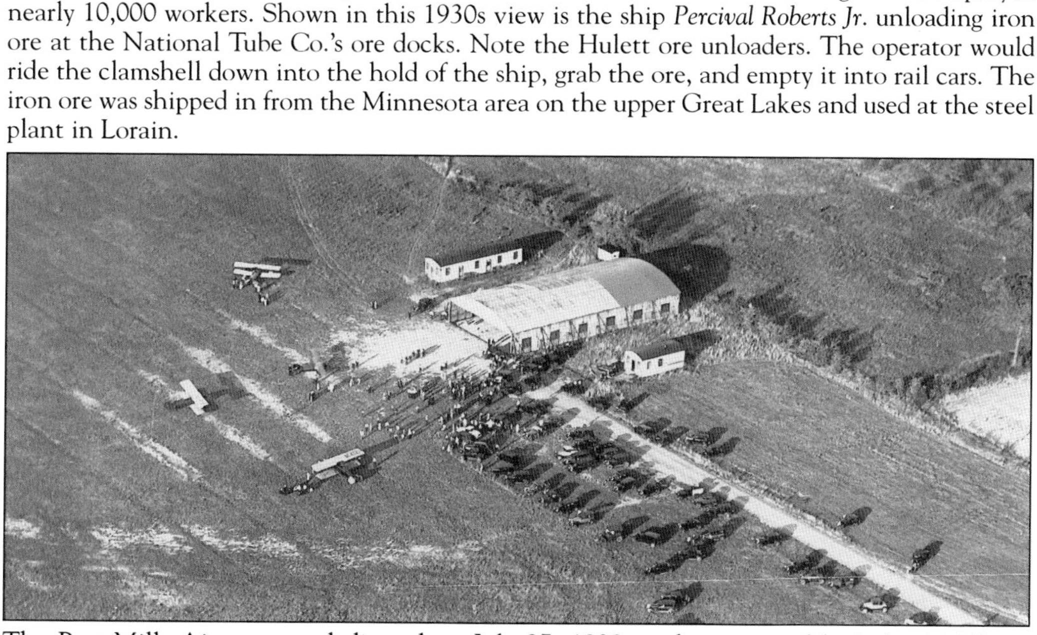

The Port Mills Airport was dedicated on July 27, 1929, and was owned by Leland Mills. It was located on 136 acres of land at the corner of Meister and Leavitt Roads. The first airplane, a Stinson-Detroiter piloted by Ed Merrit, arrived with four passengers. Buses provided by Lake Shore Electric Co. transported people from the Loop every 15 minutes to view the airport in operation.

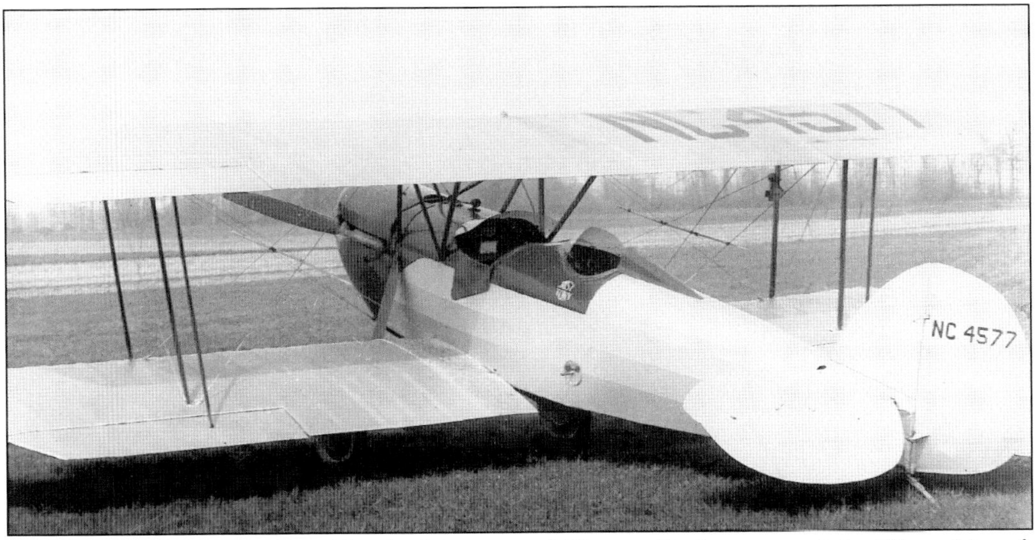

"Buck" Weaver, Sam Junken, Charley Meyers, and Clayton Brukner started the Waco Aircraft Co. in Lorain. Originally known as the Weaver Aircraft, planes were hand-made at the factory at 554 Broadway. Waco was considered a pioneer in international aviation. In 1928 the company moved to Troy.

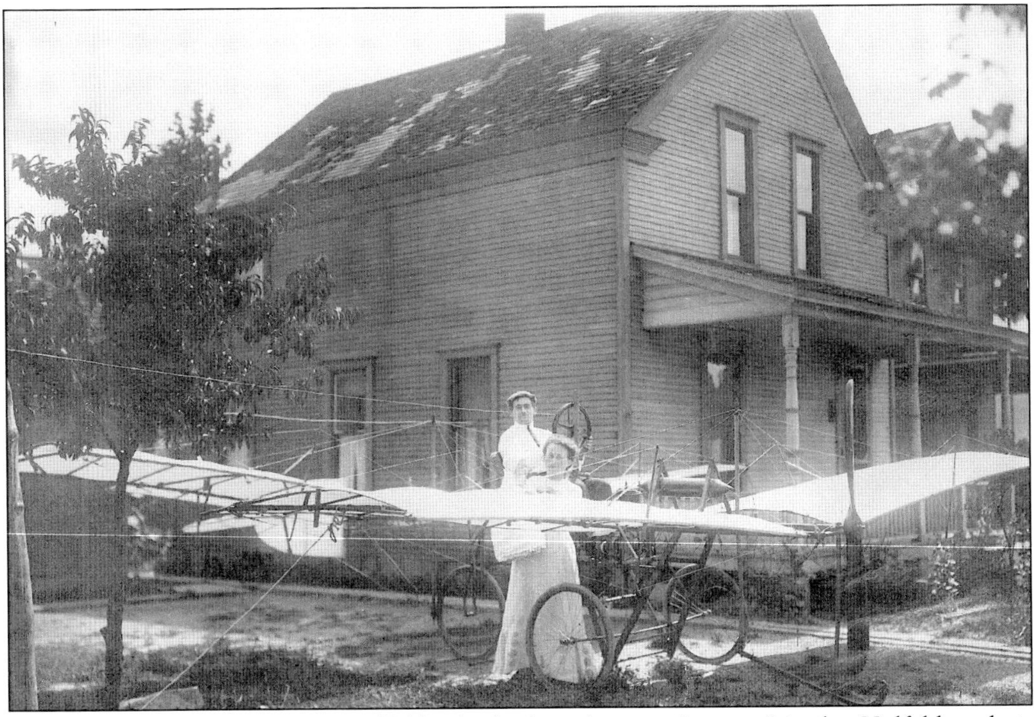

Between 1910 and 1915 Leo Holfelder built this plane in Lorain. Martha Holfelder, their daughter, said her parents took this plane down to Lake Erie and flew it from the beach. Martha said it was flown once but knew nothing else about this homemade plane built in Lorain before World War I.

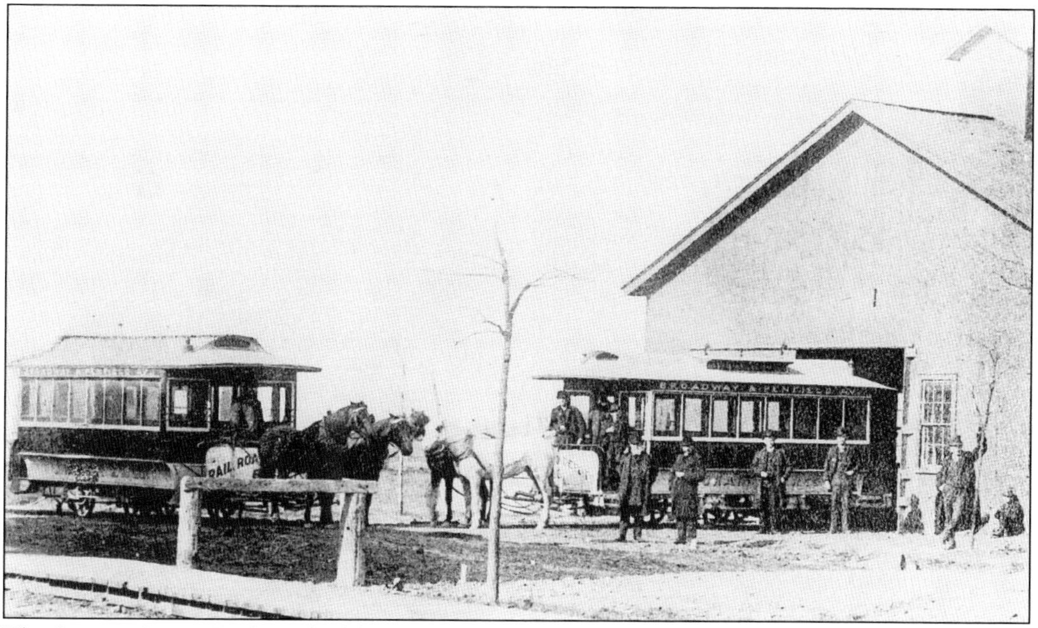

The Lorain Street Railway had horse-drawn cars that ran down Broadway from Erie Avenue south to Twentieth Street. The car barn was on the southeast corner of Eighteenth Street and Broadway. Using this line made travel down the muddy street a much easier and cleaner trip. The line lasted until 1894, when the electric streetcars came to town and replaced horses.

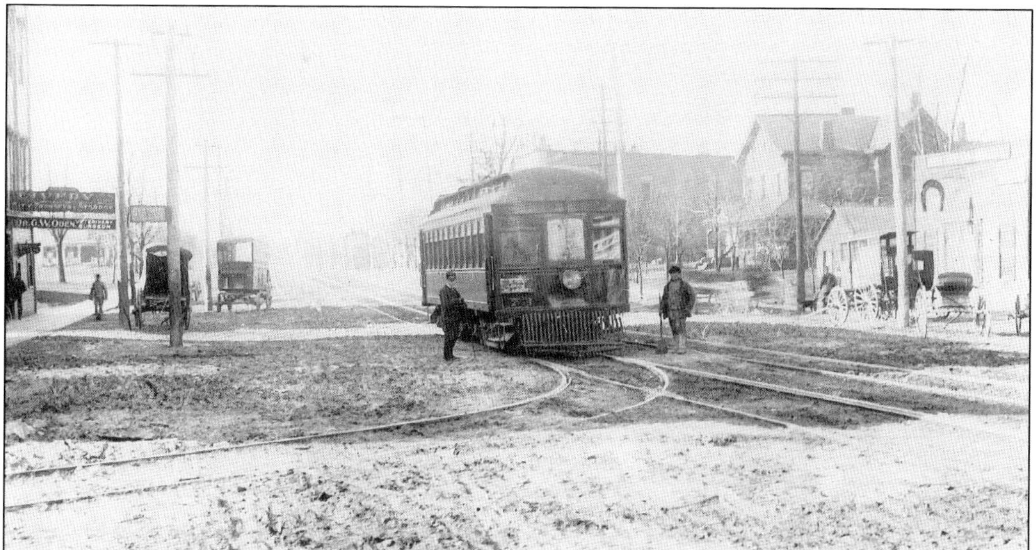

The Lorain Electric Railway (Green Line) started when Tom Johnson brought the Johnson Steel Rail Co. to Lorain in 1894. It was the start of a great system of travel. People could go from Cleveland to Toledo on the streetcars. Pictured in this view, looking west on Erie Avenue, is the "Green Line" car at the Loop. Lewis Conn's harness shop was on the right, then City Hall (barely visible), and the tall building on the right was the Wickens Funeral Home's Parkside Chapel.

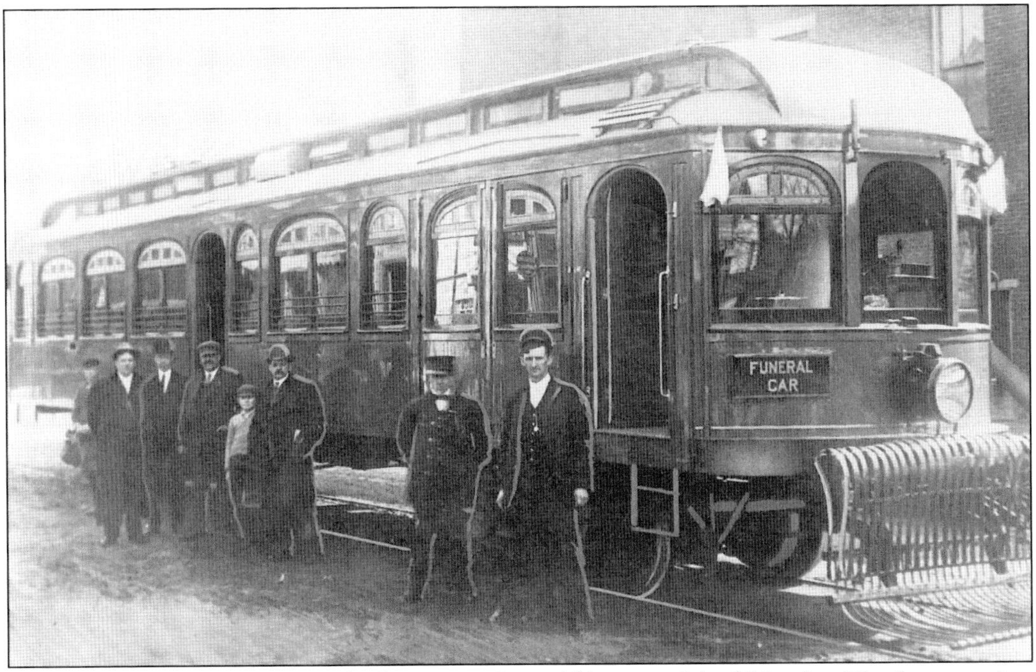

The funeral car, "Doloros," was built in 1911. It could be rented for $15 a day. The front section was large enough for two caskets, and the middle section had eight chairs for the pallbearers. In the back were 26 seats for the mourners. The car took the funeral party to the cemetery and then returned them back to town. During the 1920s, the motorized hearse came into being.

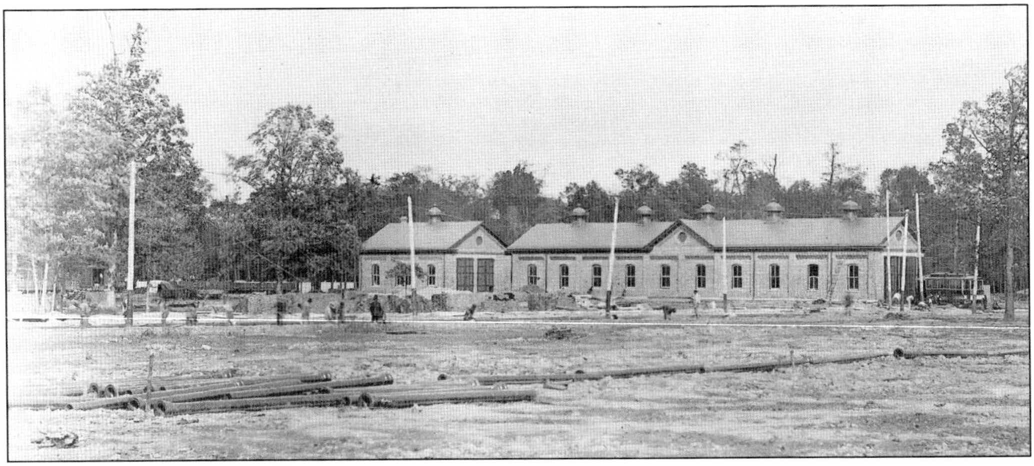

The car barns for the streetcars were located at Seneca Avenue and what is now Twenty-eighth Street. There were three competitive lines that served Lorain. The Lake Shore Electric went from Cleveland to Toledo. The Cleveland, Elyria & Western Electric Co. served Cleveland, Medina, Berea, and North Amherst, and the Lorain Street Railway went between Lorain and Elyria to serve the workers at the new steel mill. The fare for that ride was 3¢.

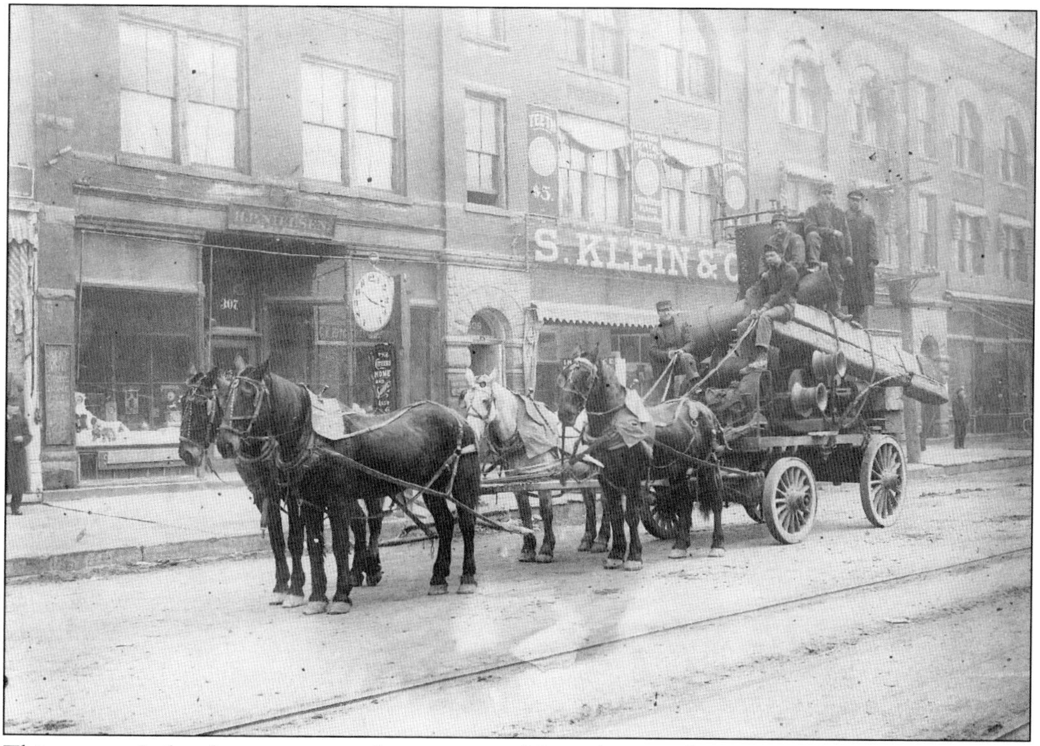

This wagon is for the streetcar rail repair crew. Note the wooden ties on the wagon. The two upper wheels above the bed of the vehicle were used to bend the rails as needed, to make them fit and for going around corners. Also note the dentist's office above the S. Klein & Co. store. Many professional people had offices on the second floor of buildings.

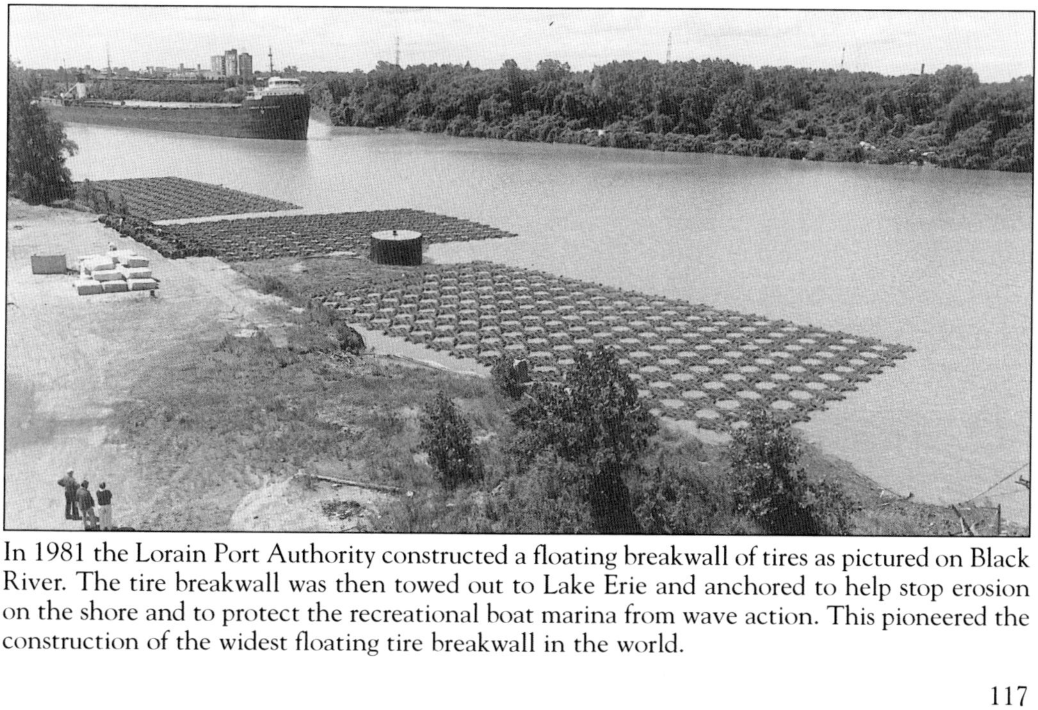

In 1981 the Lorain Port Authority constructed a floating breakwall of tires as pictured on Black River. The tire breakwall was then towed out to Lake Erie and anchored to help stop erosion on the shore and to protect the recreational boat marina from wave action. This pioneered the construction of the widest floating tire breakwall in the world.

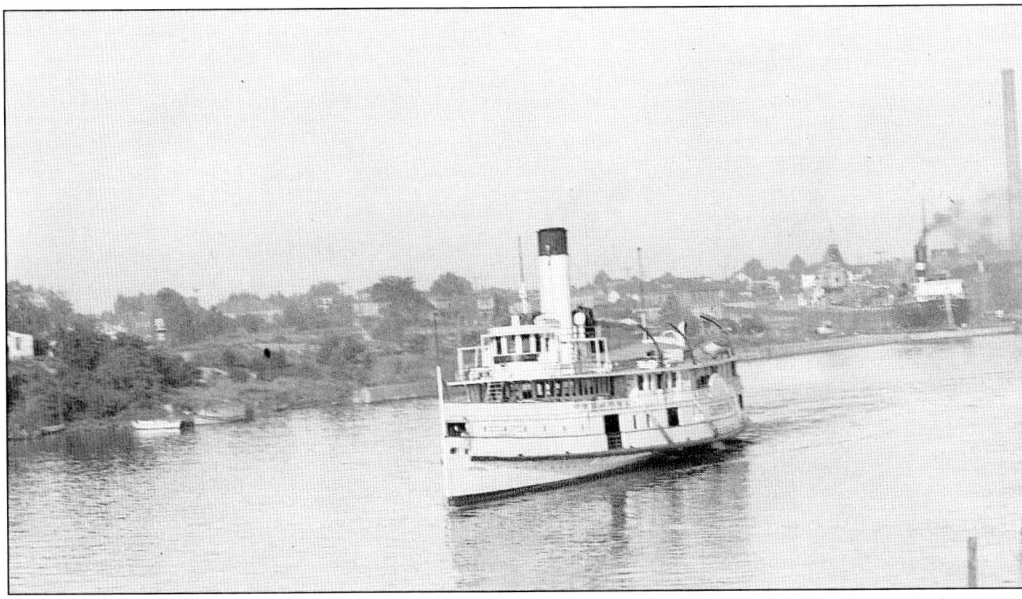

The steamer *Chippewa* was one of the passenger ships that used to ply the Great Lakes. It is shown here as it went down the Black River, with the shipyard in the background. For many years, passenger ships would provide excursions to places from Buffalo to Detroit. During the 1840s to 1860s, many escaped slaves were transported to Canada by means of these ships.

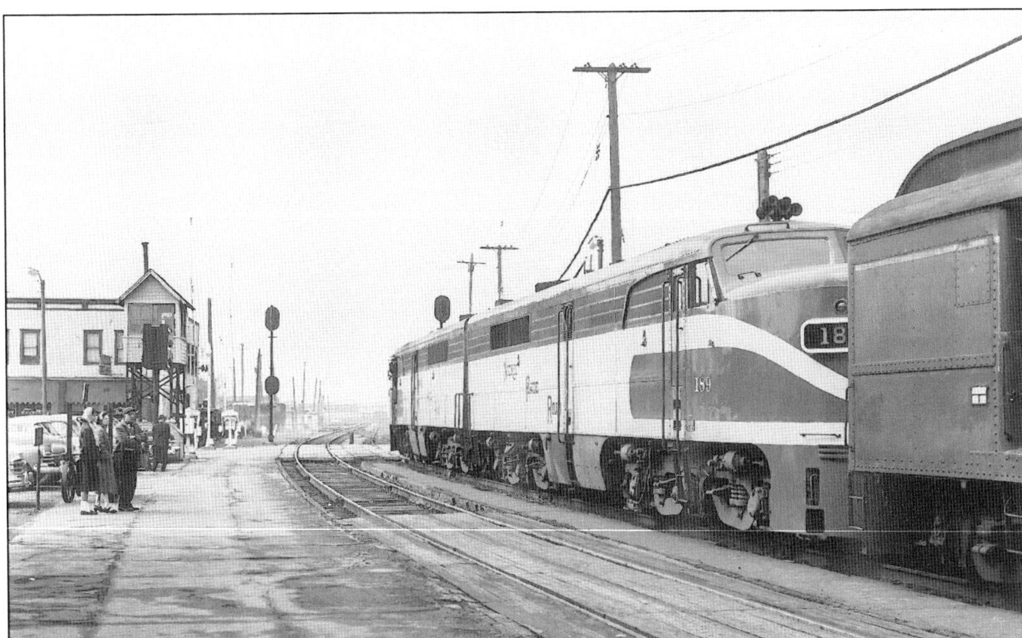

Travel by passenger train was a popular means of getting around the state and country. The picture above shows a view of the last Nickel Plate passenger train to stop in Lorain in the 1950s. The depot is behind the photographer. The "tower" on the left was where the man was stationed who controlled the gates. When a train was coming, the operator would lower the gates on Broadway to stop the traffic.

Seven

Our Famous People and Historic Buildings

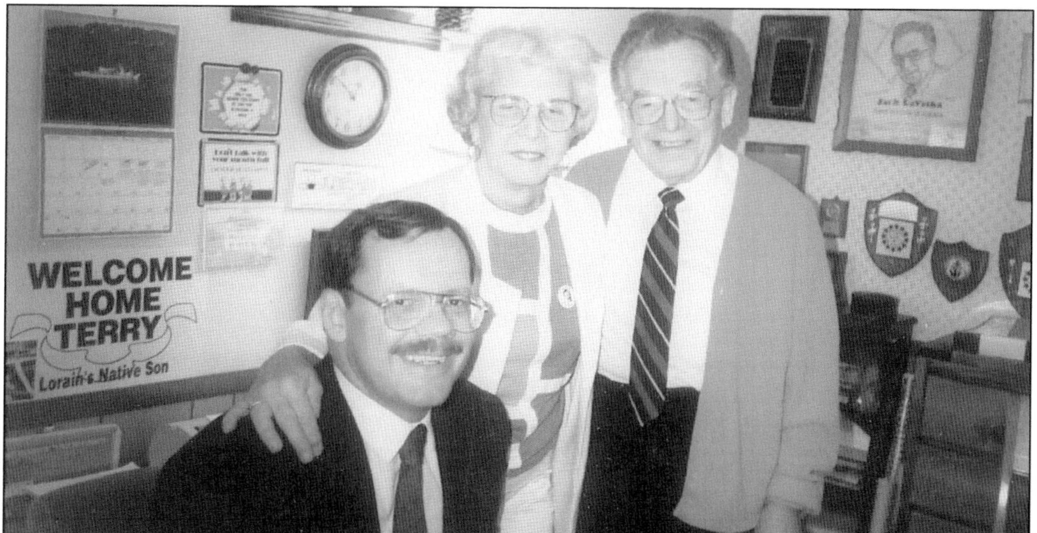

Lorain native Terry Anderson had many positions before finally working for the Associated Press. He did such a good job he was promoted to Chief Middle East Correspondent. The world knows he was kidnapped by a group of extremists called the Islamic Jihad on March 16, 1985. He was held hostage for 2,455 days and finally released on December 4, 1991. He was the longest-held American hostage. Terry Anderson returned to Lorain to be the honorary Grand Marshall of the International Parade on June 21, 1992. Pictured are Terry Anderson and Marion and Jack LaVriha, who campaigned so hard to secure his release.

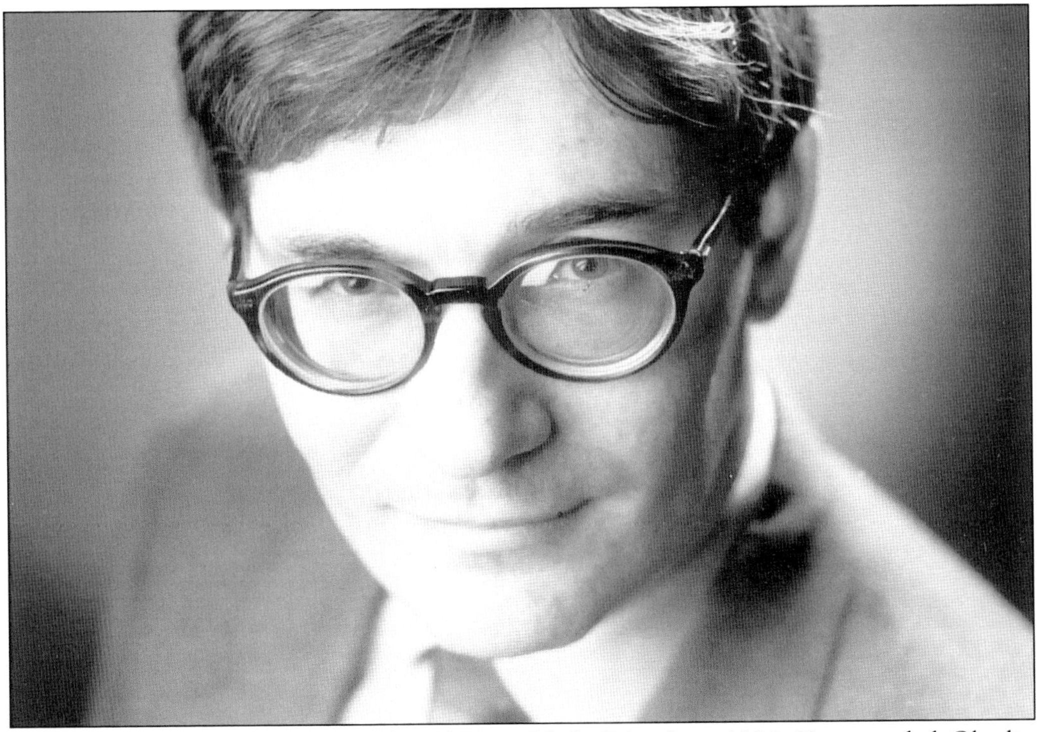

Michael Dirda graduated from Admiral King High School in 1966. He attended Oberlin College after some part-time work. He began to write book reviews for the *Washington Post* in 1977 and received the Pulitzer Prize for Literature in 1993. Mr. Dirda is the second Lorainite to win this Pulitzer Prize; the other person was Toni Morrison.

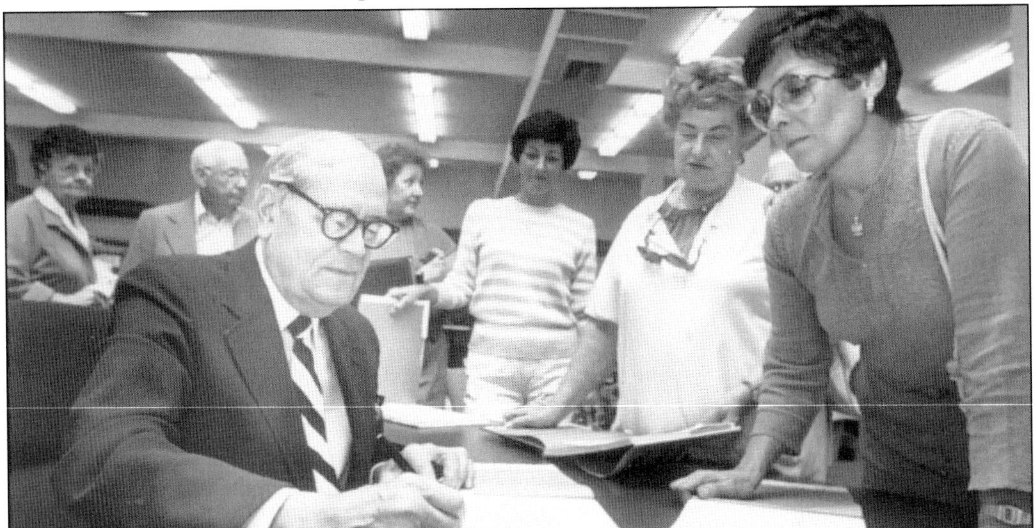

Steven Dohanos liked to draw and paint. His big break came in 1934, when he was selected as one of a group to go to the Virgin Islands for an art project to promote tourism. During his career, he designed 40 U.S. postage stamps; in 1984 the U.S. Postal Service dedicated its Washington, D.C., Hall of Stamps in Dohanos's honor. By the early 1940s he was nationally known for his illustrations on the cover of magazines such as *The Saturday Evening Post*.

Gerald Freeman brought the most passionate folk tales of all times to life as the Artistic Director of the Great Lakes Theater Festival. He was highly regarded for his productions of classic drama, musicals, operas, new plays, and television specials. A graduate of Lorain High School, he continues to work with the Drama School, which is part of the North Carolina School of the Arts.

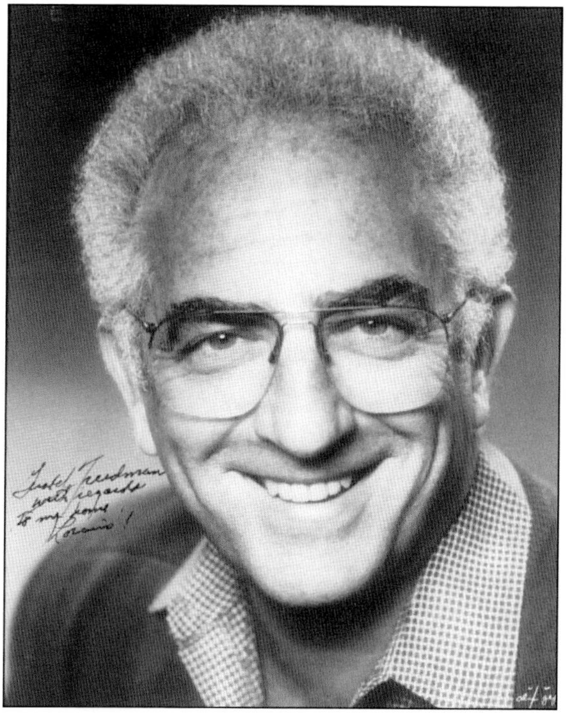

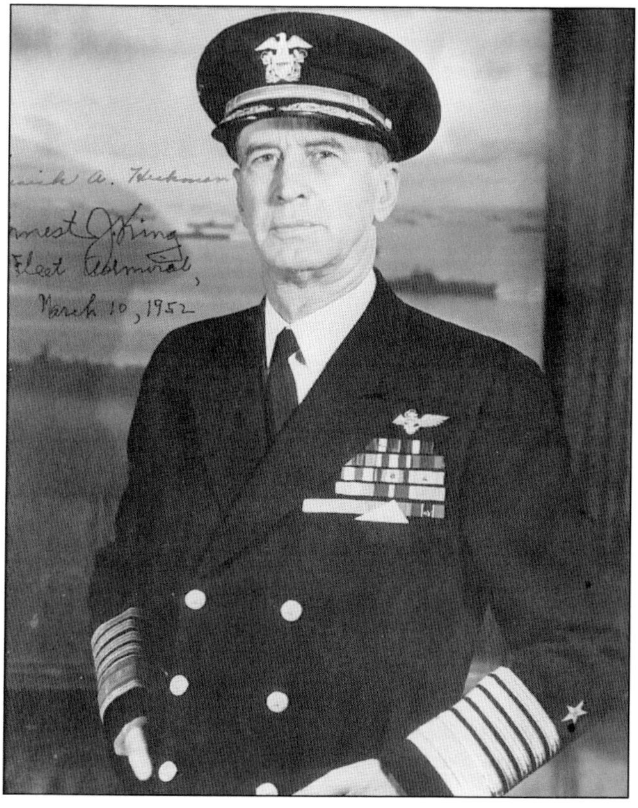

Admiral Ernest J. King was commander-in-chief of the U.S. Fleet during World War II. He was considered by many as the most powerful naval officer in the history of the United States. He was always proud of his hometown of Lorain and returned many times. He died in 1956, after a distinguished career in the navy. In 1962 Lorain built a new high school and it was named in his honor. The house where he was born is still standing at 113 Hamilton Avenue. (Official United States Navy Photograph)

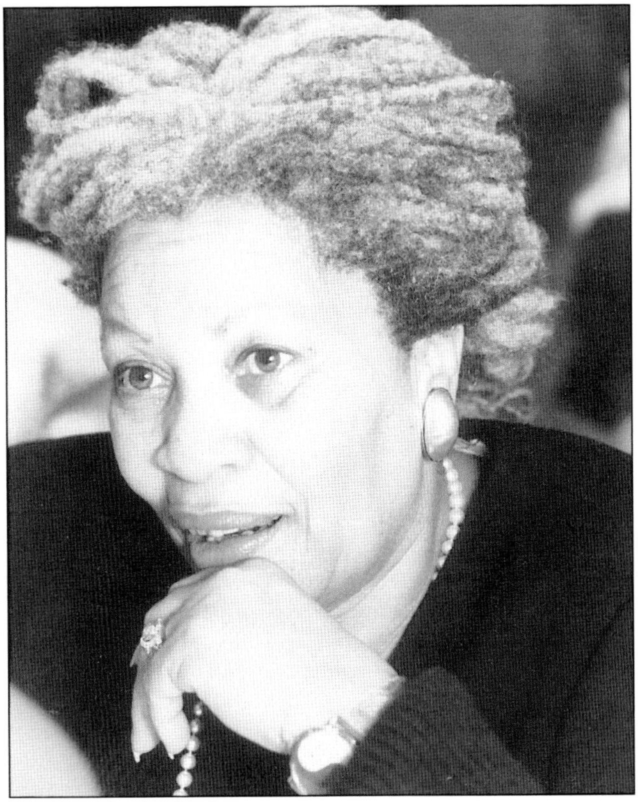

Toni Morrison was born on Elyria Avenue in Lorain. She graduated from Lorain High in the class of 1949 and became a member of the faculty at Howard University. In 1988 she received the Pulitzer Prize for Fiction and the Robert F. Kennedy Award for her book, *Beloved*. In 1993 Toni Morrison became the eighth woman and the first African-American woman to receive the Nobel Prize in Literature. (Photo courtesy of the *Morning Journal*.)

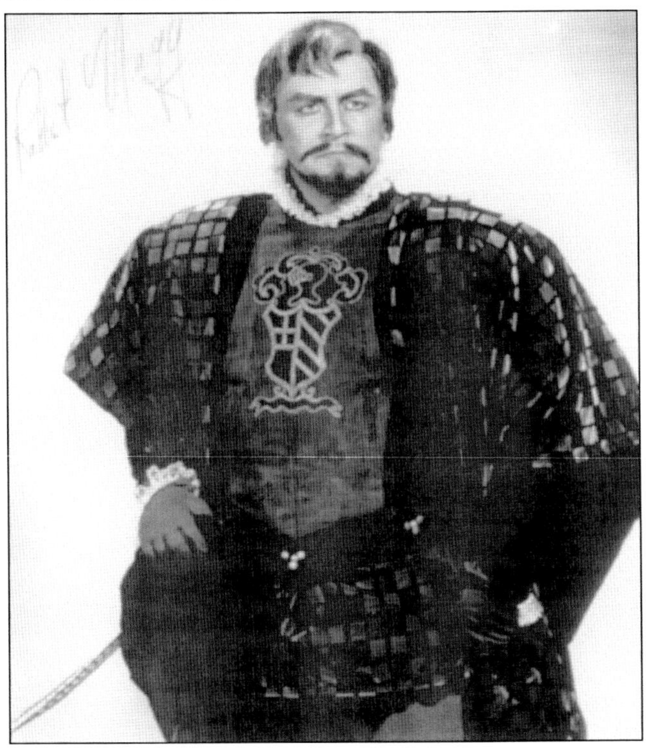

Robert Nagy used to live on West Twenty-ninth Street and attended Lorain High School. He began his musical training in his twenties and was noted for his voice. Eventually, he became associated with the Metropolitan Opera Co. of New York and sang numerous operatic parts during his career. He has sung opera in the United States and in Europe, and has received top awards in Cleveland and Chicago musical festivals.

Mark Nesbitt is a 1967 graduate of Lorain High School. He lived in Lorain until he was 21. At that time, he moved to Gettysburg, Pennsylvania, where he became a historian and ranger at the battlefield park. His first book, *Ghosts of Gettysburg*, was published in 1991. His latest book is *Through Blood and Fire*.

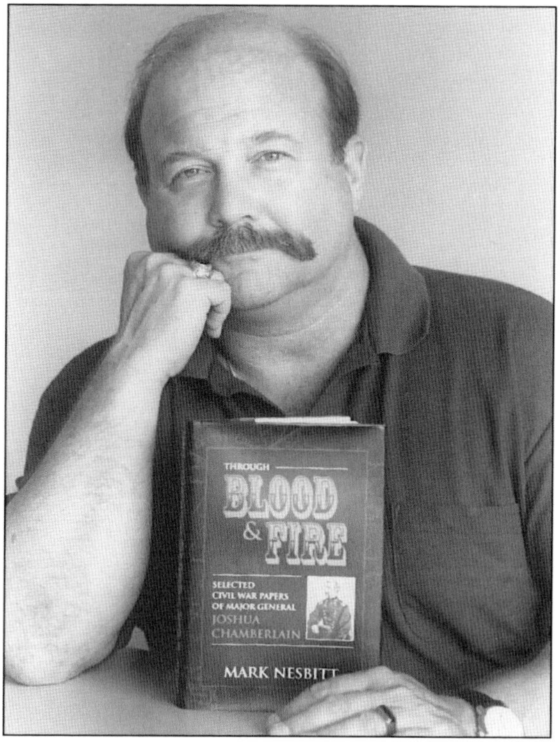

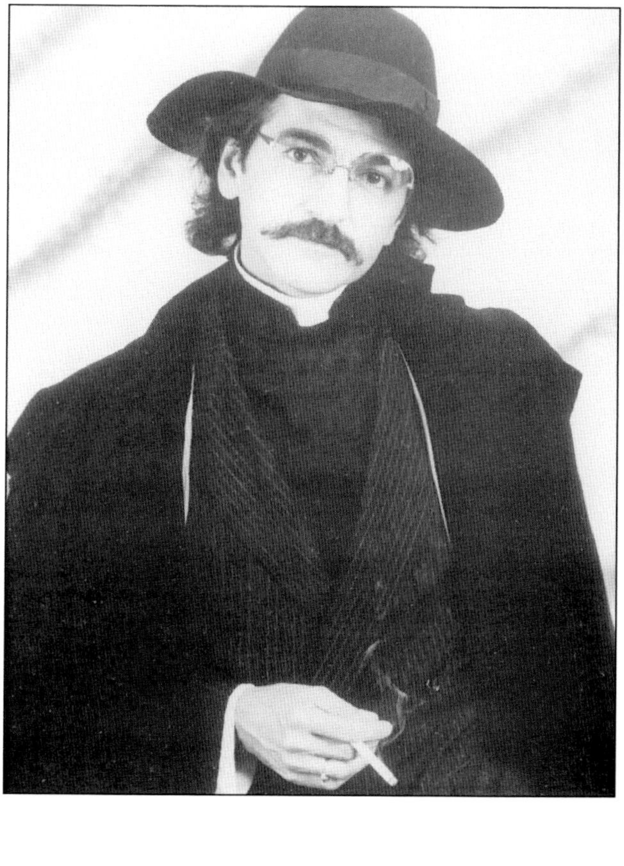

Don Novello played the part of Father Guido Sarducci, a self-styled Vatican columnist, on the television program *Saturday Night Live*. His role brought him national recognition for his humor. He is the son of Dr. A.J. and Eleanor Novello of Lorain and a 1961 graduate of Lorain High School. (Photograph courtesy of Dr. and Mrs. Novello.)

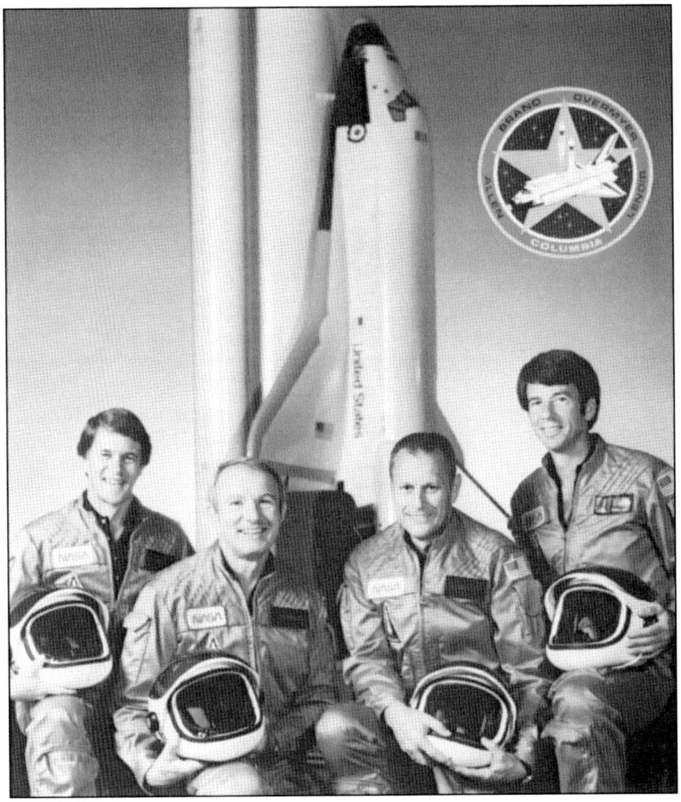

Robert F. Overmyer was the pilot of the fifth Space Shuttle Orbital flight. Colonel Overmyer was chosen in 1969 to work on the Skylab Program until 1971, and he was a support crew member for Apollo 17. In March 1996, after his retirement from the space program, he became a test pilot for the VK 30 prototype plane and was killed at the age of 59. In this picture are Joseph Allen, Vance Brand (commander), Robert Overmyer (pilot), and William Lenoir of the space orbital vehicle, *Columbia*. (Picture courtesy of NASA.)

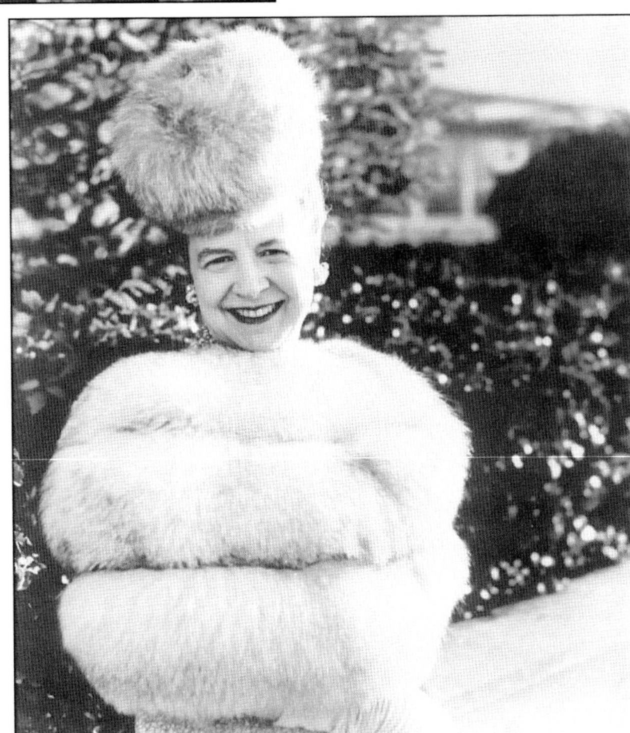

Helen Steiner Rice enjoyed writing poetry when she attended Lorain High School and continued that interest all her life. She was employed at the Ohio Public Service Co. (later Ohio Edison) and became director of public relations of the Ohio Committee on Public Utilities Information. At a convention, Helen Steiner was introduced to Franklin Rice, a banker, and they later married. When Mr. Rice died a few years later, Helen was offered a job at the Gibson Greeting Card Co. Her poems began to attract nationwide attention and she not only wrote poetry for the company cards, but published books of her poems. Born in Lorain in 1900, she died in Cincinnati in 1981.

General Johnnie E. Wilson graduated from Lorain High School in 1961. After graduation, he joined the army and became one of only ten officers wearing the four stars of the army's highest rank. He served the army and his country very well and retired in 1999 after 37 years of service.

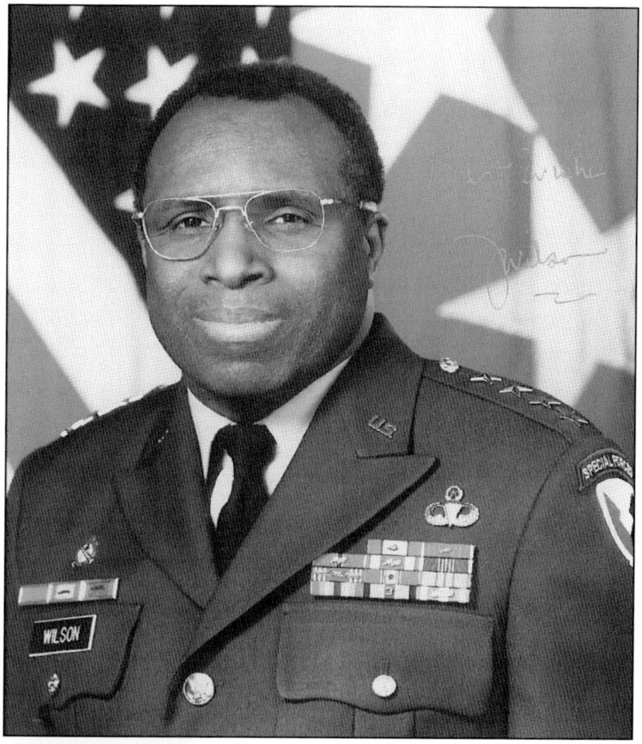

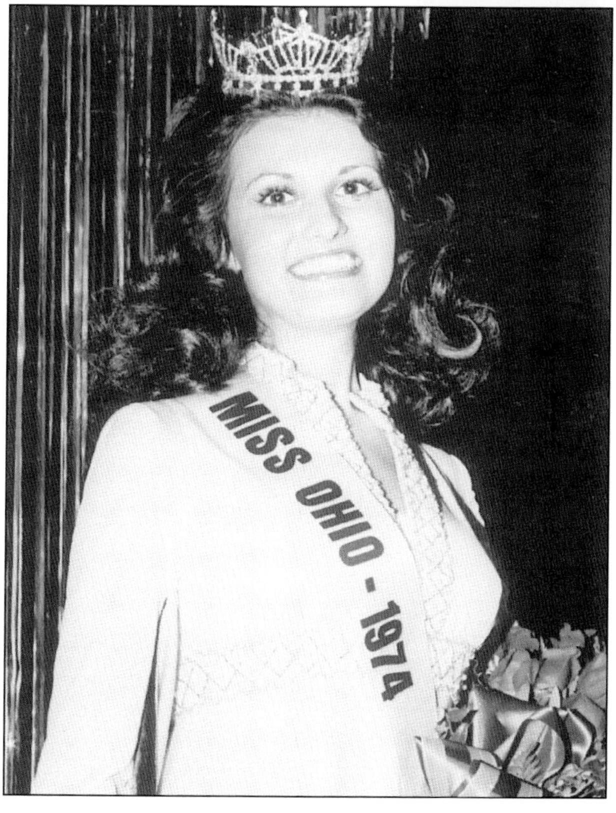

Cheryl Ann Yourkvitch was born and raised in Lorain. In 1973 she was crowned Miss Lorain County, and in 1974 was picked as Miss Ohio. She went on to represent the Buckeye State at the Miss America pageant in Atlantic City. Her crown, dress, trophy, and musical arrangement of the song she sang are on display at the Black River Historical Society in Lorain, a city that is very proud of her achievements.

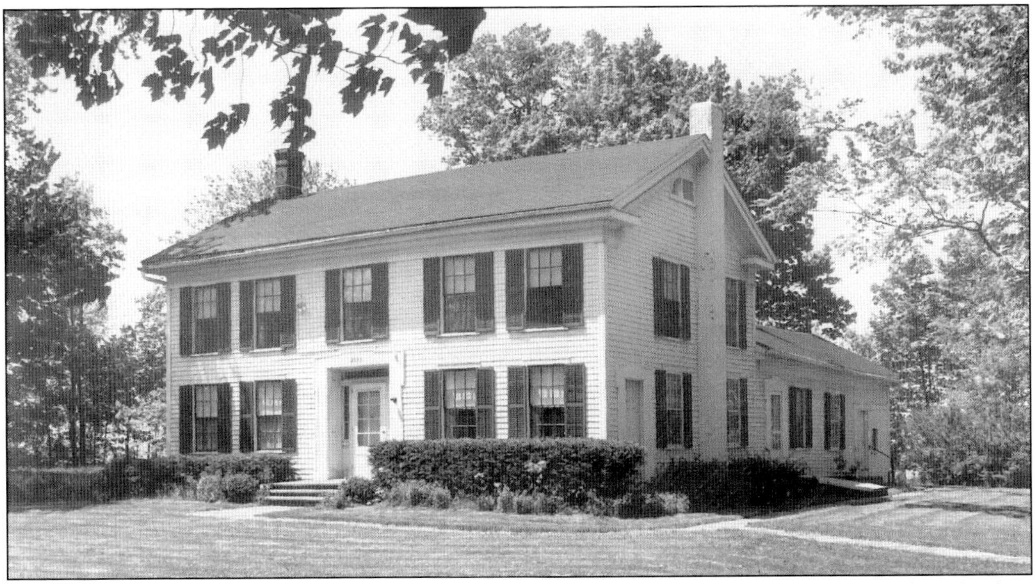

William Root and his family came from Massachusetts and settled in Lorain. They built a beautiful Greek-Revival home at 3535 East Erie Avenue. Harriet Root lived in the house for many years. During WW II, President Roosevelt asked her to head the U.S. Information Service in Washington, D.C. The present owners of the house are Ben and Jane Norton, who have preserved the home. It is now on the National Registry.

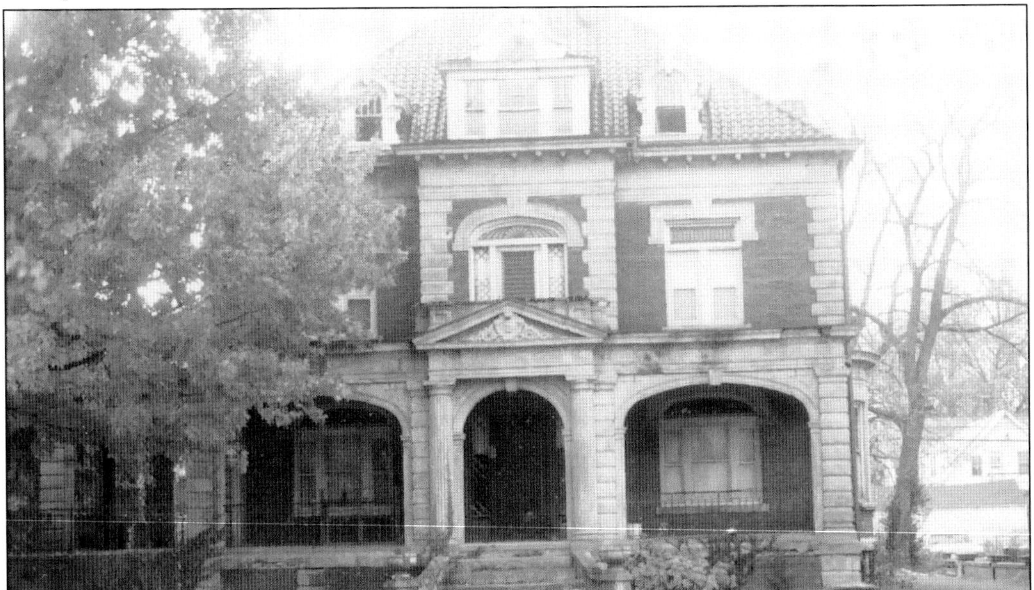

William Seher was the owner of the Lorain Brewing Co., which was located on what is now Twelfth Street. He ran the brewery in Lorain until Prohibition came along. Then he switched production to soft drinks. One of his most popular flavors was Ginger Beer. The architecture of the home is mainly Georgian Revival and was one of the most expensive homes ever built in Lorain up to that time. It cost $15,000 and is located at 329 Ninth Street. It is on the National Registry, along with other private homes previously pictured, including the Moore House at 309 Fifth Street, and the Root House at 3535 East Erie Avenue.

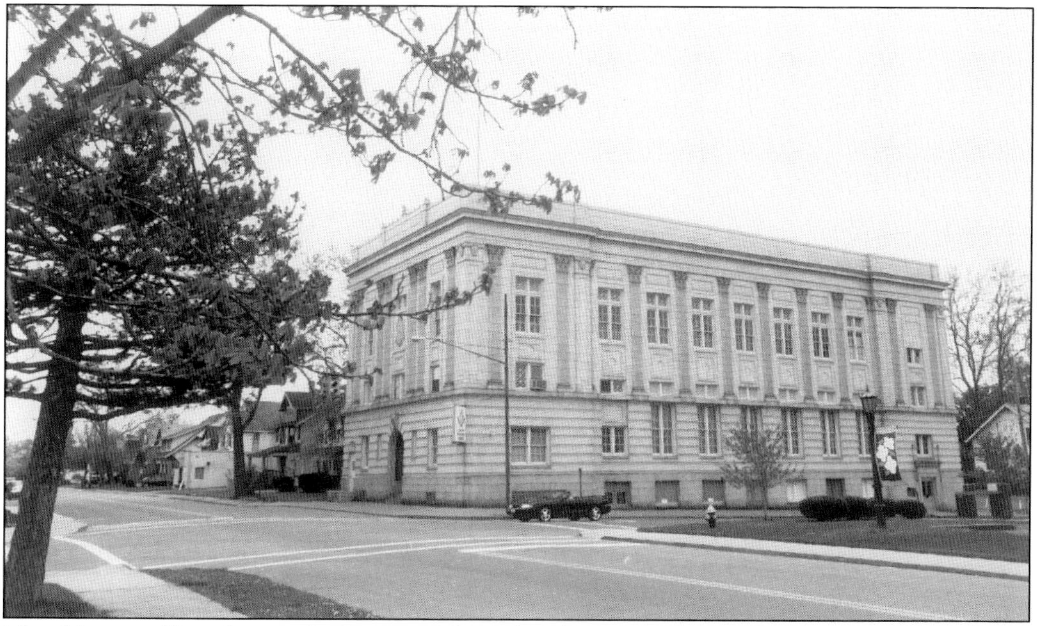

The Masonic Temple was built in 1927 in the downtown area, following the devastating tornado in 1924. It was the first permanent home of Lorain's Masonic Lodge number 552. The location is on the southwest corner of Washington Avenue and Fourth Street. The design is said to be a replica of King Solomon's Temple and has a seating capacity of over 600 people.

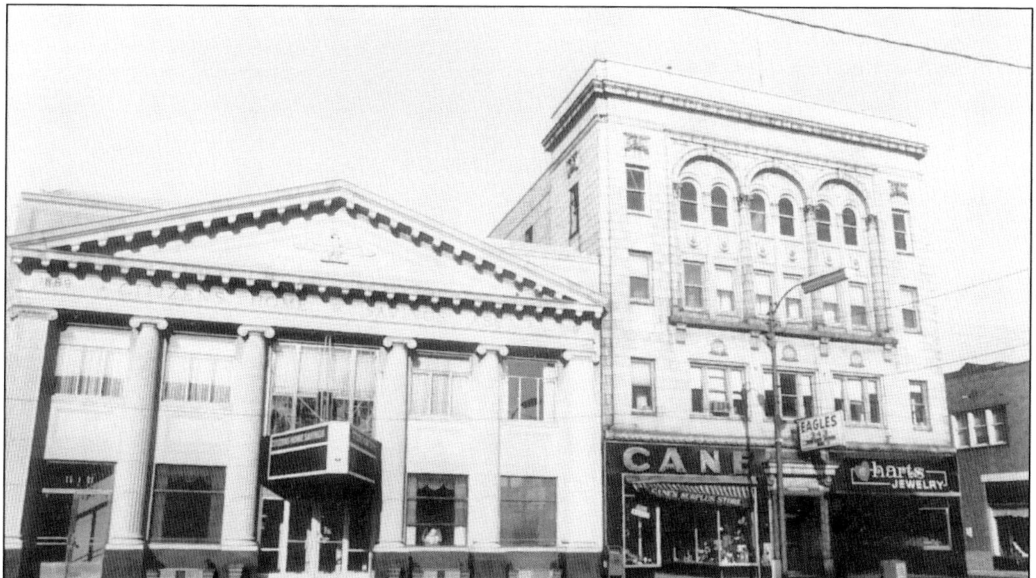

The Eagles Building is located at 575 Broadway. In 1918 it was built as a one-story building. It survived the tornado that was so destructive to the majority of the buildings of the downtown area, and it was the first commercial building in the Lorain area to employ a reinforced concrete frame. The building needed that strength because of the shortage of domestic steel created by WW I.

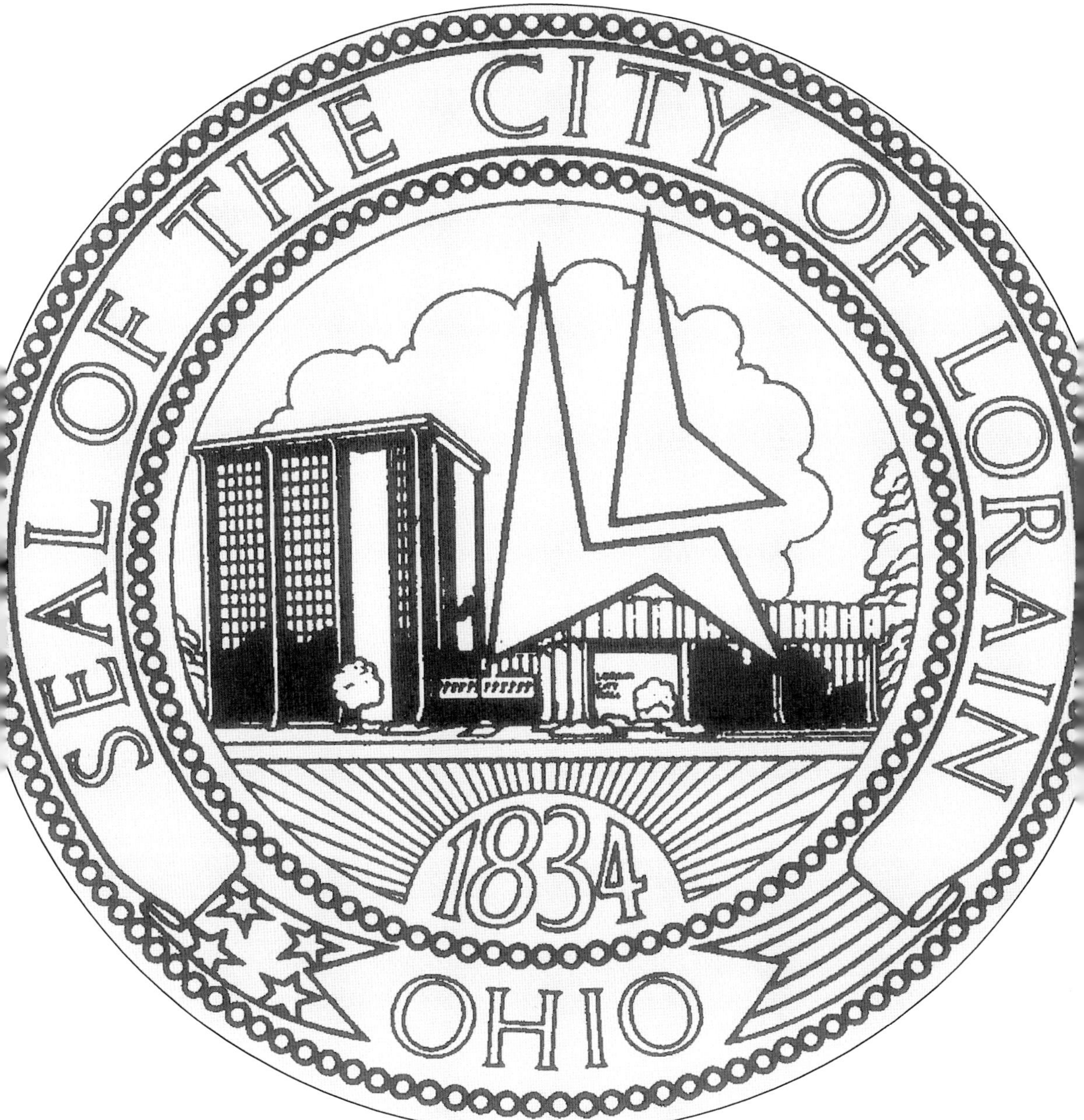

The Seal of the City of Lorain was designed by William F. Smith. At the bottom is a replica of the flag of the State of Ohio and the date of the official founding of the city. The building in the center is the new City Hall, which was completed in 1973. It includes the administration department, the police department, the justice center, and the municipal jail. The triangular symbols at the top right are the symbols, "L" and "I," which stand for the Lorain International organization and for its festival that is held each year.